Recovering Literature's Lost Ground

Recovering Literature's Lost Ground

Essays in American Autobiography

James M. Cox

Louisiana State University Press
Baton Rouge and London

96 95 94 93 92 91 90 89   5 4 3 2 1

DESIGNER: Sylvia Malik Loftin
TYPEFACE: Times Roman
TYPESETTER: Composing Room of Michigan
PRINTER: Thomson-Shore, Inc.
BINDER: John H. Dekker & Sons, Inc.

Library of Congress Cataloging-in-Publication Data

Cox, James M. (James Melville), 1925–
    Recovering literature's lost ground: essays in American autobiography/James M. Cox.
    p.   cm.
    Includes index.
    ISBN 0-8071-1491-X (alk. paper)
    1. American prose literature—History and criticism. 2. Autobiography. 3. Authors,
American—Biography—History and criticism. I. Title.
PS366.A88C69   1989
810',9'492—dc19   88-22052
                                                                                          CIP

"Autobiography and Washington" was first published in the *Sewanee Review* 85 (Spring 1977).
Copyright © 1977 by the University of the South. "Learning Through Ignorance: *The Educa-
tion of Henry Adams*" appeared in the *Sewanee Review* 88 (Spring 1980). Copyright © 1980 by
James M. Cox. Both essays are reprinted with the permission of the *Sewanee Review,* for which
the author is grateful.
    The author is also grateful to the following book publishers and to the editors and publishers
of the following periodicals for permission to reprint the essays noted. "Autobiography and
America" appeared in the *Virginia Quarterly Review,* XLVII (Spring, 1971) and in J. Hillis
Miller (ed.), *Aspects of the Narrative* (Columbia University Press, 1971). "Recovering Liter-
ature's Lost Ground Through Autobiography" first appeared in the *Southern Review,* n.s., XIV
(Autumn, 1978). "Richard Henry Dana's *Two Years Before the Mast*" originally appeared in
John D. Lyons and Nancy J. Vickers (eds.), *The Dialectic of Discovery* (French Forum, 1984).
"R. W. Emerson: The Circles of the Eye" originally appeared in David Levin (ed.), *Emerson,
Prophecy, Metamorphosis, and Influence* (Columbia University Press, 1975). "U. S. Grant:
The Man in the *Memoirs*" is reprinted by permission from *The Rights of Memory: Essays on
History, Science, and American Culture,* edited by Taylor Littleton, copyright © 1986 by the
University of Alabama Press. "The Memoirs of Henry James: Self-Interest as Autobiography"
first appeared in the *Southern Review,* n.s., XXII (Spring, 1986). "Shelby Foote's *Civil War*"
originally appeared in the *Southern Review,* n.s., XXI (April, 1985).

The paper in this book meets the guidelines for permanence and durability of the Committee on
Production Guidelines for Book Longevity of the Council on Library Resources. ∞

FOR MARGUERITE

Contents

—❦—

RECOVERING LITERATURE'S LOST GROUND

PREFACE

—⋅⋘⋙⋅—

The essays here collected were written over the past twenty-five years. They were written slowly. "Autobiography and America" began as a paper on Benjamin Franklin's *Autobiography,* which I read at Yale University in November, 1962, at the time of the Cuban missile crisis. The very title given to that confrontation between the United States and the Soviet Union was an indication of the way we wanted to see the period we were entering. Our "victory" in the encounter provided the delusionary impulse that carried us into Vietnam and all that followed. Much as the nation as a whole came to regret that drawn-out conflict, there was nonetheless the compensatory achievement of the civil rights movement that accompanied our abortive imperial efforts in the Far East. The relationship between these two conflicts—the one external, the other internal—deserves much more study than it has yet been given.

What can at least be concluded is that the Voting Rights Act of 1965 marked the long-deferred fulfillment of Grant's victory at Appomattox a hundred years earlier. Lyndon Johnson had accomplished, in the wake of an assassin's bullet, so much of what Andrew Johnson could not achieve as the successor to Abraham Lincoln. Yet even as the nation was achieving a victory over the recalcitrant southern part of itself, it was embroiled half a world away in a failing effort to defend *South* Vietnam from the northern part of itself. The failure resulted in massive destabilization at home—a breakdown of authority that finally ended with the forced resignation of a president, something that hadn't happened even to Andrew Johnson.

It should not be surprising that, during this period of social conflict and destabilization, autobiography has received more attention than it ever did in the day of the New Criticism. Not that the New Criticism was not political in its own right. It came into its own after a period when all literature had been put into the services of the state—had, in a word, been made into propaganda. We must remember that the New Criticism did not dominate the 1930s. It was a force in that decade, but so were Marxism, liberalism, the old scholarship, and belletristic impressionism. That decade eventuated in total war—World War II—and all literature was subordinated to the war effort. After the war, when the schools rapidly expanded, the New Criticism—as we have come to know it—was in an ideal position to be recognized. Far from exemplifying the elitist impulses charged to it by subsequent literary and social critics, the New Criticism was actually democratic in its practice, making literature eminently teachable for both teachers and students coming back from the war. Freeing the text from the social, political, and national interests that had held it in bondage, the New Critics offered what was essentially a practical criticism, affording what seemed—after a surfeit of propaganda—a chance for both student and text to speak to each other. The text thus became a space of volatile energy, generating not only potentialities of interpretation but also possibilities of power for the individual reader. For all its tendency to discover the special language of literature and even to emphasize the thematic presence of original sin embedded in the text, it was an Emersonian criticism even as it devalued Emerson and appreciated Hawthorne.

Still, it gave little attention to autobiography, concentrating instead on the closed forms of lyric poetry, drama, and fiction—forms sufficiently independent from history and society and sufficiently rich in language and structure to afford textual investigations of a "literary" nature. When I became interested in the subject of autobiography, there was precious little written about it. There were of course Georg Misch's monumental four-volume *History of Autobiography in Antiquity,* Roy Pascal's *Design and Truth in Autobiography,* and Georges Gusdorf's "Conditions and Limits of Autobiography." Then, too, there were fugitive pieces as well as acute remarks, made in passing, by writers and critics, but nothing to daunt a student ignorant of the subject from thinking freely about it in an indolently critical way. How times have changed! What was untilled land has been so intensively cultivated that even an ambitious student of the subject, looking down the rows of books and articles devoted to autobiography, might be discouraged from entering the field.

It is not my purpose to survey that writing or to offer my own theory of autobiography. I am no closer to a theory of the subject than I was when I began writing about it a quarter century ago. At times I think I know more about it than I did then, but such moments are usually followed by a depressing awareness that my ignorance of the subject may well have grown at a faster pace than my knowledge. This is not at all to say that the critical writing on autobiography has not been of enormous help to me. When I began writing, I held to the naïve commonsense vision that autobiography is a person's life written by that person, that it is significantly different from fiction, and that autobiographers have a privileged access to the "self" about which they write. In holding to that vision, I of course realized that there was theoretic pressure against it. The New Criticism, insofar as it dealt with autobiography at all, tended always toward converting it into a fiction of the self, since such a conversion freed criticism from the priority of historical and authorial reference into closed, "literary" form that could be dealt with as literature. Such a strategy exposed the autobiographer's inability to tell the "truth" about the self made increasingly irrelevant behind the screen of language. More recent critical theory has exposed the self itself as a fiction of language—a cumulative creation written by language. Language is thus the signifier presumptively making the self it signifies increasingly so absent that it can only be traced like a ghost between the long sequence of lines and text that make up a convention or a tradition. The convention of autobiography is the most exacerbated form of such signification, since the "I" of language, presumably signifying the individual first-person "self," is at the same time the most tyrannical convention of the linguistic system. Every person, of whatever gender or race writing in English, uses it to signify the self and is thus at the mercy, no matter how repressed, of the system.

If contemporary critical theory has destabilized the self that the autobiographer naïvely relies upon, social theorists, emphasizing autobiography as a form relied upon by minorities, have attempted to destabilize the traditional canon that has tended to exclude auto-biographies from the field of literature. Their political program envisions autobiography as a voice by means of which excluded races and genders gain access into the privileged citadel of American literature. Holding to the belief that the self does indeed exist, they see auto-biography as the avenue by which underprivileged selves gain entry into the established culture of writing. The very fact that autobiography was the chief form by means of which fugitive slaves could achieve both expression for themselves and acquire a hearing from cultivated society is evidence of the liberating as well as the socializing function of the convention.

There is neither a neat nor a difficult way to resolve these conflicting views of autobiography. The privileged writer, secure in culture, can afford to doubt the self; the underprivileged individual cannot. For the one, autobiography exposes the tyranny of language; for the other, the language of the self exposes the tyranny of society. It is precisely this undecidability about the subject of autobiography that reflects its nature. It is what we might call a transitional form of literature or a form of literature in transition. Emerson, who was himself the very spirit of a literature in transition, hoped for the day when all literature would eventuate in autobiography. Yearning for a national literature that would transcend the confinements of established English literature, Emerson exhorted writers to both touch and express the crescive self rooted in a preverbal nature that was yet the origin of language. He recognized that the domain of established literature was of necessity exclusionary, just as he realized that autobiography would be not only the beginning but the end of any American literature that could, whether reaching down toward or up from the native forces outside refined culture, make its presence felt. He knew whereof he spoke. St. Augustine had, in the autobiographical account of his conversion, reached the force of God and recovered the soul to call in question the rhetoric, the literature, and the philosophy of the ancient world.

But the writer whose work should be as compelling for the student of autobiography as it was for Emerson is Montaigne. Living through a period of religious upheaval and civil war, and living also in the age of exploration of the New World, Montaigne—a voracious reader of books—determined to make a book of himself. Seeing himself or, we could say, imaginatively positioning himself between the Old World of learning and the New World of "nature," Montaigne converted his own restless mental urgings into essays of the self. Those essays are trials or, more precisely, weighings of matter; the matter is the self; the self is matter becoming energy, the action of the mind vibrating between the present and past, the Old World and the New, the spirit and the body, the authority of books and the experience of living. The true precursor of Whitman in making the book of himself, Montaigne continuously converted his life into discontinuous essays, interpolating additional revisions in successive editions of his book.

The remarkable quality of Montaigne's essays lies in the skepticism that constantly enlarges the range of his roving meditation. By the time he reaches the final magnificent essay, "On Experience," he is commandingly in touch with the volatile relativity of the data of experience. The self he seeks is that confident source of the authority of experience and at the same time the force that generates the ever-proliferating, contradictory impulses of thought. In the midst of the essay he makes a characteristically authoritative summary of the whole issue of the self. Having noted that Perseus, king of Macedonia, was "of such a flighty and erratic character that neither he nor anyone else knew what kind of a man he was," Montaigne asserts that this condition seems to him to be true of everybody. He continues: "And above all men, I have known another of his stature to whom this conclusion would apply still more properly, I think: no middle position, always being carried away from one extreme to the other by causes impossible to guess; no kind of course without tacking and changing direction amazingly; no quality unmixed, so that the most likely portrait of him that men will be able to make some day, will be that he affected and studied to make himself known by being unknowable." The fact that, instead of "another of his stature," Montaigne had first written "another king since" has led interpreters to assume that the figure being described is presumably Henry IV of France. Yet it seems to me that the figure could well be that of Montaigne himself. Certainly the shifting, contradictory, impulsive, and wayward self described in the quote fits both the manner and the matter of Montaigne in his essays. And the aim—to make the self known by making it unknowable—seems to me to define Montaigne's great achievement, for he does make the nature of the self known as well as any autobiographer ever has and at the same time discovers its unknowability.

Montaigne is significant not only in relation to the literature of the self but also in relation to America. The New World holds an interest for him throughout the essays. He sees in "On Vehicles" that, whereas it is new to Europe, the Europeans are new to it; thus both worlds are old to themselves and new to each other. Still, Montaigne dreams of the New World as somehow simpler and less corrupt than the Old, particularly when he considers the perfidy of the Spanish explorers. He has this to say in his address to the reader at the outset of his book:

If I had written to seek the world's favor, I should have bedecked
myself better and should present myself in a studied posture. I want to
be seen here in my simple, natural, ordinary fashion, without straining
or artifice; for it is myself I portray. My defects will here be read to the
life, and also my natural form, as far as respect for the public has
allowed. Had I been placed among those nations which are said to live
still in the sweet freedom of nature's first laws, I assure you I should
very gladly have portrayed myself here entire and wholly naked.

Thus, reader, I am myself the matter of my book; you would be
unreasonable to spend your leisure on so frivolous and vain a subject.

Seen in the context of the ensuing essays, the statement makes clear
Montaigne's belief in a New World self somehow more free than the
self he portrays. Situated in the Old World, Montaigne seeks the
natural form of himself but recognizes that "respect for the public" is
a factor inhibiting full disclosure.

No wonder Emerson admired Montaigne. He recognized the
strength and readiness of the essays and could hardly have failed to
hope that he, as a resident of the New World that Montaigne had so
well imagined but never reached, might realize the possiblity of the
naked self that Montaigne dreamed possible in a New World setting.
In a very real way Emerson in his own essays sought the naked energy
of the self. He not only wrote an essay on Montaigne; he wrote one
called "Experience" in which he stripped off the "lords of life" that
the self throws forward before it. The stripping away involved Emerson in a volatile series of "disillusions" that brought him to the
"scandalous poverty" of the self—the deep subjectiveness to which
every person is subject. The sequence of disillusions, comparable
with Montaigne's skepticism, leaves Emerson with nothing but the
self to believe in. His belief is nothing less than the energy of the
self—the last illusion, the sense of presence, that keeps the mind and
heart alive. Not refusing to believe in it but helpless not to believe in
it, Emerson contends that "in the solitude to which every man is
always returning, he has a sanity and revelations which in his passage
into new worlds he will carry with him."

It is far from insignificant, I think, that Emerson felt himself an
inhabitant of the New World that formed such a deep part of Montaigne's dialectic of the mind. Whereas Montaigne, looking out of his
library for the reports on the "nature" of the New World coming
toward him, made those reports function as a skeptical counterthrust

to the authority of the books and religion he so deeply knew, Emerson sought a relation to the being of the New World nature that would free him from all the past authority his nation had tried to leave behind. His quest was for the God at once in nature and the self that constitutes the *present* rather than for the institutionalized God of the church who had been deformed into rituals and inhibitions. His exhortation to *trust* the self was, in its modification of the Socratic admonition to know the self, a mediation between the active and the passive will—between desire for and acceptance of the possibilities of existence in a New World fatally free of yet haunted by the Old World. The self he both trusted and sought was remarkably close to the one that Montaigne's brave skepticism, weighing it in the scales of thought, had found he could not know.

For both writers, the self was the inscrutable energy that generated the sallies of the mind. Montaigne's essays are exemplary in their digression, their sturdy courage to pursue even as they represent the wayward freedom of the mind. Devoted to a vast variety of particular subjects—to thumbs, to drunkenness, to sleep, to war horses, to vehicles, to cannibals—they hit their mark glancingly, as if another subject were ever at the point of distracting them. Thus, no subject can dominate the restless yet relaxed self that meets it in passing. Emerson's essays are exemplary in their sustained abruptness of insight. Their subjects are the moral and mental abstractions that have traditionally come to dominate even as they describe human experience—nature, history, manners, prudence, heroism, fate, civilization, courage. Literally seeing through these abstract categories that subject the self, the Emersonian eye at once affirms and *sentences* them. The sentences are independent in both authority and conviction. Through them, the inherited categories of morality and thought, poised always to subject the self, are in turn subjected. Because their subjection is not so much by as *with* the self, they are freed from being the object of thought and make the transparencies of vision. Thus does the Old World become the New. The Emersonian self is literally the energy of this transition.

I dwell on Montaigne and Emerson at length because, steeped in literature as they were, they sought the energy of the self outside it. "Literature" is, after all, an exclusive province. Refined and cultivated in the period following the American and French revolutions, it became an institution capable of containing even the bold Romantic

writers who had done so much to remake it. This institutionalization
of literature goes hand in hand with the specialization and division of
labor that mark the progress of the nineteenth century. The result has
been an atrophy of what, in the eighteenth century, had been the
Republic of Letters. Historians, philosophers, scientists, economists
find themselves, as writers, confined to their own realms—outside
the domain of what we call, following Wordsworth and Coleridge,
the literature of the imagination. Theirs is a literature of science and
fact, excluded from "high" literature. Realizing that the great Romantic poets actually accelerated the division should give us pause.
The literature of fact, even as it is denied the status of *imagination,*
moves the practical world, whereas the literature of the imagination,
even as it possesses purity, seems more and more driven in on itself.
Shelley had believed that poets are the unacknowledged legislators of
the world. Students of literature today—and poets, too—are more
likely to feel their study and their work simply unacknowledged.
Great writers—Jefferson, Madison, Lincoln, Grant—whose writing
moved the world barely get a hearing in courses in American literature. They are given over to departments of government and history.

I am not complaining about this state of affairs so much as making
an observation about it. Emerson was not complaining about it in his
time, but he profoundly recognized it when he wrote in the concluding sentence of "Experience": "the true romance which the world
exists to realize will be the transformation of genius into practical
power." Still, we can neither teach nor read everything. There is,
moreover, an inevitable exclusionary or hierarchical principle at the
heart of writing—a principle that both activates and accelerates the
evaluative mechanism running in the head of every writer and reader
with the speed and silence of a dynamo. Canons are formed not only
because canonized books have enduring value (which they do) or
because national and social "special interests" develop powerful
systems for supporting and sustaining them (which they do), but
because we cannot read everything and need, like slaves, all the
authority we can get to tell us what we have to read. Not for nothing
are the great artists and writers called old masters; not for nothing are
we always looking for new ones.

Autobiography is at once an act and a convention lying between the
literature of the imagination and the literature of fact—a way to get
into the culture for those outside it and a way out for those inside it. It

is an attempt both to make and record a life. Some writers make more than they record, since the making may be all the record they have; others record more than they make. No autobiographer can avoid doing both. Making a life is not the same as making one up, though memory and all the motives involved in it sway the writer toward illusion and delusion. Recording a life threatens to enslave the self that made the record possible to the hard chronology of the record. Beyond that, there is a reserve of life that either will not or cannot be written.

The following essays are concerned about autobiography but not, I dearly hope, obsessed with it. The individual writings and writers always interested me more than any wish for theory or unity I ever had. Just writing on Jefferson, Grant, and Booker T. Washington made me feel the pleasure of getting out and away from standard courses in literature. Writing on Grant led me back to a long-standing interest in the Civil War and at the same time forward to Shelby Foote's great narrative that had been published in the years I had been away from that war. I have included my essay on it in this collection because Foote's narrative, if not a work about his life, is a great life work. Then too, if there is such a thing as literature, surely Foote has written it in those three extraordinary volumes. Yet just as surely, it is history and tallies with a strong historical component in the auto-biographies I have found myself writing about. Finally, my essay on those volumes gets me out of autobiography even as the volumes speak to my abiding concern in these essays: the enlargement of the domain of literature by recovering its lost dimensions.

I could not end this preface without extending thanks to people who helped more than they know in the making of these essays: to the trustees of the Guggenheim Foundation for supporting my study of autobiography; to my colleagues Henry Terrie, Edward Bradley, and Louis Renza—the first for teaching me about the possibilities of American literature through all my years at Dartmouth, the second for literally guiding me on a line of learning leading from the classical world through St. Augustine to Montaigne and Rousseau, and the third for teaching me more about autobiography and literary theory than I thought possible; to James Olney, whose work on autobiography and whose support of my own work have sustained me all along my way; to Lewis Simpson, whose writing on American literature represents for me an ideal standard of humane learning; to George

Core, whose generous and insistent encouragement prevailed over my constitutional reluctance to collect them from their fugitive existence; to Nate Clark, whose careful typescript prepared them for publication; to John Easterly, whose able editing helped this book in more than a hundred ways; and, finally, to Beverly Jarrett, whose gracious faith and persistence made this book a fact.

AUTOBIOGRAPHY AND AMERICA

⸻⸱⸱◦∞◦⸱⸱⸻

Autobiography and confessional writing are now receiving much more critical attention than they used to, and not merely because criticism has exhausted the other genres and is moving in on a relatively virgin field. For something has happened to the whole idea of literature in the last twenty-five years. To remember that novelists such as Truman Capote and Norman Mailer have in *In Cold Blood* and *The Armies of the Night* challenged the distinction between nonfiction and fiction; to be reminded that biography and autobiography are more marketable products than fiction; to realize that *The Autobiography of Malcolm X* is somehow one of the great imaginative works of the 1960s; to recall that, in 1969, Michel Butor told an MLA audience in Denver that there is no real difference between fiction and nonfiction, between a novel and an autobiography; and to know that a conference of an English Institute session was devoted to confessional literature—to reflect upon all this is to begin to acknowledge that much more has happened than a mere opportunistic exploitation of a neglected field.

Much of this change is, I think, a result of, and a response to, the revolutionary political attitudes and feelings that fully emerged in the 1960s and early 1970s. When politics and history become dominant realities for the imagination, then the traditional prose forms of the essay and the autobiography both gain and attract power, and the more overtly "literary" forms of prose fiction—the novel and the short story—are likely to be threatened and impoverished. As such a process takes place—as politics and history tend to claim dominion over the imagination—then the literary imagination tends to respond by denying the generic distinctions that are both powerful and convenient categories in periods of stability and peace. Of course the problem is much more complicated, but these remarks may provide some sense of a developing present that can be related to my sense of the past importance of autobiography in America.

Autobiography has been important in this country. As I shall suggest, the very idea of autobiography has grown out of the political necessities and discoveries of the American and French revolutions. It is no mere accident that an astonishingly large proportion of the slender shelf of so-called American classics is occupied by autobiographies. Certainly *Walden* and *The Education of Henry Adams* would rank in almost anybody's list of the ten major American prose works, novels included. I would also include Franklin's *Autobiography,* though there would doubtless be dissenters from, as well as adherents to, such a choice. Even so, I have chosen Franklin, Thoreau, and Adams primarily because they are central and not peripheral writers, are indeed classic American writers in the sense that their acts of imagination in the form of autobiography are unforgettable imaginative experiences. Whitman offers a problem that I shall face when I reach him.

So much for preliminaries. There remains the question of just what autobiography is, and despite the present tendency to blur generic distinctions, I want to try to keep them, and not simply as a convenience but as a necessary means of clarifying the whole subject. Strictly speaking, of course, autobiography is not a genre at all in the sense that poetry, fiction, and drama are. It is a term designating a subclass of that hopelessly confusing variety of writing we place under the heading of nonfictional prose. Yet of all the subclassifications in that inchoate group, autobiography and biography are probably the clearest in our minds. We at least think we know what we mean when we speak of autobiography and biography, and we are equally sure that others mean the same thing when they speak of them. Thus, in answer to the question "What is autobiography?" I want to hold to the definition I believe we all know: a narrative of a person's life written by himself. Autobiography is in this sense the story of a life, but here there is a problem, for it is not the story but the history of a life; it is history and not fiction—which raises the further issue of distinguishing between history and fiction. Without rushing to or yearning for conclusive definitions of the two, we can at least see that both history and fiction are at base narratives, the distinction being that one narrative is based on fact, the other on invention. The one tells a story of what did happen, the other of what did not; the one can be corroborated by public and private record, the other has to protect itself against the possibility of being taken literally. All this is of course commonplace, but it is often forgotten by critics of autobiography who begin to exercise the poetics of fiction in the analysis of autobiography.

There is another striking difference between the nature of historical and fictive narrative. In historical narrative the beginning and the ending are by necessity arbitrary and unreal (perhaps *untrue* would be the better term), for history has no beginning and no end. Thus historians must set up a principle of organization that will justify a beginning and an ending, concealing their intrusion into the irreversible historical stream. Historians therefore write of the history of nations, of wars, of movements, of ideas, of governments, of decades, of explorations, always segmenting the continuous narrative line of history. Their exits and entrances are the two sure fictive aspects of their form, and though they may achieve freedom of interpretation along the way, they are bound to the fact and the sequence of past events. Writers of fiction, on the other hand, have to begin and they have to end, for fiction is all invention, and its sure truths are that it does begin and does end. That is the inescapable necessity for novelists, and their whole effort is to realize that truth—to make the beginning and the ending as fatal and as final as they truly are.

Autobiographical narrative falls between history and fictive narrative in this respect. If it is clearly historical in nature, it at least does have a beginning: the birth of its subject. True, the autobiographer, unless he has a prodigious memory, cannot remember his birth without becoming Shandean, but at least he can chronicle it from hearsay or he can begin with his first memory. In any event he has a point of beginning that is logical and incontrovertible, though of course he can deviate from such a point, beginning with a history of his parents, if he were a biographer, or at an arbitrary point in his life almost as if he were a novelist. He cannot, however, write about his death. Thus, the great event that is the goal of the biographer is forever inaccessible to the autobiographer, though he may establish a kind of pattern of his life that will enable him to treat it as if it were ended. There is another point that relates autobiography to fiction: autobiography is the life of a person, and both it and biography have subject matter that likens them to fiction, which is dependent on characters, that is, representations of persons.

These reflections, though they by no means define autobiography, do put us in a position to see rudimentary issues of autobiographical form. But there is also a historical problem about autobiography that is directly related to the subject of American autobiography. We are prone to think that autobiography preceded America, for if we know anything, we know that there were great autobiographers before the American nation existed. St. Augustine, Cellini, Montaigne, and Casanova come quickly to mind. But it is a fact worth recording that autobiography as a term did not exist at the time of the American Revolution. It was first used, according to the *Oxford English Dictionary,* by Robert Southey in a review of Portuguese literature in 1809. Before the emergence of the term, there were two categories of people's lives written by themselves: the confession and the memoir. The confession was an account of a man's private life, centering on his emotions, feelings, secrets, frustrations—essentially his private world. The memoir was more on the order of chronicle, relating to the individual's role upon the stage of history. The confession bared the inner thoughts; the memoir recounted the career. It is impossible to say just why autobiography should have emerged as a term to include both confession and memoir, but it may be helpful to note its appearance just after the age of revolution, when the modern self was being liberated as well as defined. For the American and French revolutions, whatever else they did, were the convulsive acts that released the individual as a potent political entity and gave us what we are pleased to call modern man. And each nation produced in this revolutionary period a classic account of the self: Rousseau's *Confessions* and Franklin's *Memoir* (for Franklin had only the old term with which to name his book).

In this connection it is worth noting that the corresponding classic in English literature of the period is a biography, Boswell's *Life of Johnson.* Thus, while America and France were readying for revolution, Franklin and Rousseau at almost the same moment in history were embarking on decisive accounts of themselves, while in England (which was desperately staving off revolution) Boswell was devoting himself to a biography of Johnson. Moreover, his relationship to his subject was constructed in terms of hierarchy. Yet if Boswell submitted to Johnson, Johnson in turn submitted himself to biography, and the completed work resulted in fulfillment for both men, since Boswell's remarkable revelation and recording of Johnson's talk raised Johnson's stature in English literature from a position of nobility to one of monarchy.

*　　*　　*

But Franklin and Rousseau were very great revolutionaries, and while Johnson was writing his pamphlet against the American Revolution (an act that Boswell regretted), they were engaged in liberating themselves in accounts of their own lives. These accounts were no mere records of their pasts, but genuine acts of life, not mere ways of saying but essential acts of being. Thus, Rousseau, after showing talent in a host of ways—as musician, social philosopher, pamphleteer, and novelist—at last liberated the self that stood behind yet could not be released by all the forms of expression he had tried. "I felt before I thought," he announced near the beginning of his *Confessions,* and his entire book was devoted to the generative life of feeling. The self that emerges in his pages is, with all its contradictions, something new and powerful in literature.

Instead of recording shame and later conversion in the manner of St. Augustine, Rousseau gives a nearly shameless revelation of himself, prefaced by a dare to all men to say whether they are better than he. Such a dare would be mere rhetoric if Rousseau in the course of his confessions did not exceed the wildest expectations of what an inner self might be. If his perversity and his revelations about his thwarted, devious, deviant, and frantic sexuality evoke surprise, his defenses of himself evoke outrage, and his pleas for justice by posterity are likely to provoke judgment and suppression on the part of those who wish for order. Small wonder that Johnson deplored Rousseau, for the self that Rousseau releases is the very self that Johnson's whole life was bent upon checking. Indeed Rousseau's release of such a self was the promise of the revolution that Johnson could feel in his very bones and that his whole style was both continuously and precariously subduing.

How different is Franklin's life. Johnson himself would have been hard put to disapprove it. Whereas Rousseau had released his inner life in the form of confession, Franklin chronicled his public life. Yet just as Rousseau had transformed the confession, Franklin transformed the memoir. Although Franklin chronicles his rise from obscurity to prominence, he does not suppress his emotional life so much as he shows the process of converting, using, and incorporating his desires, inner conflicts, doubts, and frustrations into a model life that in its turn can also be used by posterity. Thus, having organized a philosophical society, a university, a hospital, a lending library, and an efficient postal system, and having invented the stove, the smoke-less streetlamp, bifocals, electrical conduction, the harmonica, and a host of other items too numerous to mention, Franklin at the age of sixty-five embarked upon what one wants to call his greatest in-vention—the invention of himself, not as fiction, but as a fact both of and in history.

What is truly interesting is that Franklin's act of conceiving, dis-covering, or inventing himself almost exactly coincides with the birth of America. Franklin began his autobiography in England in 1771, just as he was becoming fully involved in the emerging separation from England, came back to work on it in France in 1784, worked on it again in 1788, and was once more involved with it months before his death in 1791. When he died, he had brought the record of his life forward to 1757—to that point when he was at the threshold of the professional diplomatic life, the life of his country, that would both occupy and preoccupy him for the rest of his days.

But Franklin is a true writer and, like Rousseau, is as interested in the act of writing as in what he writes about. He states at the outset that he is writing because he has a moment's time free from his diplomatic duties. He is therefore writing not simply out of leisure but as leisure, and his celebrated simple style, with its even tenor, equals the motive and act of leisure with which he begins. More than that, he sees his act of writing as the next-best thing to living his life over again, and he thus sees his memoir not as a record but as a second edition in which the sins of his life (which would have enormous emotional weight in the confessional form) become the mere errata of the first edition that he can point to and playfully wish to remove.

Even more important, he dates the time of his writing so that the dates of composition I referred to are not biographical information but textual reality. Thus the "life," which is to say Franklin's ac-count of his early years, is placed between the years 1771 and 1788, the years of the American Revolution, confederation, and the Con-stitution. What literally happens in the form of Franklin's work is that the history of the revolution, in which Franklin played such a conspicuous part, is displaced by the narrative of Franklin's early life, so that Franklin's personal history *stands in place of the revolu-tion.* Now the personal history that Franklin puts in place of revolu-tionary history recounts Franklin's rise from political anonymity and impotence to the position of agent for his colony, representing the people of Pennsylvania against the proprietors who reside in England. Thus, his life begins in Boston, where freedom of the press is threatened by the crown and where freedom of impulse is threatened by his older brother; it ends in London, where he is defending the colony from the attempted encroachments of the proprietors. But this represented history was not the actual revolution. There still remained the form that would realize the revolution and thus stand for it. That form was the autobiography—the life of a self-made, self-governing man written by the man himself. Although Franklin had only the term *memoir,* it is not difficult to see why, in the light of what both he and Rousseau were doing to memoir and confession, a new term would be possible as well as necessary.

We can now turn to the structure of Franklin's autobiography to see how Franklin's history reveals the man. For Rousseau, life is total crisis; his life is defined in terms of one intense feeling after another. For Franklin, there is no crisis. For Rousseau, all life is a turning point, and he thus finds himself time after time insisting that such and such an event fixed his fate. For Franklin, there is no turning point; all events are essentially equal, and that equality is not the mere inertness of a chronicle but a way of being that both reveals and reflects Franklin the man. Everything being essentially equal, Franklin is never trapped in or attached to events but is free to see them with detachment and curiosity. Thus, because Franklin sees street drainage and street lighting as being equal to lawmaking and political theory, he is free from self-absorption as he walks home from assembly sessions to think about the possibility of inventions. His detached vision objectifies ideas, equalizes all concerns, and frees him to experiment with and concentrate upon a whole variety of probabilities.

Similarly, he is free in his form, for he makes use of the very limitations of the memoir. Thus, he converts the limitation of being unable to catch up with his life and write of his death into the freedom of stopping his account whenever he wants to. After all, whenever he wants to or has to stop, whether for business or death, will be the end. That of course is Franklin's freedom of form, and we do not find ourselves dissatisfied or wishing for more when Franklin does stop. He could have stopped with the first section of the book, written in 1771 (he actually did stop and, resuming in 1784 at the request of two Philadelphia friends, he published their letters as a kind of advertisement of himself and his life), because he is not seeing his life in terms of turning point or finale, but as usable history: usable for others as a record of converting private desires into public life and private passions into rigorous self-government; usable for himself as leisure and amusement during a time of preoccupation with revolutionary duties. For the life he was able to recount in those few leisure moments was precisely the life that brought him to the fate of a career and yet remained the old free experience in which he retained the possibility of doing everything or anything. He wrote that life during the period when his career was fixed not to recapture or relive the old free life (Franklin, unlike Rousseau, does not recall or remember or yearn for his past) but to assert that life as fact and put it in place of revolutionary history.

All this may seem far-fetched speculation to those who wish to think that Franklin was just writing away on his life without any notion of writing a revolutionary book. Surely these speculations would at best amuse Franklin, but it is well in dealing with Franklin's consciousness to try to be as shrewdly calculating as he himself was. For Franklin knew he was going to be a revolutionary not only before the revolution but before he began his autobiography. Two weeks before he embarked upon the autobiography, he wrote to James Otis, Thomas Cushing, and Samuel Adams one of the most visionary letters of the eighteenth century. Acquainting them with the repressive attitude of Parliament and the crown, he forecast the steps of the revolution that was to come.

> I think one may clearly see, in the system of customs to be exacted in America by act of Parliament, the seeds sown of a total disunion of the two countries, though as yet that event may be at a considerable distance. The course and natural progress seems to be, first, the appointment of needy men as officers, for others do not care to leave England; then, their necessities make them rapacious, their office makes them proud and insolent, their insolence and rapacity make them odious, and, being conscious that they are hated, they become malicious; their malice urges them to a continual abuse of the inhabitants in their letters to administration, representing them as disaffected and rebellious, and (to encourage the use of severity) as weak, divided, timid, and cowardly. Government believes all; thinks it necessary to support and countenance its officers; their quarreling with the people is deemed a mark and consequence of their fidelity; they are therefore more highly rewarded, and this makes their conduct still more insolent and provoking.

The resentment of the people will, at times and on particular incidents, burst into outrages and violence upon such officers, and this
naturally draws down severity and acts of further oppression from
hence. The more the people are dissatisfied the more rigor will be
thought necessary; severe punishments will be inflicted to terrify;
rights and privileges will be abolished; greater force will then be
required to secure execution and submission; the expense will become
enormous; it will then be thought proper, by fresh exactions, to make
the people defray it; thence the British nation and government will
become odious, and subjection to it will be deemed no longer toler-
able; war ensues, and the bloody struggle will end in absolute slavery
to America or ruin to Britain by the loss of her colonies: the latter most
probable, from America's growing strength and magnitude.

Franklin not only saw the coming revolution; he calculated the
probable outcome. It may make him an unglamorous revolutionary to
have had such vision, since one does not seem much like a revolutionary if one has seen so much and calculated so shrewdly. It is also
worth remembering that Franklin was sixty-five when he determined
upon revolution, an old age to begin such an enterprise, but the fact
may serve as a model of possibility, a reminder that one does not have
to be young or desperate or hopeless to engage in a great revolution.

So Franklin's act of art in the *Autobiography* does not seem revolutionary; it seems even and easy and simple. But it is there in the path,
and the best one can do to those professors of English who conde-
scend to it is to say simply and innocently that it is the first American
book we have. Before Franklin there was no American literature;
there was only English colonial literature. With Franklin came consciousness, total consciousness in the form of autobiography—a history of a self-made life written by the man who made it. It is not a
fiction but a cultural fact of life, and we have to make the best of it.

To make the best of it is to see the great American autobiography that
followed not only in relation to Franklin's initial act but in relation to
the history of the country. Here it is worth noting that Thoreau's
Walden, by all admission the next great American autobiography,
appears in 1854, at just the moment the nation was moving toward
civil war, reminding us that autobiography becomes more possible
when history and politics seem to possess the very drama we seek in
stage and fictive experience in periods of equanimity and peace. In

any event *Walden* did appear in 1854, and it was much concerned
with the issues of slavery and abolition, which were splitting the
nation apart. But it was also autobiography, and Thoreau, like Franklin and Rousseau before him, was both revolutionary and writer.
Thus, writing for him was, as it was for them, not simply the record of
experience but an act of life, a making of experience. Moreover,
Thoreau, for all his differences from Franklin, does not turn inward
upon himself or his feelings but looks out upon a world of natural
fact. He, too, proposes a model life, and though it is not presented as
a model to follow but one to equal, it is a life that Thoreau, like
Franklin before him, has made for himself.

Yet this model life is much more than a making or recording of
experience. It was for Thoreau a finishing of experience, and Thoreau's experiment in form is most dramatically evident in his determination to reach a conclusion, thereby completing his life—just
what Franklin and Rousseau, by virtue of their choice of form, cannot
do. There is a cost, of course, for Thoreau in order to complete his life
has to take a part of it—the two years he spent at Walden Pond ten
years earlier—and make that part stand for the whole. He went much
further. He compressed the two years into one, letting the cycle of the
seasons stand for the completed circle of the self. To make his style
realize such a conception of the self, Thoreau sought a language at
once metaphoric and concise. Yet for all the wit and concision of his
language, there is always the fact of Walden Pond, a fact that lies
outside himself and outside language as both a seal and a promise of
his own reality. Much as Thoreau may play upon the analogies of the
pond to his own life, its existence as a natural fact is as important for
him as it is for us. That is why we cannot imagine Walden being a
fiction, even though when we visit it today, we inevitably realize that
we did not really have to go there.

What Thoreau aimed to do was to translate the particular fact of
Walden into the possibilities of being himself. Working steadily along
analogical lines with that startling clarity of his, he saw himself as
much a metaphor of Walden as it was of him. Because it was a pond,
because it was self-contained, because it had the purity and clarity to
reflect his image against the heavens, it became the reservoir of
possibilities he could realize only in relation to it. The cycle of the
seasons brooding over it was the natural time in which he determined
to cast his life. And the hut he began to construct along its shores in

the spring, occupied on July 4, and closed in with the coming of the ice upon Walden, gains significance always in relation to the pond that Thoreau, true surveyor that he was, maps and scrutinizes even as it reflects the self.

The self that emerges from the analogy is a far cry from the selves Franklin and Rousseau had discovered. Franklin, in concentrating on the externality of his past, had shown largely by implication in his style and structure the conversion of his inner self into a social and political self. Thus, his "success" is an exemplary narrative implicitly depicting the sublimation of private energies into social action. Rousseau's experiential narration is almost the inverse of Franklin's. He discloses his progressive alienation from society—the long process by which he withdrew by stages from society to his island in a lake. His island is a perfect equivalent of the embattled, moated, insular present consciousness that at once generates and releases the past that has grown inside him.

For all their difference in self-conception, however, both Rousseau and Franklin realize themselves narratively and chronologically. In *Walden* both narration and chronology tend to disappear, for just as a single year is being made to stand for a whole life, essence is always taking precedence over existence. Thoreau is neither taking over nor withdrawing from society. He stands between it and the pond in a constant attitude of seeing in Walden—Earth's Eye—an image of himself austerely and severely against society. That severity becomes Thoreau's fierce irony and makes the reading of *Walden* a humiliating as well as an exhilarating experience. The exhilaration comes from the kind of joy and independence Thoreau achieves in his insular solitude beside the pond. The humiliation comes from his almost savage criticism and exposure of the condition of man in his own time and, by ruthless implication, in all time to come. Thoreau challenges his reader like a persecuting conscience. He says at the beginning that he writes not for the strong and self-reliant souls, if such there be, but for those who find themselves somehow unhappy with their lot. He shows in the course of his revolutionary life the possibilities that lie near at hand—as near and as familiar as Walden—but he also exposes the shabby lot society has made of life, revealing in a way that no other book has revealed not only that we can do what we want but that, alas! we have already done what we wanted, that as Americans we are always free to be free but that also as Americans we always choose to be slaves. That is why he brilliantly begins with the chapter on economy, showing the minimal requirements not simply for survival but for fulfillment. Writing almost on the eve of the Civil War, Thoreau sees freedom not as Franklin's self-making but as self-possession. And he sees the self not as a means but as an end. Thus, unlike Franklin and Rousseau, he does indeed have a conclusion in which the self is completed in an ecstasy of possibility, a radiance and radiation of analogy and metaphor.

Yet Thoreau does not reach a conclusion so much as he is all conclusion, and his language is not a means to relate his history so much as it is itself his very essence—the literal translation of his being into symbol. That is why his whole direction is not to naturalize himself but to spiritualize nature, to overcome and subdue it, thereby becoming an ideal that will both afflict and elevate his reader. His language, his whole act of writing, is bent always toward finish, refinement, and purity (in the full and not the genteel meaning of those words). In order to achieve a representative life, one that will stand for a complete life, Thoreau accentuates his individuality. The tension in his consciousness and his style is thus always between universality and eccentricity, for in order to dramatize the universality of the individual, Thoreau emphasizes the uniqueness of the self. His equivalent act in language is to take such a personal hold of it that its abstractions are bent to his will and wit. Insofar as he determines to represent man, he means to render a concrete life different from the lives of others. The very burden of being an individual is to discover one's own way, which of necessity must take the individual to a land as distant, as austere, and as self-contained as the Walden Pond he keeps discovering. These are the terms as well as the burden of Thoreau's self-possession.

All this is of course self-evident, and I would not think of claiming freshness of insight into *Walden*. To approach such insight, I need the presence of Whitman. I know that his presence in my list of autobiographers must seem anomalous. It is anomalous, for Whitman is a poet if he is anything, and to begin to play fast and loose with categories is to begin to play the devil. If autobiography is narrative and history, then it is not poem and prophecy. So my chief aim is not to claim Whitman as autobiographer, but to use him to gain a perspective on Thoreau. Yet I cannot forbear a few defenses of having included him. After all, he did write a poem entitled "Song of Myself," which, considered in relation to Wordsworth's *Prelude* and Coleridge's *Biographia Literaria,* reminds us how pervasive the autobiographical form in literature became after the American and French revolutions. Moreover, Henry James, Jr., in reviewing Whitman's poetry, said that whatever Whitman's medium was, it was not poetry, though he went on to observe that it was not prose either. As far as James could make out in that early review (he happily lived to revise his opinion), Whitman's poetry was an incredibly vulgar offense against the muse herself, a blatant exhibition of self that no one concerned with the craft and glory of art could condone. Art for James was a subduing of the self through form and language. James's criticism is still remarkably apt for anyone who has not genteelized Whitman with respectability, for Whitman is and should be hard to take. Instead of the fine economy we find in Thoreau's language, the wit, the intelligence, the precision, the exactness, there is a great deal of wind, flatness, and abstraction. There is much, much more, to be sure, but one of the feelings that Whitman's poetry inspires and clearly means to inspire is that we the readers could do as well—that, indeed, if this is poetry, then what is not?

Thoreau had sought to create a sharply individualized consciousness that would stand for the possibilities of self-possession and had announced at the outset that though the first-person pronoun was dropped in many a personal narrative, he would retain it. Whitman went another way. Seizing upon the crucial fact that in the pronominal system of the English language there is no distinction in form between the second-person singular and plural, he was able to address his reader as *you* and be at once personal and general. He added to that radical formal discovery an audacious democratic program of asserting an identification between the "I" of the poet and the "you"— both singular and plural—of all to whom his poetry would prophesy. Whereas Thoreau's direction had been to translate his flesh into spirit and himself into concrete metaphor, Whitman's inspiration was to speak the word of himself, thereby creating the reader as poet. The reader would be the concrete emotional self, the embodiment of the word. Thus Thoreau's austerity and solitude; thus Whitman's constant emphasis upon love and union.

Considered in relation to their time, Whitman is the poet of union, Thoreau the voice of secession, the most powerful voice of secession in our literature. I do not mean that Thoreau was a southerner at heart. He was not. He was a Yankee, but Yankees had been old revolutionaries, and revolution had meant separation from authority. It took the genius of Lincoln to transform the old revolutionary impulse toward separation, which was as deep a part of American identity as the wish for union, into a national will for union, and it took a bloody civil war to establish the Union as an irrevocable reality. It is hardly surprising in this connection that Thoreau should have died quietly while the war raged in the South and that Whitman, who was totally prepared for the Civil War, could go to the battlefield and hospitals as a male nurse, could kiss the soldiers of the South as well as those of the North, could—best of all—write letters home for the wounded and dying, could fully see Lincoln from the moment he took the stage (even Emerson could hardly see him), and could write "When Lilacs Last in the Dooryard Bloom'd" almost the moment Lincoln was assassinated. If Milton had moved from elegy through losing civil war toward epic, Whitman moved from epic through victorious civil war toward elegy, translating the dead bodies of all his brave soldiers into the leaves of grass whose roots (as he had epically promised in 1855) came out of the faint red roofs of the mouths of the dead. The leaves of grass were nothing less than the living tongues of the dead. For if love was the impulse that would create the future reader, death was the event that Whitman had to translate. How else could there be immortality of the flesh? It is not immortality of the spirit that interests Whitman—any Baptist preacher could indulge that argument—but immortality of the flesh. Thus, that magnificent line near the end of "Song of Myself": "I effuse my flesh in eddies and drift it in lacy jags." And thus the pun on leaves of grass and leaves of the book.

To face that pun fully is to remember Walden once more. For in Thoreau's chapter on spring, just before his conclusion, he describes the breaking up of the ice on Walden and the thawing of the frozen earth. Standing before the railroad bankside, which man has cut in nature, Thoreau sees the spring rivulets tenderly eroding the fresh earth and forming miniature alluvial fans whose shape takes the forms of primordial leaves. Playing upon the analogy, Thoreau sees earth's whole excretory process as a purification into, and a promise of, the leaves to come. Almost like a savage, he tries to make a language from the very word *leaf,* expanding it into *lobe,* gutturally evolving it further into *globe,* and at last wishing that earth's primal form will be translated into the leaves of his book so that he can turn over a new leaf at last. Just as the excretion of the world's body becomes the delicate leaf above the earth, Thoreau wants his words and pages to be the purification of his flesh into pure spirit, a resurrection of the body. Whitman, on the other hand, seeks to say and be the word that will descend into the body, and his urge as well as his vision is literally to embrace the world and become it, to embrace reader and readers and become them, to be the tongue that invades every part of the body and gives every part an equal voice—a radical democratization of both body and body politic and an immortal union of himself with the world of readers he is creating, so that "Song of Myself" will, when we begin to grasp it, be true to its title—the song of ourselves, the instantaneous miracle that makes us poets, putting us at the threshold of a living faith that, lo and behold, we are the living poem that Whitman's new biblical verse has created.

It is a long way from Thoreau and Whitman to Henry Adams, largely because Adams himself sought to make the space in time as wide as possible. Yet as differently as he saw and created his life from theirs, like them he eschews the confessional element in autobiography. He does not remember, explain, or defend his past in the manner of Mill and Newman any more than he wishes to confess and reveal it in the manner of Rousseau, but like Franklin and Thoreau, he makes use of it and makes it useful. His, too, is a model life, but not a paradigm like Franklin's or a challenge like Thoreau's, for his whole notion of a model life is that of a manikin—a figure in which clothing, outline, and pattern are everything, the life nothing but plaster and sawdust, an elusive and ironic joke at the center of education, which is at once history, the thought into which life has died, and art, the narrative upon which life is spent. Being a historian, Adams saw life as history; being an autobiographer, he knew he had to make life art. Being these and being an Adams, too, he dared to identify his history with that of his country. Comprehending these strands of being in a single narrative, he left an autobiography that drew life from the autobiography that had gone before him and abundantly gave meaning back to it.

There are two striking facts of form in Adams' *Education*. First, it is written in the third person and therefore guarantees the possibility of completeness. Second, it has a gap in the center, a vacuum of twenty years about which Adams hardly speaks. We know—and such a fact of form forces us to wonder if we do not know—what happened during those twenty years. He taught at Harvard (he touches upon this fact) and was therefore not a student of life. He wrote history (he alludes to this at points along his way) and was thus a historian instead of being a part of history. And he married, only to experience the tragedy of his wife's suicide (he alludes only once to that harrowing event, telling of watching in Rock Creek Cemetery the people who came to see Saint-Gaudens' great sculpture of grief that monumentalized his wife's grave). These three acts are the silence in the midst of life, and the autobiography surrounding them is the act of mind converting them into their opposite. The teacher is converted into the student Henry Adams; the historian is converted into the victim and expression of history; the grief-stricken husband is converted into the pleasure-seeker of the mind whose whole act of play is to convert his past into a third person in an act of joyful suicide.

To see these paradoxes is to begin to grasp the consequences of Adams' third-person narration, consequences that Adams embraces with almost dismaying enthusiasm. Thoreau had retained the "I" but in order to achieve a completed self was forced into the synecdochic strategy of making a part stand for the whole. Adams, however, by converting himself into the third person, was able to treat himself not as character—for characters are in fiction and drama, not in autobiography—but as history. The consequences of such a strategy are enormous. If the self is truly history, then it is somehow past, and Adams would become merely the biographer of himself. Yet Adams is not a biographer but an autobiographer and of all things the *Education* is not, one is surely biography. It is rather a division of the self into two parts, two poles—a past and a present—in which the present self generates the past self as history. The new Henry Adams, the present generative consciousness, which in conventional historical terms grew out of the past, is by virtue of Adams' inversion actually releasing and attracting the old Henry Adams (he would be the young Adams in conventional terms) toward his source. Adams fully realizes these inversions by means of a style that can best be described as a series of paradoxes riding upon a narrative current.

The new Adams, the present Adams, who is as much the source as the end of the past, constantly exposes the descent of the old Adams, who, born too late into history from a line of presidents and fated for successes and power, steadily failed. The old Adams, always unprepared for contingency, is drawn forward—not recorded or chronicled—through the resistance of history toward the moment of the present which is the hidden "I" that he can never reach. That is the fate of Adams' form that casts the self as history. The old Adams' approach to the present is as a victim of forces beyond his control, a child amid theory, politics, technology, and accelerating history. Everything he is made to learn merely unprepares him for the past through which he is drawn. He is the great-grandson and the grandson of presidents only to feel himself cast aside from the sources of power; he goes to Harvard only to discover himself a fool in Europe; he faces the Civil War as a loyal Union man only to discover that the real treason was the betrayal of his father by Charles Sumner, the most trusted family friend; he goes to England as secretary for his father, the ambassador, in an effort to secure the balance of power they think England holds only to discover that the Civil War has already shifted the power to America and that England by remaining neutral has actually fallen behind history; he learns evolution only to return to America and find Grant in the White House; he attempts to expose the economic scandals of the Grant era only to find himself in touch with the energy of capital—which defies all his calculations; he teaches medieval history at Harvard only to discover his total ignorance of all history; he writes the history of the early years of the Republic only to recognize that the ideas of humanistic history are completely negated by the laws of physical energy. And so at last he attempts to learn the laws of science in an effort to plot force and energy in time, thereby making the art of history a science possessing predictive force, only to realize that acceleration is the law of history. Having made his predictions and seen the law of acceleration, he steps aside.

This series of belated recognitions constitutes the history and the failure of the old Adams, but it is failure generated by the polarity of the new Henry Adams in relation to the old. Indeed, the new Adams is literally *educating* the old Adams, giving the title an active and present sense that is often overlooked. Moreover, he is educating him all the time, at every instant of the narrative. For the education is nothing less than the act and vision whereby the new Adams ironically objectifies the old as a victim of history. If the old Adams is being educated by the new, the discovery is not simply one of gloomy personal failure but of the failure of all the history he has lived through—the dissolution of an old order of causation into a new energy. Thus, the nineteenth century dissolves into the twentieth, exposing in the process the fact that the men of power—thinkers, politicians, and diplomats—were not simply wrong but did not even know what they were doing, were indeed victims of the power and drift of history. Their ignorance was but one more mass of energy for the historian to measure in terms of its force.

As the old Henry Adams is attracted toward the new, his life is taken not as a loss or grief but as a conversion, and not the conversion of confessional form—the conversion of man into God, as in Augustine, or into feeling, as in Rousseau—but a conversion into historical force, so that autobiographical narrative does not displace history, as in Franklin, but becomes an ironic vision of history. The moment of conversion is, as everyone knows, Adams' vision of the dynamo in the gallery of machines at the Paris Exposition of 1900, six hundred years after Dante's vision of Beatrice. The dynamo is the beautiful objectification of Adams' act of form, for it comes into being at precisely the moment when the old Henry Adams has been attracted to the present source of his energy. True to his form at this moment when he envisions the dynamo as the end of the old Adams, the new Adams is able to see an opposite force, not forward in time but backward in history; he sees the Virgin.

These then become the poles of past and future that the old and the new Adams generate as they meet at the beginning of the twentieth century; they are at the same time the poles of energy that constitute Adams' conversion, for they make possible his dynamic theory and act of history. Because it is at once theory (an analytic formulation about past and future) and act (a literal attraction of the old Adams to the source that has generated him), it can become a genuine vision, but a vision in Adamic, not in Augustinian, terms, for it is a conversion of the self not into divine but into historical lines of force. That is why Adams' vision of the future is not so much prophetic as it is speculative.

Happily for us, the poles of dynamo and Virgin are also beautifully conclusive as a vision of autobiography and America. For Adams' discovery of the dynamo takes us directly back to our point of departure. After all, Franklin not only invented American autobiography; he also discovered—*fathered* might be the better term—electricity, and those Promethean acts bind him deeply to Adams' form and substance. More than that, there was an old family score for Adams to settle, and though Adams was terribly ironic about himself and his progenitors, he *was* an Adams through and through and had a way of dealing with the Jeffersons and Randolphs, who had thwarted his great-grandfather. Franklin in Paris during the American Revolution had driven John Adams to distraction with his social ease, detachment, and wit. While John Adams toiled, Franklin seemed to play and yet reap all the praise. The whole miserable contrast so piqued Adams that he confided his exasperation to his journal. In disclosing the dynamo as the essence of America and the future that would be American, Henry Adams was settling old scores even as he was being utterly true to his form. If Franklin had seen autobiography as self-generation, Adams would show the end of self-generation. Instead of seeing his life as the rise from obscurity to prominence, Adams saw it as the descent from prominence into obscurity and utter posthumous silence. Instead of treating life as a chronicle of success, Adams showed it as both the history of failure and the failure of history. Thus, at the moment of his conversion the old Adams feels like worshiping the dynamo, but the new Adams generates the opposite of the dynamo—the Virgin of a deeper, more primal past. For what autobiography as self-generation perforce left out was woman, the force that had moved the medieval world in Adams' illuminated vision of the past and yet the force that had been rendered irrelevant by American autobiography and revolution. There were no women in Franklin's world of the self-invented self—only the wife as helpmeet in the most practical sense and as a practical object for excess sexual energy. There were no women at all in Thoreau's world. Although there was a feminine principle in Whitman, he hermaphroditically absorbed it as he absorbed Kanada and Missouri and Montana.

And so Adams delightfully chose the Virgin, not at all as a converted Catholic, possibly as atonement and love for the wife who had killed herself, certainly as a pleasure-seeker in history, where he could be a tourist to his heart's desire.

All this is much, but it is not all. Adams declared an end to education, autobiography, and history in 1905, the year John Hay concluded the treaty between Russia and Japan. That marked the end of Adams' old eighteenth-century provincial America, the America of Franklin's invention. That America had moved from peripheral and povincial entity to become *the* treaty-making power in the West, and thus a line of force to meet the inertia of Russia and China in the East.

Thus, the city that had drawn his ancestors from Quincy and Boston and that Adams, having failed to occupy as president, had occupied as historian, was now the center of power in the West—the point from which Adams could let the energy of his mind run its own lines of force into the past and future.

But there is still more. The year 1905 was the date of Einstein's equation and the beginning of all that it has meant. Although Adams may not have known the equation, after reading the *Education,* who can say that he could not have imagined it? Even to ask the question is to answer it, for the fact is that Adams' *Education* is the heroic act of the imagination unifying history and science in an act of mind and art. To read it is to recognize the genuine pathos of C. P. Snow's cry of alarm, some fifty years later, at the perilous division between the two cultures of science and the humanities. Whatever its content, the form of Snow's "scientific" vision is, like his forms of fiction, stlll in the age of Howells. Adams had not only seen and measured the division between the two cultures but had imagined them as the poles of attractive force that, converting the inertia of life and history into energy of mind, would transform the self into a unifying con-sciousness—a third force in a new magnetic field. That is why his book is genuinely true to its title, remaining to this day an education for *any* twentieth-century reader. Of all American literature, it alone deserves to be required reading for all *students,* which is far from saying that it should be required reading for everyone or that it is the "best" American autobiography.

This, however, is an essay not about education but about American autobiography, and Adams' achievement puts me in a position to conclude the subject, which does not mean to summarize my argu-ment. A conclusion, it seems to me, ought to evoke an American writer after Adams who somehow extended the American auto-biographical tradition along the lines of force I have tentatively sketched out.

For me, that writer is Gertrude Stein. She is the woman whom Adams had tried to imagine emerging from the American scene. She drops out of medical school and the world of philosophy and science to become a dictatorial force in the world of art. She realizes almost from the beginning that America is not the newest but the oldest country in the world, since, immediately following its own Civil War, it was the first country fully to enter the modern world of steam and electricity. She leaves America to occupy Paris, the city of art, there to become an aesthetic dictator of the new art, which, emerging from the nineteenth-century dissolution of image and representation into impression, asserted clarity of line in an instantaneous perspective of abstraction. And she was, inevitably, an autobiographer. But whereas Adams had, by doubling himself, succeeded in retaining a narrative past at once generated by and attracted to a present consciousness, Gertrude Stein sought an absolute present in which not the life would be everything, the words nothing—as in Whitman—but the words everything and the life nothing. The abstraction of language would be the total present, and the achievement of the writer would lie in disconnecting language from referential reality, thereby making the words upon the page not true but real, not possessed of but possessing total reality in and of themselves. They would, in her words, be "being existing."

The only way that Gertrude Stein could even acknowledge narrative existence was to write through her companion Alice B. Toklas while speaking about herself. Thus, like the other American autobiographers, she could only reach herself by going outside. In reaching herself by being, not imagining, her intimate companion, she was not at all trying to gain an objective perspective on herself. Instead, she was uniting both autobiographical and biographical consciousness in a single creative act, thereby annihilating their priority and leaving only anecdotal perception upon the page as pure act and pure fact—not a new life in time, but a new existence in space. It has been said that she became her own Boswell, and in a sense she did, but it might be truer to say that, after writing *The Making of Americans,* she at last became one. Perhaps it was right that she should have settled in Paris, the city where Franklin had gone—in D. H. Lawrence's vision—to cut a hole in the Old World through which Europe would eventually bleed to death. Lawrence, at the end of his essay on Franklin written between the wars when Hitler was waiting in the wings of history, had cried out for Europe to let hell loose and get its own back from America. But when Hitler finally did let hell loose, it was certainly right that Gertrude Stein, who had been in Paris all those years, should have been waiting there to receive the victorious American soldiers when they liberated the city in 1945.

She—as American, as man-woman, as new Buddha—seems to

me to be both the fact and the mystery at the end of American autobiography. Her life in time, which ended in 1946, a year after the atomic bomb, is a good place to end this glimpse of the subject. Her life in words, a total present, would be the living fact on which to base a genuine vision of American autobiography as American history. That is why she is my conclusion.

Recovering Literature's Lost Ground
Through Autobiography

_____❧_____

My text is *The Autobiography of Thomas Jefferson*. It is hardly fair to
contend that devoting attention to it is to recover lost ground for
literature, since there is scarcely any evidence that Jefferson's account of his life was ever held as literary ground. Literary critics and
scholars, of course, ignore it. Historians and biographers accord it
little more than perfunctory glances. The historian almost fatally sees
the subjective element in all autobiography, since he is perforce wear-
ing his objective historical lenses. And the biographer, in self-de-
fense, has to discount autobiographical reality in order to pursue the
enterprise of biography at all. Yet despite its neglect, Jefferson's
Autobiography will provide evidence of lost literary ground.

Even to assert that Jefferson's *Autobiography* is my text raises a
problem, since that was not the original title of Jefferson's text. The
narrative, first published in 1830 by Jefferson's grandson and literary
executor, was entitled simply *Memoir*. Jefferson himself refers to his
narrative as memoranda. But in its modern reprintings (in the Putnam
Capricorn paperback, edited by Dumas Malone, and in the Modern
Library *Life and Selected Writings of Thomas Jefferson,* edited by
Adrienne Koch and William Peden) it is confidently presented as *The
Autobiography of Thomas Jefferson* without so much as an editorial
by-your-leave. This initial fact confirms what students of autobiography quickly learn—that is, that the term *autobiography* is of relatively recent usage, its earliest recorded appearance having occurred
at the end of the eighteenth century. Indeed, it was not until the
middle of the nineteenth century that it began to be widely used as a
substitute for *memoir* and *confession.* Now the term is so dominant
that it is used retroactively to include as well as to entitle books from
the present all the way back into the ancient world. Thus, Franklin
and Vico, who wrote accounts or memoirs of their lives, appear
before us with autobiographies. In addition to its triumph over time,
autobiography is imperially employed in space by those who would
apply it to novels, poems, essays, or even prefaces. Thus, we now
read that Henry James's prefaces to his New York Edition are really

his autobiography or that Freud's *Interpretation of Dreams* is his autobiography—and all this despite the fact that both men wrote narrative accounts of their own lives.

The historical emergence and domination of the term is one thing; the present critical emphasis on the subject is quite another. A collection of essays on autobiography would have been impossible as recently as a dozen years ago for the simple reason that the essays themselves did not exist. But they exist now in sufficient profusion that an editor can make a discriminating selection. This contemporary interest is a result of many factors: the relative "exhaustion" or critical exploitation of the traditional generic fields of drama, poetry, and fiction; the "political" possibility of escaping from the seemingly aesthetic or closed dimension of imaginative literature into the historical and referential possibilities of autobiography; the theoretical potentialities afforded by the problematic reference that autobiography inevitably evokes; and, I think, the growing sense or fear that the "self" upon which the imperial extension of the term *autobiography* was predicated may in fact be nothing more than a fiction that contemporary critical theory will at last expose. Language will at last be recognized as writing the self; we will give up the ego and search for ourselves in that shifty pronominal shifter—the "I" of discourse.

My choice of Jefferson's autobiography as an exemplary text is indirectly related to all these possibilities, yet my reasons for choosing it are direct and different. First of all, it is a memoir, and since I think that much criticism avoids the memoir, it is in a category of autobiography that needs attention. The memoir is, after all, pointed toward history and fact, whereas literary criticism invariably seeks after creativity and imagination. There is a distinct tiresomeness about the ease with which literary critics assure themselves that "mere" fact has little to do with the art of autobiography. The truth or falsity of autobiography is thereby subordinated to the creativity, the design, the "inner" truth of the narrative. The more we can say—and I have said it—that the autobiographer is creating and not inertly remembering his past life in the present, the more we can claim for autobiography a presence all but identical to the fictions and closed forms of "imaginative" literature both generated and mastered by New Critical literary theory.

What this procedure has meant in practice is a contraction of the imaginative orbit. Teachers, students, and critics of literature have more and more retreated from the world of fact, leaving it to the historian or the political scientist. If there is too much fact or idea in a piece of writing, it is under threat of abandonment. Look at how Ruskin, Mill, Carlyle, and Newman have faded from the field of undergraduate and even graduate study. The novel has all but routed the essay from the period course. Indeed, I think—or hope—that the present interest in autobiography is in part a hungering for a literature of content. Yet even here, the rampant "imaginative" tendency is evident. Thus, autobiographies devoted to the emotional consciousness of the writer have been much more subject to investigation than the memoir, particularly the memoir of well-known public figures. More literary attention has been paid to Frank Conroy's *Stop-Time* than to Grant's *Memoirs*. After all, Grant's book is really "about" the Civil War, and Grant himself is a "historical" figure. The same is true of Jefferson and his book. A chief reason that I have chosen Jefferson's book is that it is almost defiantly in the tradition of the memoir and therefore resistant to the aspect of mind that literary students have come to call the imagination.

The issue of choosing Jefferson's text goes beyond the matter of memoir; it goes to Jefferson himself and the relation of Jefferson to the study of American literature. All teachers and students of the subject know that lack of pure literary content (if pure literature has content!) is the norm and not the exception in the colonial and federal periods. There are few novels, no dramas to speak of, and precious little poetry prior to 1820. There are instead a host of sermons, diaries, personal and captivity narratives, histories, and political pamphlets. Yet in this very area abounding in what we are now pleased to call nonfiction prose (the very designation tells us just how utterly fiction has come to dominate literary study), it is the Puritans who hold the field. Why is this true? Why is Jefferson, for example, so essentially neglected? I imagine that Jefferson is a central figure for historians and political scientists—as central, let us say, as Hawthorne, Melville, or Whitman are to American literature. Whatever the case, he certainly is not central in any department of English. Jonathan Edwards receives much more literary attention than Jefferson; he even gets prominent presentation in an anthology called *Major Writers of America* edited by a galaxy of the most distinguished American literary scholars. Any teacher of American literature knows that the Puritans so dominate the study of early American literature that by the time the weary student gets through them in a course, there is time only to be profoundly relieved with *The Auto-biography of Benjamin Franklin*. Even Franklin is likely to be abused by any teacher who has worked himself into a state of sufficient high seriousness to endure the Puritans.

The Puritan ascension could be attributed to three causes: Harvard, Yale, and Perry Miller. Although that answer is hardly as facetious as it may sound, it is nonetheless inadequate. There is the Civil War, which consolidated, secularized, and even regionalized the original Puritan impulses into a dominant sway of American imperialism only now in the process of disintegrating. Then, too, there is probably a subliminal academic sympathy with the long, losing, embattled intel-lectualism of the Puritans; it may be an obscure donnish trade-off in which American literary scholars let the historians have Jefferson in exchange for Edwards, the grandfather of Aaron Burr; certainly it betrays the willingness of literary scholarship to link itself to morality more readily than to politics. Whatever the cause of Jefferson's slight hold on the literary mind, there is no possible way to justify Edwards as a superior writer or thinker. *Notes on Virginia* is in every way a more significant book for American literature than Edwards' *On the Freedom of the Will*—a text that, if we are to give things away, might well be surrendered to the philosophers or theologians. All this is not to demean Edwards; it is to disclose the absurd logic that has some-how placed him ahead of Jefferson. Think of the students in Ameri-can literature who have been subjected to Edwards' dreary "Personal Narrative," yet retain profound ignorance of Jefferson's memoir.

The point remains, however, that Jefferson did write an auto-biography, and Jefferson, whatever else he was, was a writer—prob-ably the most powerful writer America has produced. Despite the complaints an instructor of English might make about his tendency toward weak passive constructions, there is probably no more power-ful statement written by an American than "All men are created equal." How wise Robert Frost was to have his sensitive speaker in "The Black Cottage" observe that that Jeffersonian sentence "will trouble us a thousand years." It is the most volatile text that we know or have. And though no one really believes it to be true, who could wish that it had not been written? And written into the very concep-tion of the country?

In all probability Jefferson should not have written an autobiography; certainly his own ideas about the past constituted a strong counterthrust to whatever requests came from without or whatever impulses came from within to furnish the world his autobiography. He had spent a great part of his life trying to overthrow the past; he had even maintained throughout most of his long life that every generation had a right to its own revolt. Something of that counterthrust is evident in Jefferson's contention for privacy in the first paragraph of the autobiography: "At the age of 77, I begin to make some memoranda, and state some recollections of dates and facts concerning myself, for my own more ready reference, and for the information of my family."[1]

Beyond this blunt assertion of age, we know very little about the writing of the book, and Jefferson's biographers provide practically no information beyond Jefferson's initial declaration. He began it January 6, 1821, when he was struggling to get his last great project, the University of Virginia, into being; when the Missouri Compromise cast its dark shadow on his country's future; when he felt his own powers increasingly at the mercy of the benevolent nature his reason had imagined; and when he could see how the American revolutionary impulse had set in motion a movement eventuating in the tyranny of Napoleon and the subsequent massive conservative balance of power in the wake of Waterloo. In this connection it seems strange that Dumas Malone, in his relatively extensive introduction to the *Autobiography,* has not a word to say about the writing of the book, nor has he anything to say about it in his monumental biography. And Erik Erikson, who devoted a small book to the issue of discerning Jefferson's identity, never discusses the autobiography.

To be sure, Jefferson himself is somewhat casual in his relationship to the book. He did not "finish" it—it covers the years from his birth in 1743 until his return from France in 1790 to join Washington's administration—but here it is important to realize that first-person autobiographies cannot really be finished except with the death of the author. Jefferson is aware of the problem and keeps before himself principles of procedure sufficiently tentative to free him from the necessity of completing his project and to liberate him into the pos-

---

1. "Autobiography of Thomas Jefferson," in Adrienne Koch and William Peden (eds.), *The Life and Selected Writings of Thomas Jefferson* (New York, 1944), 3. All subsequent citations are from this edition and will be given parenthetically in the text.

sibility of quitting his book when he wants to. Midway in his text he finds himself involved with the problem of education and announces his intention of returning to the subject "towards the close of my story, if I should have life and resolution enough to reach that term; for I am already tired of talking about myself" (51). Presumably Jefferson had life enough left. But he evidently lacked the resolution. Or perhaps the resolution was directed toward completing the building and opening of the University of Virginia rather than getting to the point in his narrative where he could return to the subject of education. In any event he never recurs to the subject, but stops his autobiography with his visit to Benjamin Franklin upon returning to America.

Between Jefferson's beginning and ending, he does not pursue or cover his personal life; instead he sedulously avoids it. He offers all but nothing about his parents, having only this to say of his mother and his mother's family: "They trace their pedigree far back in England and Scotland, to which let everyone ascribe the faith and merit he chooses" (3). Although the irony here could be construed as savage, it is more likely bland. As for his father, Jefferson estimates his worth in a few measured words of praise. Nothing at all about his brother and six sisters—other than that they exist in number, not in name. And only the barest mention of his marriage to the widow Martha Skelton, daughter of John Wayles, which doubled Jefferson's property; later on there is the fact of her death, which ended ten years of what he calls "unchecquered happiness" (53). As if this were not lack enough, there is hardly a word in the book about Monticello, the passion of Jefferson's life. Small wonder that the book exists as a dead text to students of literature—dead for those ignorant of it and dead no doubt to those who, looking for the "life" of autobiography, would see only its absence in this book. Above all, it is dead to biographers, who, complacently settled in the assurance that their narratives will give us the life of Jefferson (even as those same narratives pursue him to his death), see the memoir as little more than a fund of inert facts.

This deadness in the book is actually the resistance of Jefferson's text to those who believe that personality is life. In Jefferson's hands, the memoir is not so much dead as it is a death mask—a still life molded from the outer lineaments of the face with which Jefferson faced the world. Lacking the color of a portrait, the death mask follows the lines of form rather than image. It is cold, it is hard, it is resistant, it is there. Of course, the notion of memoir as death mask is no more than a metaphor that might carry us away. Like almost every autobiography, Jefferson's is in words, and we have to do the best we can with them. The question looms: In view of Jefferson's omission of his personal life, what is his written life?

His life is, first of all, his writing. It is, as he writes in that already quoted first sentence, his beginning to make memoranda and to state recollections of dates and facts concerning his life. The acts of writing and beginning and stating are the verbs that signal both the structure and style of the book. Beginnings are more important than endings; statements are more important than narration; recollections are more important than memory; dates and facts are more important than emotion and consciousness. But it is not his present beginning to write that interests Jefferson, except insofar as that act is wedded to his past writing—and wedded in such a way as to make the past writing a present fact.

That is why Jefferson all but dispenses with his early life in a swift movement toward the key event of his life, his authorship of the Declaration of Independence.[2] To make the fact present, Jefferson gives his text of the Declaration, prefacing it with these remarks: "As the sentiments of men are known not only by what they receive, but what they reject also, I will state the form of the Declaration as originally reported. The parts struck out by Congress shall be distinguished by a black line drawn under them; and those inserted by them shall be placed in the margin, or in a concurrent column." (21). The presence of what Jefferson contends is his original text seems to me a remarkable fact in his autobiography. (Admittedly, such a fact may not offer the thrill available in *Moby-Dick* or *Huckleberry Finn* to a student of literature.) Yet one should not have to be a specialist in history or autobiography to find that text and that fact interesting. Not only is there the substantive meaning in the additions to and deletions from Jefferson's original (for example, the deletion of Jefferson's

2. In *Inventing America: Jefferson's Declaration of Independence* (New York, 1978), 167–68, Garry Wills makes the excellent point that the fire that destroyed Jefferson's home at Shadwell on February 1, 1770, also destroyed scholarly access to the world that had made Jefferson. I would add that, since it destroyed almost all that Jefferson had written, it destroyed Jefferson's own access to that world of his past. Wills makes a valiant effort to construct Jefferson's lost world, but Jefferson left it out of his life.

attribution of slavery to George III and also of his renunciation of *all* British kings forever; the addition of reliance "upon the protection of divine providence" in the last paragraph of the document), there is the enormous significance of Jefferson's fact. Whatever Jefferson is eliminating from his written account of his life—his personality, his inner feelings, his private relation—he is stating, affirming, and maintaining his original authorship of the Declaration. If, as author, he had to subject himself to the revision and censorship of a deliberative body, he is nonetheless—rather, all the more—the writer contending at the end of his life for his original text.

Much as we might want to look between the lines for Jefferson's concealed personality, it is of first importance to see that Jefferson sees his life in this book as what he had written for his country and the world. He had, after all, practically written the world for his countrymen to live in. Although it is possible to feel only the deadness of both that fact and the original text, it is equally possible to see them as possessing the energy of Jefferson's revolutionary individuality controlled by his political equilibrium. To see the original text paralleling the adopted text is to see how profoundly Jefferson had converted himself into political energy and how completely he sees that political and historical text as his life. Jefferson does not have to say anything about himself—and perhaps *cannot* reveal himself—because he originally translated himself into a text that began the history and life of a people. It is just this text that becomes the opaque effacement of the private self we continually yearn for in autobiography; yet it is worth remembering that this pronouncedly self-evident text—so publicly and so inertly part of our consciousness—guarantees our privacy even as it perpetually declares our public existence as a nation. Surely it is fitting that such an author as Jefferson—and there is only one such author—would understandably obscure the private self from public eyes, as if his Declaration, which converted the private "I" into the public "we," were the impenetrable facade at once creating and sealing off private space behind its monumental prose.

To be sure, in his autobiography Jefferson converts himself back into the "I" of autobiographical discourse. Yet the reader who has sensed the dimensions of Jefferson's Declaration can gain energy from, as well as give it to, the external and resistant structure of Jefferson's memoir. Believing that any inference about Jefferson's inner life not based on generous interest in the solid surface of his written life will be hollow indeed, I want to pursue the body of Jefferson's narrative as if it were the foundation of his being. However much I may fail to penetrate the mask of Jefferson, I will at least have given something of an introduction to the contents and organization of the book. Such a pursuit may leave us in a position to infer an inner space.

Jefferson follows his assertion of himself as author of the Declaration with an account of the two great debates that occurred during the framing of the Articles of Confederation: the debate on Article XI as to whether slaves should be counted as population in determining national taxation and the debate on Article XVII as to whether the confederated states should have equal votes or votes in proportion to their population in deciding questions. Jefferson never discloses his views on the two issues but meticulously and scrupulously summarizes the arguments of the speakers on both sides, finally indicating how the states voted. These central questions on taxation and representation, dull though they may seem in Jefferson's summary, were the perennial questions of America. They had risen to unite the colonies in division from England; they threatened to divide the United States throughout the period of confederation and constitution; and they were to haunt the nation until 1965. In writing about them in 1821 in the immediate wake of the Missouri Compromise, Jefferson was touching at the storm center of his country. Yet he never once alludes to the ominous history and significance that these questions had for the past, present, and future of his country; he vouches instead for the authenticity of his meticulous report on the basis of his having taken it from notes written *at the time* of the debates. Thus, his past writing is again claimed as the foundation of his present text at the same moment that the status of history is conferred upon the spoken opinion of more than forty years between the experience and the book. It is vital to see this process if we are to understand that Jefferson is not relying on facts but continuing to make facts. We may say that any reader can ascribe to these facts "the faith and merit he chooses." In Jefferson's text they are reported with the stillness and detachment of statements—as if, in the world announced by the Declaration, the colonies had indeed become *states* and could speak for themselves.

Conventions, Congress, Declaration, statement, states: the world of government. It is to this world that Jefferson both gave and dedicated so much of his life—with, it must be remembered, tremendous reluctance and resistance—and to which he gives practically all of it in his autobiography. Although by no means modest in relating his contributions, neither is he vain. Instead he states, or reports, his contribution to the making of government just as he reported bills to the Virginia legislature, to which he went after the Articles of Confederation were framed. Those bills—to establish courts of justice, to abolish laws of entail, to suspend importation of slaves, and to establish religious freedom—Jefferson considers the cornerstones of "a system by which every fibre would be eradicated of ancient or future aristocracy; and a foundation laid for a government truly republican" (51). The vision here is implicitly architectural, one in which democratic structure will replace aristocratic texture.

This whole portion of the autobiography recounting Jefferson's authorship of the Declaration and his work in the Virginia legislature constitutes Jefferson's contribution to the establishment of representative government; in style it reflects his own self-government—his own inner system of checks and balances. The decision to avoid declaiming or defending himself, the determination to stay in his public rather than in his personal life, and the refusal to moralize his actions are all suppressions of self in order to make a life of representation and not a representative life. It is just here that Jefferson's autobiography differs so widely from Franklin's, which is a wonderfully representative life. Franklin makes public his relatively obscure early life and shows how he succeeded in governing himself; Jefferson tends much more toward seeing his life as a result of the history he has made by writing.

From his account of "laying the foundations of a government truly republican," Jefferson moves to his contributions to that government as it entered the world of existing governments. He notes his development of a standard of currency based on the decimal system, his work in the Congress to help ratify the Treaty of Paris, his career as minister plenipotentiary in Paris as a successor to Franklin. Before embarking on this extensive sequence of material, he insistently indicates his decision not to recount his life as governor of Virginia: "Being now, as it were, identified with the Commonwealth itself, to write my own history, during the two years of my administration, would be to write the public history of that portion of the revolution within this State.

This has been done by others, and particularly by Mr. Girardin, who wrote his Continuation of Burke's History of Virginia, while at Milton, in this neighborhood, had free access to all my papers while composing it, and has given as faithful an account as I could myself" (52–53). This quotation makes clear that Jefferson sees his life as a history of himself; it also reiterates how deeply Jefferson identifies history with written documents. At the same time, it makes a clear distinction between a person's own history and his public life. As governor or president, Jefferson would apparently see his life as identical with the state or nation and therefore as available to a historian as to himself, provided the historian had "free access" to the papers of his subject.

Yet the placid clarity of the quote deserves scrutiny. After all, Jefferson's "own" history is itself largely public. What, after all, is the Declaration of Independence if not a totally public "life" of Jefferson? The very question begins to yield its answer. The Declaration is, as Jefferson sees it, his own text, and in this autobiography he can control that text even though he could not totally control it in the Congress. He can, even as he relates the history, lay claim to his authorship. As governor of Virginia he was much more the "property" of the state. Of course it would be possible—I think too possible—to point out that his career as governor was not so successful as his work in Philadelphia and in France. A better connection is Jefferson's design for his tomb, which he made during the same period that he wrote his autobiography. He directed in no uncertain terms that three, and only three, of his acts would constitute his memorial: "Author of the Declaration of American Independence, and of the Statute of Virginia for religious freedom & Father of the University of Virginia."

Author and father! these are the terms Jefferson kept somehow and somewhere for himself. To have authored those texts and to have fathered that structure were claims Jefferson felt strong enough to be engraved on his stone. These were acts that had some priority over the history Jefferson was a part of. Yet the moment he is past those acts of authorship, Jefferson is at the threshold of being merely a part of the history his very authorship has made possible. At just this moment in his text Jefferson is betraying some of the pressure his act of autobiography is beginning to put on him. Moving into areas of his life where the equilibrium between his own history and the history he has lived through is being broken, he is at the threshold of being a prisoner of his own text. His very life had been similarly threatened, for he was forever at the threshold of being the prisoner of the free country he had "written." No wonder he felt a certain freedom in France, where he was, after all, out of the country he had written.

Even so, Jefferson's account of his diplomatic years involves him in difficulties. Going to France may have seemed preferable to remaining governor of Virginia at the time Jefferson made the decision, and it might have seemed a preferable memory when Jefferson wrote his life. But it was by no means an escape. The first thing to see, however, is the disposition of Jefferson's narrative. As a diplomat, he is commissioned to negotiate treaties that will ensure commercial equity and protection for the new country that he was originally delegated to author; as a writer, he is publishing *Notes on Virginia* in Paris. He thus represents both his state and country to and in the Old World. More important, the author of a country that has literally intruded itself into the sequence of history is observing the disequilibrium caused by this new historical force in the society of nations. Jefferson writes at length of the betrayal of the Dutch republic into English hands by the Prince of Orange. Any reader with a moderate sensitivity to history will see that Jefferson's intention is to show how quickly and successfully counterrevolutionary forces (inevitably embodied by England, which had, in Jefferson's view, driven the American colonies to revolution) assaulted the forms of republican government.

At the same time, Jefferson watches the irresistible tide of republicanism emerge in and sweep through France. He not only occupies a box seat in what he earlier calls the theater of revolution as it shifts to France, but he is himself something of a center of attraction in the unfolding drama, for the republican intellectuals in France come to him for advice on how to proceed. Experienced in revolution, Jefferson was a shrewdly practical counselor as well as a diplomat who had to maintain a poised balance between his sympathies and his responsibilities. Balanced though he might be between his beliefs and his diplomacy, he was a passionately partisan republican and remained one right up to the time he wrote the autobiography. Nevertheless, at the time he was in France, he was caught in a swiftly moving chain of events that got rapidly out of control. But probably more important, at the time of writing, Jefferson faced the course of history that had intervened between 1789 and 1821. Thus, if he was caught in the chain of events in 1789, in 1821 he was confronted by the very narrative of history. Significantly enough, Jefferson's exposition of issues begins to be transformed into a narrative of events as he recounts the beginning of the French Revolution. Author as legislator is replaced by author as observer.

Although Jefferson recounts those momentous events with great authority, he clearly and inescapably knows that he is in a new relation to his narrative. Indeed, he knows much better than would many a literary critic. This is what he observes as he emerges from his extended account of events in France:

> Here I discontinue my relation of the French Revolution. The minuteness with which I have so far given details, is disproportioned to the general scale of my narrative. But I have thought it justified by the interest which the whole world must take in this Revolution. As yet, we are but in the first chapter of its history. The appeal to the rights of man, which had been made in the United States, was taken up by France, first of the European nations. From her, the spirit has spread over those of the South. The tyrants of the North have allied indeed against it; but it is irresistible. Their opposition will only multiply its millions of human victims; their own satellites will catch it, and the condition of man through the civilized world, will be finally and greatly ameliorated. This is a wonderful instance of great events from small causes. So inscrutable is the arrangement of causes and consequences in this world, that a two-penny duty on tea, unjustly imposed in a sequestered part of it, changes the condition of all its inhabitants. I have been more minute in relating the early transactions of this regeneration, because I was in circumstances peculiarly favorable for a knowledge of the truth. Possessing the confidence and intimacy of the leading Patriots, and more than all, of the Marquis Fayette, their head and Atlas, who had no secrets from me, I learned with correctness the views and proceedings of that party; while my intercourse with the diplomatic missionaries of Europe at Paris, all of them with the court, and eager in prying into its councils and proceedings, gave me a knowledge of these also. My information was always, and immediately committed to writing, in letters to Mr. Jay, and often to my friends, and a recurrence to these letters now insures me against errors of memory. (109–110)[3]

3. A point worth noting in this passage is Jefferson's emphasis on the tyrants of the North and the revolutionaries of the South. This division has particular resonance for the world that Jefferson was envisioning in 1821.

I quote Jefferson at length because the passage shows his sure consciousness of what he is about. He sees his narrative, true architect that he was, in terms of scale and proportion; he knows that the history in which he participated is utterly central and utterly continuous; he knows that he took part in its beginning and thus knows without having to insist that his written life has a priority all its own; he is sure of the truth of his account not only because he was a privileged observer with access to both sides but because he committed his experience immediately to writing. That is why he has no doubt of the cause and substance of his writing being the history of the future and why he sees history itself as a book with chapters—as if all our lives were in the process of becoming a text. Steady and measured though Jefferson's rhetoric is in such a passage, the events being recounted are violent. More important, the book of history that Jefferson envisions is also violent. Although he believes that the condition of man will be ameliorated, he just as clearly states that the process will be as violent as it is relentless.

The assurance and the detachment of Jefferson's narrative breathe a confidence that is at the heart of the stillness and purity of his life of himself. Describing the discussion with the leading patriots who came to his quarters to confer upon the revolutionary course of action to pursue, Jefferson remarks: "The discussions began at the hour of four, and were continued till ten o'clock in the evening; during which time, I was silent witness to a coolness and candor of argument, unusual in the conflicts of political opinion; to a logical reasoning, and chaste eloquence, disfigured by no gaudy tinsel of rhetoric or declamation, and truly worthy of being placed in parallel with the finest dialogues of antiquity, as handed to us by Xenophon, by Plato and Cicero" (108–109). This passage, by implication surely a direct slash at the rhetoric of Edmund Burke, shows Jefferson's own aspiration—a style cool, chaste, logical, free from ornamental texture, which will take its place with the monumental writing of the classical age in which history has been distilled back to the texts that ultimately constituted it in the beginning.

Does this mean that the time that has transpired since Jefferson committed himself to his initial text has no meaning? Of course not. The time between becomes something of a spacial perspective in that it is all but silent, yet remarkably present in its silence. Thus, intervening years do not provide a bridge of introspection, regret, nostalgia, or correction over which an erring, reconstructive, or reflective memory can pass as a rhetorical force. Neither time nor perspective are bifurcated in Jefferson's narrative. The present from which he writes is not a point from which to review the past so much as it is a point of vantage from which to stabilize it, to reinforce it as the fixed source and foundation of the present. Memory itself is, in Jefferson's eyes, inevitably erring; reflection is self-justifying. These are the faculties that, in an autobiography, generate the emotional, confessional, and defensive self that Jefferson neither wants nor believes his written life to be. He wants instead to have written his life into history at the outset, and he is clearly confident that he has so written it. That is why the text of the Declaration is so early and so completely present in the *Autobiography*.

The distinction between Jefferson's "own" self and history has its primary basis in the difference between Jefferson's text and that which the Congress adopted. And the chief difference resulting from congressional modification of Jefferson's text, as Jefferson sees history, is the presence of slavery in the United States. Although Jefferson does not openly lament congressional action, it is clear from his autobiography that he is determined to disclose that slavery is a flaw in the structure of the builder, not in the design of the architect. Yet it is just as clear from Jefferson's references to slavery that he is by no means smug about his own relation to the subject. Every time he touches upon it, his rhetoric betrays an urgency bordering on fear. Judicious scrutiny of his original text of the Declaration discloses this urgency and intensity in the accusations hurled at the king for having perpetrated the institution.[4] The fear is overtly expressed in Jefferson's remarkable discussion of the racial and social implications of slavery in *Notes on Virginia*. It could of course be argued that neither of these texts has quite the weight of the text of the *Autobiography;* that would be true for *Notes on Virginia* but precisely false for the Declaration, since it is Jefferson's original text of that document that absolutely *is* the text of his autobiography. And it is in that original text that we (as readers and as Americans) have the privilege of seeing for ourselves Jefferson's attempt to escape the issue of slavery by

4. Wills makes the striking observation that Jefferson is actually charging the king with *freeing* the slaves and encouraging them to turn against their masters. Wills, *Inventing America,* 72.

charging it to the king. The effort did not work then because the delegates could not agree on giving up slavery and so deleted that item as one of the king's crimes.

But there is another point in Jefferson's text at which he comes to grips with the issue of slavery. Just before concluding his account of the bills he "reported" to the Virginia legislature—those bills that would form the foundation for a government "truly republican"— Jefferson remarks the failure of his bill to stop importation of slaves to pass the legislature. His observations deserve quoting at length.

> The bill on the subject of slaves, was a mere digest of the existing laws respecting them, without any intimation of a plan for a future and general emancipation. It was thought better that this should be kept back, and attempted only by way of amendment, whenever the bill should be brought on. The principles of the amendment, however, were agreed on, that is to say, the freedom of all born after a certain day, and deportation at a proper age. But it was found that the public mind would not yet bear the proposition, nor will it bear it even at this day. Yet the day is not distant when it must bear and adopt it, or worse will follow. Nothing is more certainly written in the book of fate, than that these people are to be free; nor is it less certain that the two races, equally free, cannot live in the same government. Nature, habit, opinion have drawn indelible lines of distinction between them. It is still in our power to direct the process of emancipation and deportation, peaceably, and in such slow degree, as that the evil will wear off insensibly, and their place be, *pari passu,* filled up by free white laborers. If, on the contrary, it is left to force itself on, human nature must shudder at the prospect held up. We should in vain look for an example in the Spanish deportation or deletion of the Moors. This precedent would fall far short of our case. (51)

That paragraph immediately follows Jefferson's indication that he is tired of talking about himself and may not have "life and resolution" to return to the subject of education "towards the close" of his story.

Like Jefferson's inclusion of the original text of the Declaration, the passage seems to me one of the great presences in his autobiography. It is immediately vital for any reader. American history and American identity are so intricately related to it that it would be sad indeed to think that it is "history" rather than "literature." It is writing by the author of the Declaration of Independence, and it has to be faced. It would be easy to explain it away, just as it would be easy to fulminate about Jefferson's bigotry, just as it would also be easy to say that we live in a liberated time and must remember that Jefferson did not have all the advantages we have. None of these responses strikes me with anything like the force of the very presence of that paragraph. Far better to face the historical truth of the statement than to moralize or psychologize the issue. Very few modern readers would find emancipation and deportation an adequate answer to the question of American slavery. They would, however, have to acknowledge that it was an answer that was never tried. Instead, there was emancipation by force and with a violence fully equal to Jefferson's prophetic fears.

To recognize so much is by no means to claim that emancipation by force should not have been tried. It is to see instead that Jefferson was fully recognizing the violent history that the Declaration of Independence had inaugurated and was himself realizing the inevitability and the irresistibility of the force that has been unleashed. He himself is hoping that something can be done. When he says that he does not believe that the two races can live in the same government, we have to know that we are still contending that they can; that contention is nothing less than the violent course of our history. And if we are not *certain* that the two races can live "in the same government," we are nonetheless committed to the proposition that they can. It took a Lincoln to articulate that proposition on a bloody battlefield; it has taken more than a hundred years of political turmoil, breach of law, violation of civil rights, and adamantine Supreme Court rulings to sustain the proposition. That hundred years is not merely shameful, as some would have it; rather, it is violently powerful and is inseparable from a powerful and dominant central government that has become a major world power with a foreign policy by no means unrelated to the antislavery moral force Lincoln's Emancipation Proclamation incorporated into the identity of the government. It has been a foreign policy backed by fire and violence sufficient to give us pause at last. Few would want the pause to be momentous enough to cripple our contention and our hope that the two races can live together peacefully; yet surely we want it to be intense enough to give us present consciousness of Jefferson's text.

If we are students of that text and if we have consciousness to give, then the text becomes something more than dead. We can see that freedom and deportation is a conflict for Jefferson strong enough to bind him in paradox. Thus, his unforgettable observation that "nothing is more certainly written in the book of fate than that these people are to be free" is violently balanced by a counterweight, equally certain, to the effect that the two races cannot live together and remain equally free. Jefferson almost always seeks balance, but not balance as antithesis so much as balance as equilibrium. The balance that he enunciates here is all but a paralyzing stability, causing him to appeal for resolution of an unreconcilable conflict. The measure of the weakness of that appeal is located in the forbidding future prospect—a prospect so fearful that it will force human nature to "shudder." That verb, though muted in Jefferson's essentially temperate cadences, deserves all the weight the most sensitive reader can give it, for Jefferson eschews violent, florid, and hyperbolic rhetoric. His language is that of declaration, not proclamation.

Yet this very passage, coming as it does at the end of his cool account of his achievement in the Virginia legislature, shows a fear of the future. And it shows that fear at precisely the moment Jefferson is at the threshold of entering his account of his years in France— the violent narrative that he envisions as contributing to the first chapter of the new history of freedom. Before the reader can know what Jefferson will recount, Jefferson is already envisioning a future in which freedom is written in a book of fate. In other words, before Jefferson can reach that point in his past where a narrative of violent events overcame his deliberative exposition, he has, in his exquisitely restrained manner, revealed momentous anxiety about the future.

This anxiety, once perceived, is richly in the text, not beneath it. A student of literature or psychology might wish to convert it too quickly into terms of personality. I am not averse to seeing it in such terms, provided there is a determined effort to see the text first in terms of history. To have felt the life of Jefferson's history—his memoir—is to be at the threshold of surmising a mythic Jefferson, which is to say a symbolic reading of the life of the author of our country. I want to trace such a myth in its most tentative outlines— not only because such a reading is tentative but because autobiography as memoir holds itself in relation to history as well as to personality. It is to the text of his country, after all, that Jefferson gave himself; and that country which Jefferson continued to serve and in which he lived becomes in turn the book of history to which he alludes. Even so, there is a symbolic narrative to be inferred from Jefferson's form.

If Jefferson gives little attention to his parents and even to his wife, it should be remembered that his texts, this one included, are hard on parent figures. The Declaration itself, after its great steady assertions, becomes a whole series of assaults upon the king—and upon all kings. The bill for religious freedom decentralizes, defuses, and diffuses the energy of God. And Jefferson's other bills were to abolish primogeniture and entail. These monumental decisions, which are inseparable from writing this country into being, enter the stream of history and eventuate in the killing of the king and queen in France. Although he left France before they were executed, their deaths and the subsequent tyranny of Napoleon are glaring facts in the space between Jefferson's present text and the past text he is stabilizing. Was the original structure wrong to have brought such violence?

As he moves forward to the portion of his narrative in which his own ideas become a force in history, the clarity, serenity, and security of his perspective are all but brought to judgment. The anxiety, first manifestly evident in his remarks on slavery and the book of fate, is implicitly active in the form of narrative itself. Deliberation is superseded by sequence; history as text becomes history as chapter; fear of the future leads into anxiety about the past; rhetoric of declaration is brought to the threshold of becoming rhetoric of defense.

Faced with the regicide at the end of his account of the beginning of the French Revolution, Jefferson once again finds himself appealing—but appealing or wishing that an event had not happened, not that it will not happen. Separated from the king by an ocean, Jefferson and his countrymen had been spared the necessity of killing George III; they declared their country separate from the mother country, as indeed it geographically was. Yet their revolution had set in motion the much more violent French Revolution. Wishing that a constitution had been formed on the lines of limited monarchy, leaving the king "to do all the good of his station, and so limited, as to restrain him from its abuse," Jefferson sees the king as a well-intentioned yet weak victim of a vicious and violent queen: "But he had a Queen of absolute sway over his weak mind and timid virtue, and of a character the reverse of his in all points. This angel, as gaudily painted in the rhapsodies of Burke, with some smartness of fancy, but no sound sense, was proud, disdainful of restraint, indignant at all obstacles to her will, eager in the pursuit of pleasure, and firm enough to hold to her desires, or perish in their wreck" (104).

Thus does Jefferson essentially absolve the king and accuse the "wife" and "mother" of dragging the weak "father" to the guillotine. And so ends Jefferson's history—the text that he initially wrote has become the book of history in which he lived. He sees how violent that history will be; he has seen how violent it has been. Yet even here Jefferson refuses to desert the principle of revolution: "The deed which closed the mortal course of these sovereigns, I shall neither approve nor condemn. I am not prepared to say, that the first magistrate of a nation cannot commit treason against his country, or is unamenable to its punishment; nor yet, that where there is no written law, no regulated tribunal, there is not a law in our hearts, and a power in our hands, given for righteous employment in maintaining right, and redressing wrong" (105). Spiritually, or rather familially, Jefferson is willing to sacrifice or guillotine both mother and father in order to hold the principle of revolution. That means that he returns to his country from France a parricide—or a self-made orphan—rather than a self-made man.

But hold! Jefferson's text is neither history nor revelation of personality. It is memoir. As students of literature, we might want to reveal Jefferson's ego; as students of history, we might want it to provide a myth of the American self. But it is autobiography as memoir, which means that it will relate itself to the external world of the author in history, not to the inner world of self-reflection. Thus, if I have surmised a Jeffersonian myth of the "Author of the Country" as self-made orphan when he leaves France, it is a wonderful fact of Jefferson's memoir that it ends in Philadelphia—where the Declaration had been written—with Jefferson's visit to Benjamin Franklin, the original self-made man, who lies on his deathbed. What is the exchange between them? What indeed but Jefferson's narrative to an anxious Franklin about the momentous events in France; what indeed from Franklin but, upon Jefferson's inquiry about Franklin's progress on the history of his own life, the gift of a manuscript portion of that life and the double request by the dying Franklin that Jefferson keep it. Jefferson writes that he returned the manuscript to William Temple Franklin after Franklin's death. But he concludes his autobiography fearing that Franklin's grandson has somehow failed to publish it. He even suspects that he has suppressed it, since it established views "so atrocious in the British government." And Jefferson concludes his autobiography with a question and a suspicion: "But could the grandson of Dr. Franklin be, in such degree, an accomplice in the parricide of the memory of his immortal grandfather? The suspension for more than twenty years of the general publication, bequeathed and confided to him, produced, for awhile, hard suspicions against him; and if, at last, all are not published, a part of these suspicions may remain with some" (114).

Here, at the culmination of Jefferson's text, is a reemergence and even an intensification of anxiety—but revealed this time not toward future or past so much as to the text of autobiography itself. It is certainly worth knowing that four years before Jefferson wrote his memoir, William Temple Franklin had actually published the portion of his grandfather's memoirs to which Jefferson alludes. That portion was no small fragment of Franklin's life but a crucial and extended account of his negotiations in London in 1774–1775. In A. H. Smyth's edition of Franklin's works, the narrative account, addressed to Franklin's son, comes to eighty long printed pages. Jefferson, usually meticulous in such matters, had ample time and opportunity as well as every reason to check his suspicion rather than doing what he did, which was to end his memoir with his recollection of the contents of the "lost" manuscript. Perhaps even more revealing, Jefferson himself had written a letter to William Duane in 1810 giving a significantly different though essentially parallel account of his visit with Franklin. Julian Boyd, in an extended and informative editorial note, gives what must be forever the definitive account of the transaction. As Boyd sees things, Jefferson is in error about William Temple Franklin because of his suspicion that the young man was in British pay, but he is remarkably accurate in his memory of what was in the document.[5]

A commonsense account of this ending might well see it as Jefferson retiring from the effort to check every statement against past letters and other archival evidence. I think such a possibility not unlikely. At the same time, to see Jefferson yielding to his long-held suspicion allows us the indulgence of a symbolic reading of the ending. If Jefferson returned from France (in the text of his memoir) a self-made orphan, he finds his true and strong father in the self-made Franklin, the oldest of the founding fathers. In giving Jefferson the manuscript he has originally written to his illegitimate son, Franklin bequeaths his text to his "legitimate" son in order to ensure it from possible carelessness or abuse by the illegitimate grandson (Franklin,

5. Julian P. Boyd et al. (eds.), The Papers of Thomas Jefferson (20 vols. to date, Princeton, 1950–), XVIII, 87–97.

true to his revolutionary identity, founded a firm line of illegitimacy!).
Jefferson, who had no sons, sees in his own failure to protect his
bequest a betrayal of his patrimony as well as the possibility of
parricide by the grandson—and not only Franklin's parricide by
William Temple Franklin but his own by his grandson. This seems to
me an extraordinarily apt ending of the life of a true revolutionary, the
Author of Our Country, who believed all his life that there should be a
revolution every twenty years. Such a belief would have been weak
indeed had it lacked the power to generate such a fear.

Similarly, such a symbolic reading of Jefferson would be weakly
literary if it failed to recognize that Jefferson's conclusion to his own
memoirs actually serves to destabilize the definitive text of Franklin's
Autobiography, that wonderful first book of American literature.
Anyone who reads Franklin's account of his negotiations with the
British will see how much that text belongs with any edition of
Franklin's *Autobiography.* Carl Van Doren, almost alone among edi-
tors of Franklin's autobiographical writings, saw how essentially a
part of the *Autobiography* it was. Written on shipboard as Franklin
returned from England in 1775, it is by an author who, having recognized the adamantine hostility of the British government to its American colonies, is himself committed to hot-hearted revolution. No
wonder the old man gave it to Jefferson upon *his* return from Europe
to assume the duties of secretary of state in Washington's cabinet; no
wonder Jefferson could have felt that, in having it, he had a part of his
"father's" life as original as his own original text of the Declaration.
And having let it slip through his fingers, no wonder he trembled at
the loss of a *text,* this author who was so truly an Author. Although he
may have been wrong in his suspicion of William Temple Franklin, he
was right in his memory of that text being a part of "the history of his
own life," which Franklin on his deathbed was preparing for the
world.

If we reclaim that text from the obscure burial it suffers in the
Franklin papers, we will see Franklin's account of himself at the
moment he departs from England to become a revolutionary American. He is the true expatriate that Jefferson, almost alone of all the
revolutionaries, believed all Americans to be. Seeing so much, a
student of American autobiography might begin to experience the full
capacity of the Author of Our Country to destabilize everything fixed
before him.

RICHARD HENRY DANA'S
TWO YEARS BEFORE THE MAST:
AUTOBIOGRAPHY COMPLETING LIFE

Whoever looks at the bibliographies of articles and essays written since 1950 on American literature will find it difficult to believe that *Two Years Before the Mast* could ever have been chosen by D. H. Lawrence to appear in his extremely select list of *classic* American literary works. Of the thousands and thousands of items on American writers and writings, only four or five are devoted to Dana—and here it is well to note that there are significantly *fewer* articles devoted to him after 1950 than before. To be sure, there is John Haskell Kemble's extremely helpful 1964 edition published by the Ward Ritchie Press; there is Robert Lucid's excellent edition of Dana's journals (1968); there are two books—Samuel Shapiro's *Richard Henry Dana, Jr.* (1961) and Robert Gale's *Richard Henry Dana* (1969); and there is William Spengemann's intelligent emphasis on the book in his *The Adventurous Muse* (1977). Yet, aside from Spengemann, there is a perfunctoriness about the attention—a perfunctoriness that in itself tells us that the book is slipping from academic consciousness. Whatever struck Lawrence about it in his arresting chapter—and his treatment of Dana, like his treatment of every writer in his remarkable book, is arresting—no longer strikes anthologists. The leading American literature anthologies now run toward five thousand pages, but not a page is Dana's.

It would be possible to attribute Dana's slippage to the academic institutionalization of the New Criticism, which has in turn caused the decline of nonfiction prose (as it is now called) in the face of ever-increased emphasis on poetry, drama, and fiction. Yet the rise of women's studies, black studies, and Native American studies has been attended by renewed interest in discursive prose. Even more important, the social and theoretical interest in autobiography in the last twenty years has brought that form very much into the foreground. And *Two Years Before the Mast,* as I shall try to show, is in a profound way an autobiography. Yet in this very period the book has, if anything, lost ground.

So we have to find better reasons, a primary one of which is that, for all of Dana's attempt to be before the mast, he has come to be associated with the genteel tradition. He was, after all, a Harvard man at the very time he made the trip, a Harvard law student at the time he wrote the book, and a Boston lawyer at the threshold of a Brahmin career at the time the book was published. Although his defense of fugitive slaves in the early cases around 1850 made him feel estranged from proper Boston society, it came to constitute a new basis for respectability as New England, finding itself more and more against the South, provided much of the moral spearhead in the war for the Union. It was precisely this respectability that came under attack in the twentieth century. Thus, Lowell and Whittier came to be classed with Holmes and Longfellow as the Schoolroom Poets. Insofar as they were poets, they could and can still be anthologized as representatives of "literary" New England's effort to equal at best or to imitate the culture of old England. But insofar as they were prose writers, who reads them? Lowell's only claim to attention is that he wrote a negative essay on Thoreau. And what American literature class is exposed to *The Autocrat of the Breakfast-Table?* Put Richard Henry Dana, with his one book and that a long one, into such a context, and his disappearance into obscurity becomes much clearer.

But there is a second and much more important reason for Dana's decline: the rediscovery of Herman Melville. It is a matter of no small importance that Melville had been fully rediscovered in 1922, when Lawrence wrote *Studies in Classic American Literature.* Indeed, I think the rediscovered presence and immediacy of Melville—Lawrence devoted two chapters of his book to Melville's work—are very much culturally related to Lawrence's whole enterprise. For there is a Melvillian quality in Lawrence's style—an insistent Ahabic intensity coupled with a bluff Ishmaelean exuberance. The subsequent rise and all but enthronement of Melville in American literature seems to me exactly paralleled by Dana's slide into obscurity. The tolling of Dana's bell might have been unknowingly struck by Bliss Perry's essay "Dana's Magical Chance" in *The Praise of Folly* (1923). Perry wrote much in praise of Dana and in the confident manner of the later genteel tradition (members of which were for the most part by that time quartered in the academy); he was himself literary and judicious, realizing that Dana's book was somehow his essential life in that it liberated him from the proper Bostonianism of his time—Perry was precisely genteel enough to be critical of the old-fashioned proper Bostonians—and provided the magical moment that converted Dana's literary romanticism into the romance of the real. Yet Perry did no more than intelligently approve the book, just as he intelligently approved some of Dana's later writing. When all is said and done, Perry views Dana as part of the fabric of the post–Civil War New England civilization that forgot Herman Melville and led more or less in a straight line to . . . Bliss Perry.

Be all that as it may, the rise of Melville has without question cast Dana into shadow. Thus, the most likely way a graduate student today encounters Dana is through Melville's letter to him praising *Two Years Before the Mast*. Dana's readers will remember his remarks on meeting the whaleship *Wilmington & Liverpool Packet* of New Bedford: "A 'spouter' we knew her to be as soon as we saw her, by her cranes and boats, and by her stump top-gallant masts, and a certain slovenly look to the sails, rigging, spars, and hull; and when we got on board, we found everything to correspond,—spouter fashion."[1] When we think of *Moby-Dick* and the grandeur Melville brought to whaling, it is difficult not to direct a condescending literary judgment upon Dana's critical scrutiny of the dirty whaler, which he views with scarcely less aversion than the greasy Russian brig he encounters in San Francisco harbor. When we think of the long, lonely, forlorn, yet incredibly lofty struggle of Melville's creative life, then Dana's retreat from his one book into a Boston law office seems downright pathetic.

But Dana's life is not his work—or perhaps it would be better to say that his work, *this* work, is his intenser life. And it is much too easy to use Melville to devalue Dana. Anyone who knows Dana's book knows that it is a match for anything Melville wrote before *Moby-Dick*. Melville himself knew that best of all and never tired of praising Dana's work. Nor is there in his praise the slightest note of condescension. It was in a letter to Dana, after all, that Melville first

---

1. Richard Henry Dana, *Two Years Before the Mast*, ed. John Haskell Kemble (2 vols.; Los Angeles, 1964), I, 208–209. All subsequent citations are from this edition and will be given parenthetically in the text. Unfortunately, this edition does not include the chapter "Twenty-four Years After" which Dana wrote for his revised edition of 1869. The best edition available in paperback is the Penguin edition, edited by Thomas Philbrick.

mentioned his writing of *Moby-Dick*. A sustained look at Dana's book is an effort well worth taking.

Everyone knows or should know the dimensions of the book—this account of a nineteen-year-old Harvard student going to sea in a two-year voyage around Cape Horn to California. The title of the book makes clear both the novelty and achievement of the journey, for it was life before the mast and not aft that Dana lived and wrote about. His motive in taking ship had been to give his strained eyes a rest, and so there was, or is, a particular resonance in that common phrase "going to sea," as if the element into which Dana went were sounding the very sense he sought to strengthen. Returned from his trip with healed vision, Dana graduated from Harvard in 1837, attended law school and emerged with his narrative at the same time that he was ready to set up as a lawyer. His announced aim in his narrative was to bring to the world the experience of the common sailor; his unannounced purpose was to gain public identity in such a way as to strengthen his possibilities as a maritime lawyer. Thus, his original concluding chapter was devoted to the possible reforms that might be considered regarding the relation between ship captains and crew—or, we might say, between masters and men.

Even to make such an equation is to gain a much fuller perspective on the book in its own time. For *Two Years Before the Mast* is devoted to two paramount subjects: the relations between captain and crew aboard an American merchant ship and the possibilities of life in California in the mid-1830s. Published in 1840, the book was in its way a profound expression of the culture. First of all, it was adventurous—written by a young man, an easterner, who was finding his manhood in going west. Second, it was informative, giving a detailed and intelligent account of the customs and culture of California—that Catholic, Spanish-Mexican space toward which the Protestant-ethic United States was expanding more rapidly than it could quite know. Dana saw the economic, if not the manifest, destiny of that expansion in the very facts of voyaging around Cape Horn for California hides and returning to Boston to manufacture shoes that in turn would be shipped back around the Horn to California to be sold to Mexicans and Spaniards. In fact, Dana, remarking on how little holiday the Yankee captains gave their crew in relation to that granted by Italian ships, could compute the number of extra work-days Americans got from their workers per year. He saw even further that, but for religious observances on Sunday, the crew would have no leisure at all if matters were left to shipping companies and their captains. At the same time, he saw the readiness with which secular Americans were beginning to settle in a Catholic country, and he recorded the beautiful phrase they had for the removal: "to leave one's conscience at Cape Horn." The very resonance of the phrase, coupled with the polar plunge and resurrection that stood behind it, presaged the world to come. If settlers could brave Cape Horn on hermaphrodite brigs, how much more readily they would move once a true overland trail were secured that would cut the distance from eighteen thousand to three thousand miles.

But there was more than the adventurous outreach so expressive of American expansion and eventual war with Mexico that lay ahead in the decade after the book was published. There was also the matter of the captain's absolute authority aboard ship—authority that could either express or indulge itself by means of corporal punishment, which is to say flogging. The dramatic high point in Dana's narrative comes when, shortly after arriving in California, two members of the crew are flogged by Captain Francis Thompson. The first man flogged was Samuel Sparks, hesitant of speech and hailing from the middle states (actually Westmoreland County, Virginia). Somehow exasperated by Sam's behavior, Thompson increasingly badgers him until a response is drawn.

"I'm no Negro slave," said Sam.

"Then I'll make you one," said the captain; and he came to the hatchway, and sprang on the deck, threw off his coat and rolling up his sleeves, called out to the mate— "Seize that man up, Mr. Amerzene! Seize him up! Make a spread eagle of him! I'll teach you all who is master aboard!" (I, 103)

Seeing the full fury of the captain, a second sailor, John the Swede (whom Dana calls the best sailor on board), objects and is also seized up.

When he was made fast, he turned to the captain, who stood turning up his sleeves and getting ready for the blow, and asked him what he was to be flogged for. "Have I ever refused my duty, Sir? Have you ever known me to hang back, or to be insolent, or not to know my work?"

"No," said the captain, "it is not that I flog you for; I flog you for your interference—for asking questions."

"Can't a man ask questions here without being flogged?"

"No," shouted the captain. "Nobody shall open his mouth aboard this vessel but myself," and began laying the blows upon his back. . . .

The man writhed under the pain, until he could endure it no longer, when he called out, with an exclamation more common among foreigners than with us—"O Jesus Christ! O Jesus Christ!"

"Don't call on Jesus Christ," shouted the captain. *"He can't help you. Call on Frank Thompson!* He's the man! He can help you! Jesus Christ can't help you now!"

At these words, which I never shall forget, my blood ran cold. I could look on no longer. Disgusted, sick, and horror-struck, I turned away and leaned over the rail, and looked down into the water. A few rapid thoughts of my own situation and of my prospects for future revenge, crossed my mind; but the falling of the blows and the cries of the man called me back at once. . . . Everyone else stood still on deck at his post, while the captain, swelling with rage, and with the importance of his achievement, walked the quarterdeck, and at each turn, as he came forward, calling out to us,—"You see your condition! . . . You've got a driver over you! Yes, a *slave-driver—a negro-driver!* I'll see who'll tell me he isn't a negro slave!" (I, 104–105)

I quote the passage at such length because it vividly dramatizes as well as summarizes the issue of tyranny in the book—and summarizes it upon lines of slavery at the very moment the antislavery movement was becoming the country's major concern. Moreover, in the very act of becoming the flogging master, Thompson also becomes a blasphemer, as if he were fitting himself for the very role of plantation tyrant that antislavery pamphlets and slave narratives were going to depict. It is a short step from the factual Frank Thompson to the fictional Simon Legree twelve years later.

Yet if these aspects of the book—the youthful adventurousness, the western "matter," and the issue of absolute tyranny—give hint of the book's expression of and relation to the cultural and political issues of nineteenth-century America, they are but the beginning of the book's power. Other aspects of the book are equally important in measuring Dana's strength and depth. But the flogging scene remains the dramatic high point of the narrative—and remains so, I contend, because it *precedes* in Dana's own mind the antislavery cause he himself was later to become involved in. The scene's great power, in other words, derives not from the subsequent stereotype, but from the profound priority it had in Dana's mind and narrative. It is just here that D. H. Lawrence is very helpful—because he goes against the grain of so much that has been and still may be written about the book. For Lawrence, it is not the flogging, but the idealism of both Dana and John the Swede that is offensive. The idealism mucks up what would have been a simple and swift punishment, and so John's interference results in making Sam ashamed when he should have been simply hurt. Forced to see the sacrifice his shipmate has made, Sam finds his pain becoming misery, and the couple comes to humiliation and confusion, rather than to the clarity of a master-man relationship. But let Lawrence speak in his inimitable way:

> As a matter of fact, it was John who ought to have been ashamed for bringing confusion and false feeling into a clear issue. . . . The case was one of passional readjustment, nothing abnormal. And who was the sententious Johannus, that he should interfere in this? And if Mr. Dana had a weak stomach as well as weak eyes, let him have it. But let his pair of idealists abstain from making all the other men feel uncomfortable and fuzzy about a thing they would have left to its natural course, if they had been allowed. No, your Johannuses and your Danas have to be creating "public opinion," and mugging up the life-issues with their sententiousness. O, idealism![2]

The great strength of Lawrence's vision is that it arrests us at the verge of our usual academic mistake of subjecting ourselves to the antislavery conscience. For Dana, that ideal is primarily rooted in experience; for us, it is primarily imposed by history. Surely there are few readers who can agree with Lawrence, *really* agree with him on this matter; yet surely also there are few who, however intensely they might disagree with him, would refuse to acknowledge that *Studies in Classic American Literature* is one of the greatest books—perhaps the greatest—ever written on the subject. It is great enough to deserve a real criticism. If we have made an effort to place Dana in his time, it is well to remember that Lawrence's book, appearing in 1923, opened with the unforgettable attack on (and appreciation of) Benjamin Franklin. That attack concluded with these lines: "Now is your

2. D. H. Lawrence, *Studies in Classic American Literature* (New York, 1923), 178–79.

chance, Europe. Now let Hell loose and get your own back, and paddle your own canoe on a new sea, while clever America lies on her muck-heaps of gold, strangles in her own barbed-wire of shalt-not ideals and shalt-not moralisms. While she goes out to work like millions of squirrels in millions of cages. Production! Let Hell loose, and get your own back, Europe!"[3]

To feel the genuine force of Lawrence's assault is to know that Hitler at that moment was waiting in the wings of history. Is it too much to imagine him, upon hearing Lawrence's apostrophic plea, saying, "Would you repeat that just one time so I can be sure I heard you right?" Do not mistake me. I do not indulge such fancy in order to smear Lawrence with an association to Nazism, but to suggest both the burden and consequences of his vision. For if we cite the implications of that sentence, we also have to remember that Lawrence also said, in reference to Cooper's Natty Bumppo, "The essential American soul is hard, isolate, stoic, and a killer," at just the moment Hemingway was waiting in the wings of American literature.

To see just how good Lawrence is on Dana, one merely has to see how the very people who would most deeply disagree with his easy approval of flogging nonetheless wind up complaining of Dana's idealism on other counts. There is a long tradition of lamentation about Dana's bowdlerizing primness. There are hints that, for all his polite presentation of himself in the book, Dana actually drank, swore, and even womanized in his western sojourn. And much can be made of Dana's Americanized Victorian disposition (which he exercised in later life) to go to cities, frequent red-light districts, and find himself engaging prostitutes in conversation, most likely to urge them to go and reform. Whereas Lawrence upbraids Dana for vomiting over the side rather than facing the flogging, these high-minded opponents of Lawrence's blood vision lecture Dana on being squeamish about sex and the true hurly-burly of maritime life. It is just here that Lawrence shines. He never complains, because he realizes that Dana's idealism gives him what we might call the mysticism of the factual. It is no fuzzy or foggy mysticism, but a special kind of clarity. Lawrence puts it this way: "It is in the dispassionate statement of plain material facts that Dana achieves his greatness. Dana writes from the remoter, non-emotional centers of being—not from the

3. *Ibid.*, 31.

passional emotional self." And at another point, after quoting Dana's description of a thunderstorm at sea, Lawrence observes: "Dana is wonderful at relating these mechanical, or dynamic-physical events. He could not tell about the being of men, only about the forces."[4]

Because Lawrence has the daring to affirm master over man against Dana's idealism, he sees the strength of that idealism itself, sees how it is determined to master facts and culture and hides and trade and even the elemental ocean itself. Put another way, Dana's decision to avoid or censor sexual matters is precisely what liberates him to write the narrative he does. That sense of self strong in moral idealism keeps him distant from the crew, enables him to take pleasure in reading Sir Walter Scott's *Woodstock* to them, lets him see with assured detachment that they respect his education, and frees him to see, describe, and confront the forces of sea and sky and land. No wonder that Henry Adams memorably sketched Dana in *The Education*.

> Dana . . . affected to be still before the mast, a direct, rather bluff, vigorous seaman, and only as one got to know him better one found the man of rather excessive refinement trying with success to work like a day-laborer, deliberately hardening his skin to the burden, as though he were still carrying hides at Monterey. . . . Dana's ideal of life was to be a great Englishman, with a seat on the front benches of the House of Commons until he should be promoted to the woolsack; beyond all, with a social status that should place him above the scuffle of provincial and unprofessional annoyances; but he forced himself to take life as it came, and he suffered his longings with grim self-discipline, by mere force of will.[5]

Adams' characterization catches the contradiction that has come to work against Dana in the minds of the very people who, inheritors and even progenitors of gentility—as the whole academic establishment perforce must be—come down hardest on him. I am not thinking merely of scholars, but of students. They seem to resent Dana's ultimate retreat from the sea; they resent his literariness, his refinement, his decorum, and his return to genteel Boston society. Part of the resentment arises from the luxury that 150 years of historical

---

4. *Ibid.*, 169, 189.
5. Henry Adams, *The Education of Henry Adams*, ed. Ernest Samuels (New York, 1973), 29–30.

perspective affords. The strong vernacular tradition was only beginning in American literature at the time Dana wrote, and even then
only in the comic mode of Jack Downing and the early Southwest
humorists. But the deeper clue to the resentment lies in the students'
recognition that Dana's betrayal of his experience is their own future
betrayal writ large—writ large because at least Dana left behind him
on the trail of retreat a written testimony of his resistant experience.
This whole response is related to the emotional alienation on which
American middle-class society thrives. Give a person a leg up the
cultural ladder of social mobility, and he either apes high culture or
consciously plunges into the muck, as if the very law of the middle-
class mind lay in displacing the present space with an acquisitive
grasp of future possibility (there is the idealist aspiration) or a nostalgia for the "experience" from which the aspiration has averted itself.

There is no need to complain about this state of affairs other than to
know that the complaint is but one more example of middle-class
displacement. The point is that, whatever his refinement censors,
Dana is aware of the true middle-class drama of his life. He does not
repress that drama in order to show off his experience. There is no
more point in upbraiding him for returning to Harvard and Boston
society than there is in scolding him for concealing the "true" chaos
and vulgarity of life at sea. Dana knows in the profoundest way that
his very language of seeing and charting his course is that of a
straightforward description that necessarily expresses his refined
identity even as it adheres sufficiently to objects to require both
fidelity and lucidity of exposition. Dana is not so much committed to
experience or facts as he is apart from them; his very detachment
gives his narrative its fine objectivity. The facts—whether they be the
sails of the ship, the men on board, the storms at sea, the coast of
California, or the hide-curing process—are narratively thrown forward to displace the true chaos Dana felt at the heart of the romantic
adventure that had drawn him out of Boston society. This narrative
displacement is the literal conversion of the submissive fear that had
caused Dana to return to Boston into the authority that seals his
identity as a writer. For Dana the writer, the facts are themselves the
forces. Thus, men and ships and coasts and hides are facts sufficiently
stripped of moral idealism or informational inertia to seem accelerating into naked action.

At the heart of this action is the writer Dana, not in any way functioning as rememberer or celebrant or confessor (though the book is an act of memory, a tribute to the experience and a harbinger of loss and guilt), but as recorder—and himself almost a record, as if he were marooned between his text and context. No wonder Dana later called the experience a parenthesis in his life, as if he recognizes that his life was a sentence in the sad, full meaning of the term and his book was somehow at once interpolated into, yet exempt from, it. The action of the book, therefore, does not happen to Dana so much as it happens. He is part of the happening in the sense that the narrative recounts his presence in the field of forces and, in the sequence of events, lets the presence take shape as part of the ship.

To see the force of the book and how it takes shape to reveal Dana, it is necessary to go back to the relation between him and Captain Thompson, for Thompson, of all the figures in the book, is the one most recurrently present. He is the down-east johnny cake who makes things happen—the master of the ship and perforce the figure of authority who assumes in the flogging scene the character of tyranny. The fact that Thompson has died between the time of Dana's experience and the time of the writing frees Dana to expose his tyranny. Dana's narrative discloses, almost immediately after the flogging scene, Thompson's losing control of his ship, just as, in the flogging, he had lost control of himself. Thus, in San Diego the *Pilgrim* gets out of control and drifts into the *Lagoda*. Once freed, it drifts down upon the *Ayacucho,* whose captain has to come and assist Thompson in maneuvering his vessel. Later, when Thompson is announced on board the *Lagoda,* her salty old skipper inquires whether he has brought his brig with him, a remark that elicits enormous amusement from Dana's tyrannized shipmates.

However much Dana's sequence exposes Thompson, his account of the action always takes precedence over the psychology of the characters. Indeed, the men in this book, even Thompson himself, cannot become characters; the action of the book *includes* them; they belong to it as units of force and presence. Of those units of force, Thompson is the one who most threatens to become a dramatic character, only to have the full encounter with California force him into the background. To be sure, he does not disappear. He shows his hard-bitten lack of sympathy by refusing to give medicines from the ship's stores to Dana's sick Kanaka friend, Hope—and Dana at this point rather piously remarks almost outside the narration: "This same man died afterward of a fever on the deadly coast of Sumatra; and God grant he had better care taken of him in his sufferings, than he ever gave to anyone else!" (I, 243).

Yet the captain is never again released into the dramatic identity of the flogging scene; rather, he remains as resistant fact and force. Thus, when the ship *Alert* is about to return home with Dana on board and Thompson commanding, Thompson calls Dana aft and requires him to get one of his shipmates to take his place on the *Pilgrim* in exchange for his chance to go home. Dana here reveals to Thompson that he has connections back in Boston and that he also has information that Thompson has orders to bring him home and so stands his ground: "But it would have all availed nothing had I been 'some poor body' before this absolute, domineering tribunal. . . . But they saw I would not go, unless 'vi et armis,' and they knew that I had friends and interest enough at home to make them suffer for any injustice they might do me" (I, 261).

At first a sailor, English Ben, is brought forward in great dejection to take Dana's place.

> Ben was a poor English boy, a stranger in Boston, without friends or money; and being an active and willing lad, and a good sailor for his years, was a general favorite. "Oh yes!" said the crew. "The captain has let you off because you are a gentleman's son and have got friends, and know the owners, and taken Ben because he is poor, and has got nobody to say a word for him!" I knew that this was too true to be answered, but I excused myself from any blame, and told them I had a right to go home, at all events . . . yet . . . the notion that I was not "one of them" which, by participation in all their labor and hardships, and having no favor shown me, had been laid asleep, was beginning to revive. But far stronger than any feeling for myself, was the pity I felt for the poor lad. (I, 262)

So much of value is in that brief sequence. There is, first of all, the resistance of the captain. We never see his mind at work, because his interior space is never opened, but we can imagine him. He has figured out Richard Henry Dana and has forced him into the truth of his identity: that he is privileged, is separate, is a gentleman's son with influential connections. And Thompson is determined that

Dana's return to society—despite all his fine sentiments—is going to be at the expense of a poor sailor. How good that Dana does not repress this detail of his life, and how good that the captain's character must be *inferred* here. That is at once an example and a revelation of Dana's economy.

The only way Dana can extricate himself from these toils is to publish an offer giving "an order upon the owners in Boston for six months wages, and also the clothes, books and other matters, which I should not want upon the voyage home" (I, 263). Harry May, a Boston boy, accepts the offer, and Dana is let off the hook, though not without full exposure. Moreover, in Dana's concluding chapter, he notes that Harry May went to ruin as fast as ever he could. It is not that Dana is merely to blame; rather, it is a sequence in which he is implicated, and the implication is both articulated and reinforced in the sequence itself.

To begin to see this relation between Thompson and Dana is to see that Thompson has indeed measured his idealistic, subversive crewman and drawn him out of the berth he had made for himself among the crew. But the figure of Thompson, though ever at the threshold of independent dramatic identity, nonetheless remains submerged in the force of authority. It is law itself, from which there is no appeal, and Thompson is merely the agent. To see the relation is also to see how the other figures in the book function. They emerge in Dana's field of vision as related to, yet separate from, Dana. He is attracted to them because he sees how they reflect aspects of his own "civilized" self-image; yet, adrift in the boundless life of the sea, they are separate, external embodiments of the fragility of civilization in the face of the tyrannical force and freedom of oceanic experience. Thus, George Marsh, a sailor from apparently good English family, is about to ship into the infinite Pacific, where Dana will never again see him; there is Bill Jackson, the most handsome figure Dana has ever laid eyes on, yet who is unaccountably not an officer; there is Tom Harris, possessed of the finest mind Dana has ever encountered, yet a man who has been to the bottom of every sin and every experience; and there is the Kanaka, Hope, Dana's friend who all but perishes to venereal disease. Marsh hails from the gentility of the English life to which Dana is attracted; he has even kept an interesting journal of his experiences. Jackson is the very image of handsome yet rugged innocence—a mirror of what Dana imagines himself to be. Harris, possessing the intelligence, at once practical and theoretic, to excel in argument, is capable of being the lawyer Dana intends to be. Hope is the frail and sensitive victim of civilization whom Dana's Christian idealism wishes to appreciate, protect, and defend. These individuals are not characters but figures facing him from the world before the mast. They are his future writ large should he remain before the mast; they are recorded indelibly because he is returning to the civility of civilization. Dana never asserts the relationship; the figures appear, asserted prominently into the record. But for this assertion, they would be unrecorded points of consciousness. The full relationship they bear to Dana must be inferred from their essential presence in the factual space of Dana's account. To see Dana's presentation of these figures is to begin to grasp fully the purity of Dana's narrative. They remain in the record as evidences of humanity in the element of relatively unconscious nature. Had Dana imagined them further into being, he would have pursued them into a more novelistic structure; had he imagined them beyond a certain point in relation to himself, he would have headed into conscious self-revelation and confession and lost the clarity of fact and force he gains by remaining outside the objectivity of drama and the subjectivity of imaginative inner space. The record of the external journey assumes sequential dominion, subordinating plot on one hand and self-reflection on the other. They are tendencies, impulses, potentialities held in thrall by the force of sea and ship and land.

All of which brings us to what we can call the travel matter in the book. This matter—the matter of California—occupies the middle portion of the account and is itself a presence of fact, information, and escape for Dana. As source of fact, it provides him with assurance that he is conveying useful information to his audience, and it also possesses the kind of referential reassurance that he is not merely recounting his emotional life or the "excitement" of his adventure at sea. Just as it provided a space into which Dana the sailor could escape onto ground ungoverned by the tyranny of the master, the presence of California is the expository space by means of which Dana can elude the dramatic and novelistic closures that constantly threaten him. The flogging scene seems to me to represent those forces in their purest and most powerful form. Readers remember it because its vividness, arising out of its purely dramatic dialogue between captain and men, thrusts aside the recorder. It is of great interest, I think, that the next chapter of the book describes a liberty day in California. In that chapter Dana recounts the particular joys he and his friend Stimson had in getting away from ship and crew. But the point is that California actually exists as a landed space—a place of horses and customs that Dana the writer can occupy, thereby freeing himself and his narrative from being overrun by the tyranny of plot that the flogging scene so powerfully generates. The freedom— for Dana the sailor *and* Dana the writer—gives both psychic energy and thematic economy to Dana's descriptions of California, making them a strong part of the narrative rather than mere information filler in his account. Confronting the Spanish culture, as it almost idly and lazily presents itself before the fierce aggression of Protestant energy, Dana can feel the leisure and grace of civilization absent even in Brahmin Boston, underpinned as it is by the ruthless and vulgar capitalistic energy that sends out a hide-hunting ship captained by the Yankee Thompson. It is hardly surprising that Dana somehow finds a wistful sympathy for George Ballmer, the English sailor who falls overboard and is lost, and for George Marsh, who is very possibly an aristocrat abandoned into the Pacific infinite. Moreover, both Tom Harris and Bill Jackson, whom Dana idealizes, are Englishmen. To be sure, these are implications more than they are explications of the text, yet they inevitably buttress Dana's determination to return to civilization.

California is, after all, the place where European civilization, which has already conquered a primitive civilization, is about to be defeated once again by aggressive Yankee capitalism, and in this book the matter of California and the adventure of the journey meet in the action of getting hides for the return to Boston. That action—the journey and the hide gathering—is nothing less than the relation between the industrial civilization of Boston and the agricultural civilization of California. Although the California civilization seems sleepy and lazy to Dana, it nonetheless furnishes the raw material that the ship has come in search of. Hide gathering, more than being part of the "nature" of California is, in relation to Boston, the reality of the place. At the very end of his California stay there is a passage on the subject that seems to me to represent the essence of Dana's factual

matter. It at once describes and defines the process of loading hides
for the homeward journey. First, the lower hold is filled with hides
laid one atop the other to within four feet of the beams, and then:

all hands were called aboard to commence steeving. As this is a
peculiar operation, it will require a minute description.

Before stowing the hides, as I have said, the ballast is levelled off,
just above the keelson, and then loose dunnage placed upon it, on
which the hides rest. . . .

Having filled the ship up, in this way, to within four feet of her
beams, the process of steeving commenced, by which an hundred
hides are got into a place where one could not be forced by hand, and
which presses the hides to the utmost, sometimes starting the beams of
the ship, resembling in its effect the jack-screws which are used in
stowing cotton. Each morning we went ashore, and beat and brought
off as many hides as we could steeve in the course of the day, and, after
breakfast, went down into the hold, where we remained at work until
night. The whole length of the hold, from stem to stern, was floored off
level, and we began with raising a pile in the after part, hard against the
bulkhead of the run, and filling it up to the beams, crowding in as many
as we could by hand and pushing in with oars when a large "book" was
made of from twenty-five to fifty hides, doubled at the backs, and put
into one another, like the leaves of a book. The opening was then made
between two hides in the pile, and the back of the outside hide of the
book inserted. Two long, heavy spars called steeves, made of the
strongest wood, and sharpened off like a wedge at one end, were
placed with their wedge ends into the inside of the hide which was the
center of the book, and to the other end of each, straps were fitted, into
which large tackles were hooked, composed each of two huge purchase blocks, one hooked to the strap on the end of the steeve, and the
other into a dog, fastened into one of the beams as far as it could be got.
When this was arranged, and the ways greased upon which the book
was to slide, the falls of the tackle were stretched forward, and all
hands tallied on, and bowsed away until the book was well entered;
when these tackles were nippered, straps and toggles clapped upon the
falls, and two more luff tackles hooked on, with dogs, in the same
manner; and thus, by luff upon luff, the power was multiplied, until a
pile into which one hide more could not be crowded by hand, an
hundred or an hundred and fifty were often driven in by this complication of purchases. When the last luff was hooked on, all hands were
called to the rope—cook, steward, and all—and ranging ourselves at
the falls, one behind the other, sitting down on the hides with our heads
just even with the beams, we set taut upon the tackles, and striking up a

song, and all lying back at the chorus, we bowsed the tackles home,
and drove the large books in chock out of sight. (I, 255–56)

This passage might well stand for the very form of the book—and it is
surely no accident that the metaphor applied to the hides also applies
to Dana's narrative. I do not mean that Dana is always so minute in his
description of process but that this passage, like the flogging scene,
represents the essence as well as the extremity of Dana's factual
prose. Moreover, we might well say that Dana's own book has about
it the charged compactness of the stowed hides, as if the matter of the
journey were being driven home.

The manner in which the book of hides is made and then driven into
and between the piled hides as if it were a wedge seems to me an apt
description of Dana's composition. Instead of seeing expansion or
compression as his dynamic principle, Dana here discloses it to be
insertion, which at once produced both expansion and compression.
That act could very well express the nature of the book. Surely the
chapter on liberty following the flogging is in a real sense inserted,
which is to say wedged in, in such a way that the discontinuity of the
process is largely concealed by the increased compactness. The result
is a swiftness of sequence that greatly reinforces the *active* element of
the factual descriptions. The matter and culture of California are, in
effect, invaded with process.

Here again we can see how this form at once invites and resists
whatever logic of direction we might wish to put on it. There is, of
course, the master trope and master fact of departure and return. And
there is the archetype of the *Bildungsroman* much present, so that we
might well see Dana growing up or passing through crises. There is,
for example, the fierce and lengthy passage of Cape Horn on the
return voyage, the terrible storms of which could be seen psychologi-
cally to represent Dana recovering the conscience he had left at Cape
Horn. The outward voyage around the Cape had been a relatively
easy summer passage, but the midwinter return passage near the
Fourth of July is perilous in every respect. There Captain Thompson
seems to lose his courage, but then Dana comes down with a paralyzing toothache, leaving him no way to be smug about the captain, if
indeed the captain is afraid. Such psychologizing of the narrative is
too easy, too dramatic, too novelistic for the current of Dana's prose.
Dana *is* sick, so sick he cannot stand watches and is sentenced to lie

miserably in his bunk at the very height of the crisis—he who had all his life a superb constitution. Yet this inner space is never really allowed to open, because of Dana's interest in the ship, the waters, and the weather. An object like an iceberg thus displaces whatever interior logic we might wish to impose.

> And there lay, floating in the ocean, several miles off, an immense irregular mass, its top and points covered with snow, and its centre of a deep indigo color. This was an iceberg, and of the largest size, as one of our men said who had been in the Northern ocean. As far as the eye could reach, the sea in every direction was a deep blue color, the waves running high and fresh, and sparkling in the light, and in the midst lay this immense mountain-island, its cavities and valleys thrown into deep shade, and its points and pinnacles glittering in the sun. . . . But no description can give any idea of the strangeness, splendor, and, really, the sublimity, of the sight. Its immense size;—for it must have been from two to three miles in circumference, and several hundred feet in height; its slow motion, as its base rose and sank in the water, and its high points nodded against the clouds;—the dashing of the waves upon it, which, breaking high with foam, lined its base with a white crust; and the thundering sound of the cracking of the mass, and the breaking and tumbling down of huge pieces; together with its nearness and approach, which added a slight element of fear,—all combined to give to it the character of true sublimity. (II, 291–92)

This passage, filled as it is with active verbs, gives a clue to how much motion means in this narrative of travel. In this instance it is the slow motion that Dana's description is at once catching and arresting, but there are times when the currents and clouds seem to rush toward the ship until it careens like a racehorse. In this narrative all things seem in motion, the sun running low in the heavens, the great storms bearing down upon the frail ship, the wind lashing the rigging, the sea running astern, a dark cloud looming on the horizon. If we wanted to choose a passage in which this movement is captured in its muted purity, it might be this one: "When all sail had been set, and the decks cleared up, the *California* was a speck on the horizon, and the coast lay like a low cloud along the northeast. At sunset they were both out of sight, and we were once more upon the ocean, where the sky and water meet." (I, 270). Here the verb, which is held to the end, embraces the inertial might of moving forces that all but exclude the ship.

Then there is the ship itself, which figures so prominently in the book. If Dana's passages on the factual matter tend to pervade description with active process, his passages on ships pervade the act of sailing with description. Full of technical terminology that is never really explained, these passages become expositions of rife activity. Dana knows—and even happily knows—that most of his readers are landsmen and can scarcely know half the verbs and nouns he uses to describe the elaborate activity of rigging and reefing and furling in the face of ever-shifting winds; he even observes in his preface that this ignorance has never seemed a hindrance to novel readers of Cooper and Marryat because, as he says in the preface, he "has found from my own experience, and from what I have heard from others that plain matters of fact in relation to customs and habits new to us, and description of life under new aspects, act upon the inexperienced through the imagination" (I, xxii).

Dana is no doubt right in his contention, but the imagination to which he refers is not novelistic. For in his world, as we have seen, men appear almost like sketches lacking both causal force and vivid portraiture of characters. They are given only an outline and a bare life history either inferred or reported by Dana. And so in this narrative the activity of sailing is the very process of movement. This entire matter, which constitutes so great a portion of the book, like the matter of California, lies between the expert sailor (who presumably could explain and verify every movement) and the ignorant reader, who feels the mysterious terminology as *facts in action.*

Here, at this moment in mid-1840, Dana instinctively grasped a matter of great importance. Any reader today at once feels the "romance" of this movement—a romance all but depending on his own ignorance—and senses the elaborate technology of a sailing ship. The ignorance functions as the great *unconscious* power of movement, just as the actual sails and the terminology attending them are the highly conscious technology of dealing with the true unconscious forces of nature that propel the ship. The ship itself, as described by Dana, is thus a displacement of all the human unconsciousness into which Dana does not voyage. His own voyage chronicles his mastery—a highly conscious mastery of every line and sail on the vessel—yet his narrative converts that conscious mastery into descriptions clearly designed to evoke vague comprehension (except to the most privileged insiders who have actually spent years at sea).

There is a fine passage on the homeward voyage—after the *Alert* has rounded the Horn and is rushing north toward home—that both represents and sums up the large narrative component of a ship at sea.

> One night, while we were in the tropics, I went out to the end of the flying-jib boom, upon some duty, and, having finished it, turned round and lay over the boom for a half an hour, admiring the beauty of the sight before me. Being so far out from the deck, I could look at the ship, as at a separate vessel; and, there, rose up from the water, supported only by the small black hull, and towering up almost, as it seems in the indistinct night air, to the clouds. The sea was as still as an inland lake; the light trade-wind was gently and steadily breathing from astern; the dark blue sky was studded with the tropical stars; there was not a sound but the rippling of the water under the stern; and the sails were spread out, wide and high,—the two lower studding-sails stretching out on each side twenty or thirty feet beyond the deck; the topmast studding-sails like wings to the top-sails; the top-gallant studding-sails, spreading fearlessly out above them; still higher, the two royal studding-sails, looking like two kites flying from the same string; and, highest of all, the little sky-sail, the apex of the pyramid, seeming actually to touch the stars, and to be out of reach of human hand. So quiet, too, was the sea, and so steady the breeze, that if these sails had been sculptured marble they could not have been more motionless. Not a ripple upon the surface of the canvas; not even a quivering of the extreme edges of the sail—so perfectly were they distended by the breeze. (II, 320–21)

Here, as the ship approaches home, Dana finds it at last motionless upon a silent ocean, and so almost consciously he produces a piece of set description, as if he were painting or sculpting the ship. Yet the passage is much more than a set piece of description, for Dana literally builds the ship before our eyes, moving from the water to the stars. And Dana at such a moment is characteristically separate from his scene, located as he is on the prow of the ship, looking aft upon the image of the fact that is literally sending him home backward.

To see and sense such a passage is to understand the particular apathy Dana felt in actually arriving in Boston. He had had the anticipation of home as if it were to be the climactic ending of a novel. Yet the movement and arrival leave ship, shore, and ocean somehow behind him like an iceberg of attraction. In building this image of the ship, Dana brings to rest all the furious action of making and reefing sail. And in a deeper way he is, I think, completing the life of the

great sailing age. He is much aware of steamships; indeed, he has had
to confess to his readers how inept he was in explaining to the Kanaka
sailors the technology of steam power.

Be that as it may, the image of the completed ship at full sail might
well stand as the ending of the book. As an ending, it would give the
lie to any interpretation that put the flogging as the central action of
the book. We might conclude instead that, unlike the Californians
who had left their conscience at Cape Horn, Dana had actually found
his conscience upon the western passage, only to lose it on the difficult return voyage. It is well to remember in this connection that, in
the course of the wonderfully smooth voyage north toward Boston,
there is another flogging. This time it is the black cook who receives
the captain's blows for having become involved in a vocal and physical altercation with the mate. In this instance, Dana treats the matter
as if he had been instructed by D. H. Lawrence himself, which is to
say that he treats it as a matter of passional readjustment. Since the
cook is black, it would, of course, be possible to see Dana's treatment
of the incident as a manifestation of the barely submerged racism
running just beneath the surface of liberal Boston gentility. The possibility is certainly there (it is remarkable how little critical attention
has been devoted to this second flogging), yet Dana's writing cannot
be reduced to such a strait. Rather, Dana, in the moment of at once
constructing and arresting the image of the ship—and in that action
literally turning his back on Boston even as the ship drives him
home—is affirming the imaginative dominion of the external journey
as his true life and subject.

There remains, however, the fact that the imagined ship is not the
ending of the book. Instead, Dana, like the Dickens of *Great Expectations,* had two endings. The first was a concluding chapter focusing
on the possible legal and moral reforms that might be effected between captain and crew. That ending, rooted in Dana's socially reasoned fear of the passionate drama of elemental human conflict—the
fear that enabled him to concentrate objectively on the much more
elemental and unconscious forces of nature—led him directly out of
the book into the life of law that lay before him. Nineteen years later,
Dana returned to California on a steamship, and twenty-nine years
after writing his book, he secured the copyright and displaced the
original concluding chapter with an account of his return visit. And so
Dana actually ended his book by returning to it, as if the book itself

had attracted him back into it and literally annihilated the link he had
originally wrought to connect his experience to his professional life.
The book *was* his life and had fatally identified him. Thus, as if he
were in a Victorian novel, he told what had happened both to California and to the sailors and captains he had sailed with or met upon his
voyage.

Dana's return to his book discloses how completely he had actually
completed his life in his early voyage. He had thought, when he
finished the book, that he was ready for his life in law—and indeed he
was. Yet even as he began his legal career, he also began in 1842,
married and living in Boston, to keep a journal. His first act in his
journal "life" was a brief narrative account of his life up to the time of
taking ship to California, as if he were, in the manner of *Two Years
Before the Mast,* completing the early portion of his life. Significantly
for our purposes, Dana saw his early life at school much as he had
written of his life at sea. The chief event is a flogging he received
from a schoolmaster—and a fine problem for anyone writing about
his life would be to decide how much his writing of *Two Years Before
the Mast* actually *shaped* his whole prior life.

However much his written narrative may have thrown his early life
into focus and form, it left his later life to the mercy of the law. Thus,
having narratively accounted for his early life at the outset of his
journal, Dana drops into a discontinuous (and conventional) record of
his thoughts and activities. As his years at law wore on, so did the
journal. Dana could not give up the law, or at least he did not; he even
achieved distinction in it through conscientious labor and meticulous
attention to detail. These years of professional work told on his
constitution, and in 1859 his doctor advised a long vacation. The
opportunity afforded Dana a chance to fulfill a life-long dream of
making a voyage around the world. And around the world he went, as
if he were at last going into the infinite expanse of the Pacific that he
had somehow fled from when he made the deal with Frank Thompson
to return to Boston. It was on that trip that he returned to California
and got the material with which to complete the book of his life. From
California he went on to Japan and China—and to Penang in Sumatra, where he visited the grave of his cousin, George Edward Channing, who had shipped with Francis Thompson. When Thompson
caught the fever that killed him, Channing—who, according to

Dana, had not "consulted me as to the captain"—in nursing the dying Thompson, also contracted the disease and lost his life.[6]

If this cousin lived out the destructive life at sea that Dana had retreated from, it was another cousin, Francis Dana, who lost all but a small portion of the journal Dana had entrusted to him upon his arrival in Boston on the *Alert,* forcing Dana to reconstruct largely from memory the book of his life.

These two "losses" left Dana with his two "lives"—the life of the book he was to write and the life of the law he was to live. The addition of his final chapter had the practical value of providing a distinctly new edition of the book of his life, as he at last secured the copyright from Harper's, who had never given him a penny of royalty beyond the flat fee of $250 they paid him for his manuscript (Dana estimated that the publishing company had made fifty thousand dollars from the sales of the book in their twenty-eight years of possession). More important, it brought him back into the book that had completed his life more than he could know.

All that remained for Dana was to practice law in a more leisurely style, enjoy the High Church Episcopalianism to which he was more and more devoted, and finally go to Rome, where he died in 1882. He is buried there—in the Protestant Cemetery.

6. Richard Henry Dana, *Two Years Before the Mast,* ed. Thomas Philbrick (New York, 1981), 527.

R. W. Emerson:
The Circles of the Eye

Emerson is doubtless as visible as he has ever been in the university. Before the advent of American literature as a "subject," he may have enjoyed a wider reputation as venerated presence in the society at large. Before the existence of that venerated presence there had been Emerson, a venerable presence himself, no longer brooding over Concord but dying in it after the Civil War; before that, there had been Emerson the lecturer, spending himself on lyceum circuit forays as an apostle of culture; and before the lecturer there had been the original Emerson, the preacher and writer who had, sixty years after the Declaration of Independence, set out to liberate the imagination of himself and his countrymen. It is surprising how quickly we are led back through these generations of Emerson as object of study through Emerson as genteel cultural presence through Emerson as Concord Sage through Emerson as cultural circuit rider to Emerson the Seer— the veritable eye of God and Self and Nature. How quickly, in other words, we are led back to the transparent eyeball through which Emerson originally declared his vision.

That figure was in its way everything for Emerson. It was as much, let us say, as Whitman's outsetting assertion

> I celebrate myself
> And what I assume you shall assume
> For every atom belonging to me as good belongs to you

was to be for Whitman. Having imagined so much, Emerson must have felt that everything was possible. Of course everything *was not* possible; if so much had not flowed from Emerson's outsetting announcement, the whole passage in *Nature* might be little more than a fine instance of a young idealist's whistling in the dark. Yet even if nothing had followed, surely, were we to encounter the passage among the papers of an unknown theological aspirant, we would hear the ring of prophetic assurance in this announcement of a symbolic identity. Indeed, when the passage in its earliest form takes shape in

Emerson's journal (March 19, 1835), the eyeball metaphor is significantly absent.

> As I walked in the woods I felt what I often feel, that nothing can befall me in life, no calamity, no disgrace (leaving me my eyes) to which Nature will not offer a sweet consolation. Standing on the bare ground with my head bathed by the blithe air, and uplifted into the infinite space, I become happy in my universal relations. The name of the nearest friend sounds then foreign and accidental. I am the heir of uncontained beauty and power. And if then I walk with a companion, he should speak from his Reason to my Reason; that is, both from God. To be brothers, to be acquaintances, master or servant, is then a trifle too insignificant for remembrance. O, keep this humor, (which in your life-time may not come to you twice,) as the apple of your eye. Set a lamp before it in your memory which shall never be extinguished.[1]

Harold Bloom believes that the fear that "the humor may never return creates the extraordinary image of the transparent eyeball, an image impatient with all possibility of loss, indeed less an image than a promise of perpetual repetition."[2] This is good as far as it goes, but it does not go far enough. For the fact is that in the passage in *Nature,* the metaphoric eyeball *displaces* the fear—which is quite different from saying that it is created by the fear. Moreover, the fear in the original passage, far from being what we might call an anxious fear, is really a commonsensical fear, laced as it is to the logic of probability. The ringing proclamation of the self as eyeball is an eloquent conclusion, a poetic hyperbole, serving as a concrete seal of the experience that has just been described. It is a conversion of the "I" into the Eye, of the self into the Seer.

Ever since Christopher Cranch caricatured Emerson as a monstrous eyeball on two spindly legs, there has been no shortage of persons ready to bear witness to the outlandishness in Emerson's original conception. Even Jonathan Bishop, who has written one of the finest books on Emerson, feels that the metaphor represents a lapse in style from the fine description of the "bare common" that

1. Ralph Waldo Emerson, *The Journals and Miscellaneous Notebooks,* Volume V: *1835–1838,* ed. Merton M. Sealts, Jr. (Cambridge, Mass., 1965), 18–19.
2. Harold Bloom, "Emerson: The Glory and Sorrows of American Romanticism," in David Thorburn and Geoffrey Hartman (eds.), *Romanticism* (Ithaca, 1973), 158.

initiates the passage.[3] Yet just as Bloom seems to want the original
fear to take a higher intensity than the journal passage warrants,
Bishop wants the "realistic" or "concrete" Emerson to prevail over
the oracular and transcendental prophet. In its immediate context—
the context of *Nature*—and in the context of Emerson's whole career,
his figure of himself as transparent eyeball at once released and
defined his act of imagination. If the figure did not cause Emerson to
be what he was, it nonetheless reveals to us, in the light of what he
turned out to be, *who* he was—and the passage in which it first
appears is therefore worth concentrated attention.

> Nature is a setting that fits equally well a comic or a mourning piece. In
> good health, the air is a cordial of incredible virtue. Crossing a bare
> common, in snow puddles, at twilight, under a clouded sky, without
> having in my thoughts any occurrence of special good fortune, I have
> enjoyed a perfect exhilaration. I am glad to the brink of fear. In the
> woods, too, a man casts off his years, as the snake his slough, and at
> what period soever of life, is always a child. In the woods is perpetual
> youth. Within these plantations of God, a decorum and sanctity reign,
> a perennial festival is dressed, and the guest sees not how he should tire
> of them in a thousand years. In the woods, we return to reason, and
> faith. There I feel that nothing can befall me in life,—no disgrace, no
> calamity (leaving me my eyes), which nature cannot repair. Standing
> on the bare ground,—my head bathed by the blithe air and uplifted into
> infinite space,—all mean egotism vanishes. I become a transparent
> eyeball; I am nothing; I see all; the currents of the Universal Being
> circulate through me; I am part or parcel of God. The name of the
> nearest friend sounds then foreign and accidental: to be brothers, to be
> acquaintances, master or servant, is then a trifle and a disturbance. I am
> the lover of uncontained and immortal beauty. In the wilderness, I find
> something more dear and connate than in streets or villages. In the
> tranquil landscape, and especially in the distant line of the horizon,
> man beholds somewhat as beautiful as his own nature.[4]

In its immediate context, the context of the paragraph in which it
appears, the figure is the climax of the description of the writer's
perception of Nature—the section of Nature that is itself entitled

---

3. Jonathan Bishop, *Emerson on the Soul* (Cambridge, Mass., 1964), 10–15.
4. Ralph Waldo Emerson, *Essays and Lectures*, ed. Joel Porte (New York, 1983), 10. All
subsequent citations of Emerson's essays are from this edition and are given parenthetically in
the text.

"Nature"—and is thus the "nature" of *Nature*. In one sense, the figure is the symbolic transformation of the subject, the writer, into an identity equivalent to the state of being, a heightened gladness to the brink of fear, which has been experienced on the twilit bare common. As equivalent, it is metaphoric in the traditional sense. Or we might, following Bloom, call it an image. But in another sense, it is an *action* that instantaneously transforms being into seeing; if it does not annihilate personal consciousness, it reduces the personal identity to zero by virtue of the expansion and uplift of the essential self into infinite space: "I am nothing. I see all." Moreover, there is a paradoxical relation between the eyeball and the infinite space it occupies. Since the eyeball is transparent and cannot be seen—is in effect an invisible organizing filmic globe presumably containing the universe, through which and in which the currents of the Universal Being circulate—it should be coextensive with the infinite universe. Yet the figure is nonetheless concrete, an assertion of infinite existence in a definite image. That paradox was not something Emerson sought to realize as an aspect of style—he particularly disliked that characteristic of Thoreau's writing. Rather it was an expression of the essential relation between language and Nature. It was the inevitable and miraculous necessity of a true—that is, a poetic—language to assert the radical relationship between thought and thing. That is why Emerson did not, at his best, use metaphor decoratively and why, in this crucial instance, he did not say he became *like* a transparent eyeball. The figural transformation is, for Emerson, the active spiritualizing power of language—it is the God acting as language—and Emerson's becoming a transparent eyeball is his primary metaphor. This transformation is a fatally idealizing process in which mean egotism becomes nothing, whereupon "nothing can befall me in life. . . . The name of the nearest friend sounds then foreign and accidental: to be brothers, to be acquaintances, master or servant, is then a trifle and a disturbance." Yet for all the idealizing in Emerson's act of vision, the metaphor keeps the vision from being totally subjective. It is subjective in the sense that the consciousness in the form of the eyeball in effect contains everything. Still, there *is* the metaphor, which carries Emerson outside himself. The mean ego has vanished in order for Nature to exist. To be sure, it is impossible to tell whether Eye or Nature comes first. In the sequence of the entire passage, Nature precedes the Eye, though it is clear that, by becoming part and parcel of God, the Eye sees Nature—as if God passed through the Eye to create Nature. All three entities—God, Man, and Nature—clearly interpenetrate one another, and Emerson's logic throughout the essay wants to place them in an equal relationship. That is why both the argument and direction of the entire essay bend to embrace that equality; it is also why this initial figure is the instantaneous enactment of the whole idea of Nature. It is, after all, both image and act of the imagination seeing nature, and the essay is both elaboration and consequence of that vision.

If Emerson's logic is equalizing, or attempting to equalize, God and Man and Nature, his rhetorical bias, his inheritance of traditional religious language, and his transformation via transcendence relentlessly combine to form a vertical and hierarchical idealization of Nature. Thus, Emerson's movement in the essay is from the "low" commodity of Nature up through aesthetic to moral and intellectual beauty, through language, through discipline, and on to idealism. These terms constitute the very ladder of his aspirational vision. Yet for all his impulse to idealize Nature, Emerson has to reject idealism because it would degrade Nature into phenomena, thereby denying the existence of the very entity he has set out to redeem; it would, as he says late in the essay "leave me in the splendid labyrinth of my perceptions to wander without end" (41).

For that reason, Emerson moves from idealism to the realm of spirit, the active principle of idealism—what we might call thought in motion—which sends up and illuminates the universe. Spirit is, of course, God—the Supreme Being that, according to Emerson, does not build up nature around us but puts it forth through us (41). But Nature is, by virtue of the passage through us, like the human body, an inferior incarnation of God, a projection of God in the unconscious. Spirit is the impulse that organizes and gives direction and purpose to Nature; its equivalent in style is the imperative, hortatory, moral tone that characterizes Emerson's prose, inspiring him to radical metaphor yet constantly threatening to weaken the power in Nature he seeks.

For Nature, that which the transparent eyeball at once sees and contains, must be, like the eye that sees it, radically there. And like the eye that sees it, the limits of nature are infinite; indeed, despite the solitary pastoral setting in which Emerson sees it, Nature really can include society. Although the solitude has the benignant aspects bestowed upon it by the equally benignant and idealized Nature, there is outside the perimeter of the eye the negative world of the vanished ego—the world that Emerson can, as the mood moves him, cast outside or inside nature. It is the world of talent rather than genius, convention rather than originality, the past rather than the present, the church rather than God, institutions rather than men—in a word it is society rather than the essential self in Nature. It forms the negative but highly necessary background that affords Emerson an instantaneous perceptual dialectic, enabling him to pour positive energy into his charmed field of vision and thus dramatize the original power so necessary to invigorate the idealizing impulse.

So what we have in *Nature* is a declaration of independence not so much from society as in society—for it is society that surrounds Emerson. After all, it is a *bare common* from which Emerson soars into his identity. Moreover, the bare common was not present in the journal entry. To be sure, Emerson allows himself free passage from bare common to Nature's woods in his movement toward his ultimate assertion. Even so, he clearly has that bare common much in mind when he says, at the very threshold of translating himself into a visionary, "Standing on the bare ground . . . all mean egotism vanishes."[5]

Thus, in his first essay, however much Emerson sought to define Nature, he meant to possess the ground from which he could see society. This twilight walker is occupying the space at the center of the village, not to reject the village, not to reform it, as much as to envision it in the fullest sense of the word. For all the infinite space Emerson figuratively occupies, he is still on that bare common, and his whole aim, located as he is at the center of society, is to free himself to become the center—to possess the *common* nature possessed by the village and make it something more than bare. The possession is not of course in terms of legal, material ownership—the village and town already own it materially—but in terms of a vision that will discover the force of Nature that exists not only on the bare common but also in the heart of the sleeping society. By being the

5. Emerson had, at the very outset of *Nature*, shown his disposition to move freely between the *common* and the *philosophical* sense of nature, a point I shall emphasize later in the discussion. His movement here from the bare common to the sanctified transcendental woods, though it can be seen as the vagueness of rapture, seems to me to exemplify a determined freedom from being fixed in nature as place.

veritable pupil of Nature, Emerson will be the true teacher of society. The bare common is therefore the crucial ground on which Emerson stands; to realize it is to recover the full meaning of Emerson's decision, at the outset of *Nature,* "to use the word [*nature*] in both senses;—in its common and in its philosophical import." The *common* sense of Nature is, as Emerson says, those essences unchanged by man, whereas all those constructions of man—houses, roads, canals, towns—fall under the heading of Art. By deliberately refusing to deny this common sense of Nature, even though it would *exclude* the bare common from the realm of the natural and place it in the realm of the artistic and social, Emerson means to subject the common sense of Nature as well as the bare common to full re-vision.

The whole argument of Emerson's first essay is thus rooted in the instantaneous act of the figure that grounds the argument. Jonathan Bishop, in discussing Emerson's style, wisely observes that Emerson knew that a man's metaphors mean what they say.[6] Surely this one, as much as any Emerson never imagined, bears witness to that observation. It literally foresees the conclusion of *Nature,* in which Emerson says: "The problem of restoring to the world original and eternal beauty is solved by the redemption of the soul. The ruin or blank that we see in nature is in our own eye. The axis of vision is not coincident with the axis of things, and so they appear not transparent but opaque" (47).

And he goes on to say that once we have integrated spirit and matter into their original unity, then we will look at the world with new eyes. He even evokes his Orphic Poet to proclaim in the last sentences of *Nature:*

> As when the summer comes from the south the snow banks melt and the face of the earth becomes green before it, so shall the advancing spirit create its ornaments along its path, and carry with it the beauty it visits and the song which enchants it; it shall draw beautiful faces, warm hearts, wise discourse, and heroic acts, around its way, until Evil is no more seen. The kingdom of man over nature, which cometh not with observation—a dominion such as now is beyond his dream of God,—he shall enter without more wonder than the blind man feels who is gradually restored to perfect sight. (49)

6. Bishop, *Emerson on the Soul,* 119–28. Bishop's entire discussion of Emerson's concern with, use of, and commitment to metaphor is excellent.

Although the poetic utterance gives us once again the metaphor of vision, it is perilously close to the threshold of flaccidity. The "as when . . . so shall" construction is far from the swift, spirited oracular language of the essay. Of course Emerson could say—really does say—that it is not himself but his Orphic Poet speaking, but that is an insufficient defense. If the Poet is Bronson Alcott, then why choose Alcott, if he can do no better than this? Besides, it is not Alcott; it is Emerson, run beyond his true ending into weak vision and weak language. Here is indeed vapidity, and it occurs the moment Emerson enters a "heavenly" realm in which there is not the sharp resistance of those opaque things. In such a realm Emerson is in the resistless air of spirit, and the world of Nature is always at the threshold of becoming a weakly poeticized prospect rather than a strongly imagined figure of spirit.

If we take Emerson, standing on the bare common, become an eye at the natural center of society to see and thereby re-create it, we have the essential Emerson—the Emerson of *Nature* imagined by himself at the outset of his career as the fixed center of the existent universe. He had his essential thought, as Kenneth Cameron has shown.[7] He had a style to match his vision, a style in which metaphor (itself the visible presence, in language, of thought in the act of becoming image) at once preceded and made possible his argument. And he had his role, that of teacher and preacher to the townsmen he would instruct and exhort. Finally, he had his form, the essay, which through his eye was an experiment in vision—an urgent perception intent upon disclosing the unity of man and nature. Since Emerson was a writer, not an artist, his seeing perforce had to be saying. What Emerson sought in style was a rhythm and a decisiveness that would equal the perception he proclaimed. Discursive argument was largely closed to him, for his initial position put him out of linear logic, a point Sherman Paul decisively made thirty-five years ago.[8] His poetic, symbolic, or metaphoric identity—call it what we will—kept his language constantly charged with affect. His denial of time, in favor of circular repetition, drove him toward compression and epigrammatic execution of thought and away from expansion, discur-

7. Kenneth Cameron, *Emerson the Essayist* (2 vols.; Raleigh, 1945). The first volume amply documents the influences upon and development of Emerson's thought up to and including the publication of *Nature*.

8. Sherman Paul, *Emerson's Angle of Vision* (Cambridge, Mass., 1952), 5–26.

siveness, exposition, and narrative, which he felt were enslaved to clarity, the mere light of the understanding.

His vision sought to pierce the surface of Nature and Man and literally review the traditional terms, the essential generalizations that form the permanent structure of man in society. The very titles of his successive series of essays display his central concerns: "History," "Self-Reliance," "Compensation," "Spiritual Laws," "Love," "Friendship," "Prudence," "Heroism," "The Over-Soul," "Circles," "Intellect," "The Poet," "Experience," "Character," "Manners," "Gifts," "Nature" (not the original essay but a subsequent and quite subordinate attempt on the term), "Politics," and "Nominalist and Realist."

These are what I choose to call the Circles of the Eye. It is no more an accident that the one geometric form to which Emerson devotes an essay is the circle than that that essay should begin with the following sentences: "The eye is the first circle; the horizon which it forms is the second; and throughout nature this primary figure is repeated without end. It is the highest emblem in the cipher of the world" (403). There is the Emersonian style at its finest—a strong, unqualified assertion, followed by another. The second two assertions are in one sense restatements of the first one, though they are just as clearly consequences of it. And the fourth is at once declarative and metaphoric. That word *cipher* does a world of work. For the cipher is of course a zero, an empty arithmetic circle that, placed at the right of, or following, a number, increases its value tenfold. It is also a coding, a symbolic reading, which discovers meaning. The sentences, sufficiently independent to be epigrammatic, create a momentary yet decisive gap between each other, which the eye and ear of the reader and listener bridge with a responsive intellectual leap of energy. Moreover, the metaphoric second sentence is not illustrative but equivalent, as if it were inevitably called forth. In a fine way, the metaphor is buried, or rooted in the very sense of the passage. It is, in other words, a third and final circle of the primary eye. How quickly all this is done, and how completely. Begin an essay this way, and how can you fail?

Well, you can fail even so, and Emerson sometimes does fail, though certainly not in this essay. It is one of his best—short, fierce, and utterly complete. The "I" of the author is fully converted into the reading eye of the reader. Emerson does not see for us but sees

through, by means of us. The connections we have to make to discover the full sequence are by no means free association; they are the
fated spatial silences between the sentences, instinct with implicit
energy—dots, we might say, which, when connected, form the circle
of the essay. Emerson ends on the following note:

> The one thing which we seek with insatiable desire is to forget our-
> selves, to be surprised out of our propriety, to lose our sempiternal
> memory and to do something without knowing how or why; in short to
> draw a new circle. Nothing great was ever achieved without enthusi-
> asm. The way of life is wonderful; it is by abandonment. The great
> moments of history are the facilities of performance through the
> strength of ideas, as the works of genius and religion. "A man," says
> Oliver Cromwell, "never rises so high as when he knows not whither
> he is going." Dreams and drunkenness, the use of opium and alcohol
> are the semblance and counterfeit of this oracular genius, and hence
> their dangerous attraction for men. For the like reason they ask the aid
> of wild passions, as in gaming and war, to ape in some manner these
> flames and generosities of the heart. (414)

I have not quoted the passage for the presence of a final circle in it,
though it is good to see Emerson strongly return to his primary figure.
Nor is it quoted for possessing the utterly typical absolute assertion:
"Nothing great was ever achieved without enthusiasm." That is an
example of the Emersonian sentiment of assurance executed as epigram; yet for all its absoluteness, it is nonetheless the expression of a
mood, and Emerson has already said in this very essay that "our
moods do not believe in each other." Emerson knows quite well
outside the circle of this essay that something great might be achieved
without enthusiasm. But that would be another circle—possibly the
circle of Prudence or Wealth or Manners or Politics.

No, not for these is the passage exquisite, but for the rare, and in its
movement, the daring ending—the abrupt illumination of Cromwell's somewhat grandiose utterance in terms of drunkenness,
opium, and alcohol. Here is a swift and pungent explanation of rankly
sensual behavior under the aegis of the idealized statement. The
abruptness, which is to say the instantaneous decision, of the move
sends life and meaning in both directions. For Cromwell's statement
depicts a stage of drunkenness—a not knowing where one is going—
just as the state of actual drunkenness is also some effort to get out of
oneself. Such a fine blunt move seems to me a genuine realization of

Emerson's contention at the outset of the passage that "we seek with an insatiable desire . . . to be surprised out of our propriety." The sudden juxtaposition of the two activities; the sequence, which is to say the direction, from high to low; and the relationship, so much of which is left implicit or silent in the charged space between the sentences—all combine to charge the field.

These sentences of Emerson are like atoms; they are striving to be worlds of their own; they bear out again and again in the action of their form his endless plea for the present to prevail over the past, and are thus repeatedly executing his central theme, just as their self-containment repeats his central figure. The high mind—even the high-mindedness—of Emerson is always present, even dominant; it is the resonance of his tone. But its swift reach into the so-called material and instinctual world is richly audacious. These descents of the spirit are as fraught with ecstasy as any ascent Emerson could make. They not only promise but recover wild nature. Such conversions of spirit to Nature are the perceptions of the transparent eye.

The Emersonian sentence, charged with its atomic independent impulse—he once referred to his sentences as infinitely repellent particles—is the analogue of the essay struggling to contain it. The essays are the larger self-contained circles that stand by themselves, yet are bound to one another by the larger silent spaces between them. In a way they are all repetitions of *Nature,* for Emerson is an alarmingly repetitive writer. And these silent spaces between the essays are the vanished mean ego—the first-person pronoun of Emerson— which has become the charged space wherein we connect or leap the gap from essay to essay. We might even say that the vanished mean ego, the *biography* of Emerson, which has literally dissolved into the spaces between the intense intuitional moments of vision that literally are the essays, is admonished into silence by the voice of vision, the sayings of the seer. After all, Emerson's essays are self-directions as much as they are directions to an audience. No, not quite as much, for the hortatory tone of the preacher attempting to lift us out of ourselves represents a balance of admonition flowing outward in the form of address.

This vision of the essays as circles of the central eye is of course nothing but a metaphor—yet I mean for it to have consequences. First of all, the repeated conversion of the "I" into the Eye cannot be taken lightly. There is enormous psychological cost in such an idealizing process. If the "I" and all the personalities that existed around Emerson in time and place—his parents, his brothers, his wives, his children—are not annihilated, they are threatened with consumption by the vision. There is a sense in which Emerson literally feeds off the death of those around him. Before he wrote *Nature,* he had already lost two brothers and a first wife, all victims of tuberculosis, and he himself hovered at the threshold of consumption during his early life. Breath, which is our literal physical experience of the spirit of life, was thus crucial, even desperate, to Emerson; hence the astonishing literal force in his use of the verbs *inspire, transpire, conspire, expire, aspire.* There is, for example, a felt relation between his bursts of inspiration and the death of his first wife. If he does not exult in her death, there is nonetheless an influx of energy consequent on her passing—an imaginative energy boldly evident in the journal. Her spiritualization, which Emerson's traditional religious attitude embraces, makes her a part of the air he breathes. And the clear despair he records on the loss of his brother Charles is but a prelude to the strong assertion of *Nature.* Getting out of the "I," the personal pronoun, and getting over the deaths of loved ones is no tired or traditional "spiritual" vision for Emerson, precisely because it is a literal breathing in, or inspiration, of the death in life.

Moreover, there is in Emerson's bold assertions of self-confidence a threat to everyone around him. In the face of prior disasters and griefs, even if we grant that his second marriage and the birth of a son may have given him needed assurance for launching himself as a writer, Emerson's assertion of an idealized metaphoric self that, short of blindness, would be impervious to any evil, has about it a ferocious element of provocation. If Margaret Fuller had proclaimed her acceptance of the universe, Emerson had both stared and dared it to its face. Implicit in his contention that no evil can befall him in his form of transparent eyeball is a challenge to the Universe to do what it will, since he can see by himself. How glad we should be that he at least had the grace and wit and common sense to exempt his eyes, both of them, from his all but absolute act of pride! Looking at the statement from another point of view, we could say that if we had been little Waldo and had been precocious enough, we would have wished to say before we were five years old, "Father, *why* did you say such a thing?" For if Emerson was austerely coming out of evil, he was at the same time asking for more. It would be the fuel for his flame. How have pride and not be stricken? And no amount of transforming pride into obedience can quite charm Emerson's circle unless rude Nature and violent spirit are surging within it. Otherwise, it will be just a charming circle in the form of a decorative metaphor.

There is thus, I think, in Emerson's fine sentences early in *Nature,* an implicit sentence of death for little Waldo. And indeed, can we, looking at Emerson's life, wish that Waldo had lived? Can we really imagine he would have grown up to be a flaming independent imagination? Emerson's other children hardly fared well. There was Ellen Tucker Emerson, named for the dead first wife, as if she were to be an admonition to Lydia (who had herself suffered a renaming as Lydian to get her out of the unfortunate New England vernacular pronunciation), who took care of the Concord Sage in his declining years. There was Edith Emerson, whose husband, W. H. Forbes, helped Emerson with his finances and securities. And finally there was Edward Waldo Emerson, inheritor of the sickly Emersonian constitution, who could not go to the Civil War—was indeed actively denied his wish to go by his concerned parents—and who was left to edit Mr. Emerson's journals. He did creditable work, I think we could say, but every line of his prose affirms his role as undertaker of the body of Emerson's work. Whatever vengeance was in the children lay in building a sepulcher for the father. The true children of Emerson were elsewhere. Born of the seeds of language, Thoreau and Whitman, Emily Dickinson and Robert Frost (and Frank Lloyd Wright and Charles Ives, too), were wild, recalcitrant embodiments of the Emersonian spirit, flaming by the ponds and in the cities, villages, and fields of the Republic.

I am not higgling about Emerson's failure to be a good parent— whoso would higgle, let him dare to have children and know what it is to possess them. I simply wish to welcome the fate that was in Emerson's freedom, the death in his life. Already in *Nature* he had said at the end of the section on discipline (which precedes the section on idealism): "When much intercourse with a friend has supplied us with a standard of excellence, and has increased our respect for the resources of God who thus sends a real person to outgo our ideal; when he has, moreover, become an object of thought, and whilst his character retains all its unconscious effect, is converted in the mind into solid and sweet wisdom,—it is a sign to us that his office is closing, and he is commonly withdrawn from our sight in a short time" (31). Biographically considered, that passage clearly refers to Charles, who had just died. But it just as clearly looks forward to the passage in "Experience," which deals with the death of Waldo. Logically considered, the passage unremittingly defines the terms of the transparent eyeball. Seeing a friend is at once a conversion of life into thought, a *taking* of life. And if such seeing is to continue, more life is going to have to be taken. To be sure, in the sweet dialectic of transcendence, thought has preceded life anyway and can be declared as the more intense conception and conclusion of life. Yet Emerson's prose is never as sweet as it may look. He himself wanted bite and sting and decision in prose.

This vision of Emerson's Eye in relation to his personal life may seem appalling, yet I think much of the writing on Emerson discloses attitudes that could well be considered expressions of precisely this vision held *unconsciously*. There is, for example, a distinct wish expressed by critics of Emerson that his personal life should have been more of a trial of his ideas than it actually was. Thus, there is even a downright resentment about his "success," his too serene middle years. Similarly, there is, on the part of those who praise Emerson, a slight lament that he lost something of his early fire when his house became warm and comfortable.

All of which brings me to the second consequence of seeing Emerson's essays as the circles of his Eye. For all the change that Emerson celebrated—remember that the currents of the Universal Being are constantly circulating through the transparent eyeball—the Eye is just as constantly fixed. Although Emerson can look on the faces of Nature, the tyrannous Unity must assert itself and be asserted again and again. I do not see Emerson as "developing" or "progressing" or "declining." Of course he declined into old age; of course he finally lost his energy (he had always maintained that he had never been given enough to begin with). But he lived long enough as a writer to make it necessary for those who posit a decline to bury him prematurely in order to confirm their vision.

Nor do those who see Emerson as somehow discovering more reality than he first bargained for fare much better. If the one party tends to see Emerson as a revolutionary who slumped into society, the second tends to see him as an emerging Realist whose initial dream was superseded by experience. Stephen Whicher, who regretted a bit too much the absence of evil in Emerson, wishes to rescue the later

Emerson, the Emerson who faced the fate of his earlier freedom. Jonathan Bishop, on the other hand, finds the early Emerson sounding the bolder note and receding through the crises of Waldo's death into the practical world of *The Conduct of Life*. And now Quentin Anderson appears to applaud Bishop's evaluation of the early Emerson as the more revolutionary, but to assert that the revolution was a mistake. Anderson has seen the student riots, the Vietnam War, the imperial American expansion into Asia, and implicitly as well as explicitly relating this recent history to the Emersonian imagination, he deplores the imperial Emersonian self, which he sees as what he calls a "coming out of culture."[9]

There is no doubt that the early Emerson is central. Emerson was in effect all there at the beginning, and all that he was to do was implicit in the metaphoric identity he proclaimed for himself. Of course, he had experience; of course he saw things in life that he could not quite have foreseen at the outset. But visions of Emerson's career in terms of crises and turning points, of ups and downs, of directions from revolution to compromise or from idealism to realism have their own distortion. That there was entropy of energy I am delighted to acknowledge, but there was never the kind of entropy that could not produce the old flame from the slow decay.

Indeed, locating Emerson's revolutionary power in his early years causes Anderson to distort the image of the outsetting Emerson. Emerson never was so revolutionary as Anderson wishes to have him. He had from the very beginning a deeply conservative quality. He was right on that bare common in the center of village culture. It was the eccentric Thoreau who occupied the ground at the edge of the village. If Emerson had revolted against the church, it was nonetheless a one-man revolt that Emerson never wanted vulgarized into a movement. Thus, he was asking the divinity students not to leave the church but to be themselves within it and thereby renew it. Emerson is always aware that society exists; he very much wants it to exist; he has no real doubt that it will continue to exist; he knows that the isolate position he assumes in relation to it is just that—in *relation* to it, and therefore in a deep way, deep enough to be rooted in instinctual consciousness, dependent upon society as an entity all but equal to whatever self he can ever assert.

9. Quentin Anderson, *The Imperial Self* (New York, 1971), 201–44.

It is true that he is always determined to affirm the self over society, but the affirmation always has the ring of exhortation. The appeal in Emerson's imperatives is a recognition that the balance of power is on society's side and must always be proclaimed for the self precisely because it has been so fatally surrendered. There is from the beginning a margin of safety on the bare common that has somehow been secured by law and is therefore a sanctuary, a new church to move into. Thus, Emerson is calling to us to rely on ourselves out of a profound recognition that we will not and have not; the ringing of his bell is a reminder of what we could but will probably never be. What keeps Emerson strongly present beneath the ringing of that bell is his solid grasp of the fate—the persistent and repeated form—of society. By getting out of history, Emerson wants to see the external stability of change almost as much as he wants to accomplish the change of getting out. The self he proclaims has about it no small measure of tradition; it is a recovery as well as a departure.

Emerson's very language embraces the traditional aspect of speech. He does not want a new language so much as he wants a renewal of the existing language. He loves proverbs and is delighted to see new experience conform to the traditional, proverbial, common wisdom. If he earnestly desires to lodge his own proverbs in the language, he nonetheless knows that he has chosen the proverb and the epigram as the desired form into which to cast himself. That is an inextricable aspect of his aphoristic and oracular style. For all his ringing insistence that man is innocent instead of originally sinful, Emerson wants the innocent self to be a conscience—a new conscience to be sure, but withal a conscience. Hence the admonitory aspect of his essays. Emerson's blessed encouragement is, as everyone knows who reads him, both accompanied by and charged with admonition. His uplift is not without squelch. Consciousness is forever at the threshold of becoming conscience. The teacher is always about to be the preacher; the lecture or the essay is never far from being the sermon. The Emersonian sentence is sufficiently instinct with judgment to carry conviction.

Emerson's whole drive toward unity, toward circularity, illustrates this conservative element in his imagination. For the circle, however much it may be impelled to expand, is seeking both to include and to contain all of experience rather than to reject and destroy it. The two eyes that become one in transparent sight inte-

grate rather than divide the field of vision. The very fact that vision
is Emerson's metaphor of thought makes him know the aspect of
illusion that dwells in the realm of what he would call reality. If it is
inevitable that he should have written an essay on circles, it is equally
inevitable that he should have written one on illusions. What is great
about Emerson is his willingness to expose and thereby anticipate the
illusoriness of his own thought. The bulletlike force of his self-
relying sentences always threatens to put the reality of the preceding
sentence in jeopardy.

There is a deep impulse in Emerson to declare everything as an
illusion—everything. The question that then stands up to this hard
Yankee pressure is "What is the most powerful illusion?" The answer
is, I think, the central self, that transparent eye of consciousness. Yet
because even it is ultimate vision it has an element of illusion in it—
which is far different from saying that it is necessarily unreal or
illusory. Surely Emerson's repeated and memorable admonition to
trust the self betrays in its very terminology the appeal at the heart of
the imperative. The appeal is for every man to believe in and assent to
those momentary flashes in experience when issues appear clear,
when emotion is translated into adequate action, when thought seems
the very double of the body. The motion of the body is, when it moves
instinctively beneath the sway of mind, the double of the will and is
our primary experience of Nature instinct with thought.

This illusion of a central self is so persistent that Emerson is willing
to risk all on its being a reality. And so the central self is the anchor of
essays so apparently disparate as "Self-Reliance," "Experience,"
and "Fate." "Self-Reliance" is a buoyant call to trust those intuitional moments when perception—which for Emerson is instantaneous thought—yields total presence, blotting out the image of the self
in relation to society (which is conformity) and the image of the self in
relation to past experience (which is consistency). "Experience," on
the other hand, instead of exhorting to self-trust, rushes headlong
through the categories of perception, which Emerson denominates
Illusion, Temperament, Succession, Surface, Surprise, Reality, and
Subjectiveness. These are the lords of life, the very illusions by
means of which man creates his existence. Indeed *experience* is, as
Emerson sees it in what seems to me the most exhilarating of all his
essays, the swift exposure of these dominant categories of perceptions—what we rely on as our ideas of life—as illusions. These

forms of perception are the means by which we temporarily fix Nature only to see it burst into another life. Without the fix, the *idea* of Nature or Life, we cannot see it, yet the moment form gives our vision identity, Nature dances into life again. There is nothing left at the last—after the successive disillusions—but the sanity of the self that creates the illusory lords of life. Thus, if "Self-Reliance" was a ringing exhortation to trust the self, "Experience" turns out to disclose that, after the last disillusion of experience, there is nothing else to rely on *but* the self, of which Emerson bravely says: "We must hold hard to this poverty, however scandalous, and by more repeated self-recoveries, after the sallies of action, possess our axis more firmly" (490). That axis is surely the volatile line relating Experience to Self-Reliance, and the two essays are really its poles. If the one is positive and the other negative, they are the alternations of a single current of energy. And surely "Fate," far from being a change in Emerson's central philosophy, is a change in perspective. Once Fate is seen— and Emerson burns with all his original energy as he sees it—then Self-Reliance is once more possible. For the man who can humbly accept his destiny can even recklessly obey his impulses.

To believe in the self enables a person to see society more than it makes him wish to reject or even reform it. Every person must see it by and for himself; otherwise he merely joins a movement and is engulfed by a party of society. And the seeing is likely to be as brief as it is sure—as brief as a sentence or an essay. The solitary intensity of vision predicates a stubborn conservative, persistent society that will perennially occupy the interstices between the moments of intuition.

Is Emerson then a conservative? Not on my life. After all the admonition, the exhortation, the relentless and even fearful idealization, there is a buoyant hope in Emerson—and buoyant not because it is hope but because it is shown by Emerson to be a state of mind that practically exists in every waking day—as near as the air we breathe. Of course Emerson can be weak and distant—not merely in his late years but in his early ones, too. He is, as John Jay Chapman astutely remarked, weak on the fine arts. His overwhelming belief in language prevented him from being able to see visually. Seeing is really always saying in Emerson; perception is always thought. And if Emerson is not weak on love, he is certainly hard on it. Because he sees every self as a circle, two selves can touch at only one point. The more intense the point of contact, the more appetency and hunger are aroused at other points along the vast perimeters of the two selves. Thus, after all is given to love and particularly when all is given, the self can and must come into its own. Such a view goes hard with romance, with narrative, with the novel. And though Emerson could write on the Comic (how pleasantly surprising that he made the attempt), he hasn't much of a sense of humor. He has no patience with anyone who giggles, and says so in a way to chill the playful heart. He can, after a long session of reading him, seem to have enough moral seriousness about him to make a reader, or this one at least, embrace Mark Twain's contention that the Moral Sense makes us the lowest rather than the highest creatures in God's Kingdom of Nature.

Yet count over his weaknesses as we will—count them over with savage delight—Emerson still sees us, really makes us possible. He was, after all, a prophet, not in predicting the future but in making it happen. He called for a scholar, and there was Thoreau. He called for a poet, and there was Whitman. Reading Emerson at his best is always a reminder as well as a recognition that I am. I do not know his work well enough. I have not read it all. I have not devoted myself long enough or hard enough to the task of understanding him. But there he is to tell me that there are better things to do than to read him, that I have read enough of him, that I am as good as he is, that I, too, at this instant, shall prevail. And all in a voice at once exacting and exhilarating, a voice that, when heard, is proof as well as prompting of my inmost character. Here is no coming out of culture, but a making culture possible.

U. S. Grant:
The Man in the *Memoirs*

---··<∞>··---

Since my larger subject is autobiography and my particular subject is
U. S. Grant, let me begin with a touch of personal autobiography.
Here at Auburn in the Deep South I can only hope that my southern
accent can be at least faintly heard, for I am from the South—the
"Upper South," I suppose I should say. Virginia is my native state,
but I was not born just anywhere in Virginia. My home is in southwest Virginia, in the mountains. The farm on which I was raised—I
use the word advisedly—is 2,800 feet above the sea, a higher elevation than any farm I know of in New England, where I have taught for
twenty years. So I think it might be better to say I am from the High
South—though from the perspective of the Deep South it might seem
more like the Shallow South. Politically, it was certainly "shallow"
at the time of the Civil War.

Every true Virginian cannot forget that western Virginia went with
the North when the war began and was made a state as part of the
political effort to add free states to the Union. In the mountainous
parts of southwest Virginia, western North Carolina, eastern Kentucky, and east Tennessee there was great sympathy with the North.
Even so, my people went with the South. My grandfather was a
captain in the Confederate Army and was wounded in the battle of
Gauley Bridge early in the war; he was brought home along two
hundred miles of rutted roads for a semiparaplegic life that lasted
until 1906. I say semiparaplegic with a certain emphasis, because he
married and had eleven children.

I cite these facts not as credentials but perhaps as an explanation for
my long-standing interest in the Civil War. There was not, as I remember, much talk in my home about that war. My mother, who had
come from Pulaski County, just to the east of my native Grayson
County, could remember her uncles—one of whom had fought with
Lee, the other with Joseph E. Johnston—arguing over the merits of
those two commanders. My father knew, and knew well, the broad
outlines of the struggle but rarely stressed the Civil War as a subject of
conversation. Yet somehow I was more interested in the war than any

of my schoolmates were. I can remember reading Mary Johnston's *The Long Roll* and Clifford Dowdey's *The Bugles Blow No More* early in high school and then going beyond fiction to read Douglas Southall Freeman's four-volume biography of R. E. Lee. And I can never forget what for me was the strongest passage in Faulkner's *Intruder in the Dust,* because, reading it at the University of Michigan just after returning there from World War II, it seemed to sound some depth of my emotional life. The passage is part of Chick Mallison's remembrance of his uncle Gavin's voice, speaking for him the truth it no less seemed for me.

> It's all *now* you see. Yesterday won't be over until tomorrow and tomorrow began ten thousand years ago. For every Southern boy fourteen years old, not once but whenever he wants it, there is the instant when it's still not yet two oclock on that July afternoon in 1863, the brigades are in position behind the rail fence, the guns are laid and ready in the woods and the furled flags are already loosened to break out and Pickett himself with his long oiled ringlets and his hat in one hand probably and his sword in the other looking up the hill waiting for Longstreet to give the word and it's all in the balance, it hasn't happened yet, it hasn't even begun yet, it not only hasn't begun yet but there is still time for it not to begin against that position and those circumstances which made more men than Garnett and Kemper and Armstead and Wilcox look grave yet it's going to begin, we all know that, we have come too far with too much at stake and that moment doesn't need even a fourteen-year-old boy to think *This time. Maybe this time* with all this much to lose, and all this much to gain: Pennsylvania, Maryland, the world, the golden dome of Washington itself to crown with desperate and unbelievable victory the desperate gamble, the cast made two years ago; or to anyone who ever sailed even a skiff under a quilt sail, the moment in 1492 when somebody thought *This is it:* the absolute edge of no return, to turn back now and make home or sail irrevocably on and either find land or plunge over the world's roaring rim.[1]

I have always liked the fate in my life that took me north to read that passage, just as I now like the fate that has brought me south to speak of U. S. Grant—a hard figure to face, even for an American, let alone a southerner. Both southerners and northerners saw him as a killer during the Civil War; even worse, remembering that he had grown up the son of a tanner, they saw him as a butcher. At Shiloh and in the

---

1. William Faulkner, *Intruder in the Dust* (New York, 1949), 194–95.

assaults before Vicksburg, he had shown how prepared he was to endure large losses of men. And in the Wilderness and again at Spotsylvania, he sustained losses in direct confrontation with Lee that no prior commander could stand without retreating. Finally, at Cold Harbor, when he lost seven thousand men in a little over eight minutes, northerners as well as southerners, though they could see that he would never turn back, had to wonder whether anyone on either side could endure the arithmetic of such a victory.

In the 120-year aftermath of that struggle, the nation has tended to see him as the stubborn and relentless figure who plunged from Shiloh to Appomattox, seemingly careless of the cost of lives, "to fight it out on this line if it takes all summer."[2] Lincoln and Lee, the other two men who live in the national memory as the central triumvirate, have been largely exempted from responsibility in the slaughter. Lincoln's martyrdom and Lee's surrender have left them with an increasingly benign image. Yet we have to know, if we have read Shelby Foote's magnificent narrative of the Civil War, that it was Lincoln who, long before the Wilderness, had realized that what the northern army required—what *he* required—was a general who could withstand such arithmetic.[3] Moreover, it is well to remember that Grant tells us, in his *Memoirs,* that about the only subject in which he was good at West Point was mathematics (I, 39). As for Lee, his gentle face in all those portraits obscures the fact that he was as much a killer as Grant. From the moment he took command of the Confederate forces in the Seven Days east of Richmond, he showed a disposition to attack—and often to attack entrenched positions. Thus, if Grant's strategy at Shiloh and at Chickasaw Bluffs prefigured the Wilderness and Cold Harbor, Lee at Malvern Hill prefigured Pickett's charge at Gettysburg. To think about Lincoln and Lee and Grant this way, it seems to me, is to begin to comprehend how prepared they were to bear the responsibility of killing in the war. Bearing that kind of killing was what McClellan and his Confederate counterpart, Joseph E. Johnston—both of whom were profoundly loved by their men—could not quite bear. They lacked that ultimate willingness to give battle.

---

2. Ulysses S. Grant, *Personal Memoirs of U. S. Grant* (2 vols.; New York, 1885), II, 226. All subsequent citations are from this edition and will be given parenthetically in the text.
3. Shelby Foote, *The Civil War: A Narrative* (3 vols., New York 1958–74), II, 119.

Looking at the war with hindsight, as we must, we see the fatality of Grant ultimately facing Lee—and where but in the *Wilderness,* only fifteen miles wide and eight miles deep, and not in the West or in the mountains but in the East, only fifty miles from Washington. It is as if that term *wilderness,* so integral to anything we could think about America, were to be contracted, confined, and concentrated into an area where two men—one from the South and East, from a great American family related by blood and marriage to the immortal Washington, and groomed to lead a ragged army of revolution not altogether unlike the one that Washington led; the other from the North and West, from obscure stock and an even deeper obscurity into which he had withdrawn, or sunk, to emerge into prominence through a series of victories at Fort Donelson, Shiloh, Vicksburg, and Chattanooga—were to face each other as battle-tested representatives of their societies. The fierceness of that encounter still has power to exhilarate, but it also makes us tremble, no matter where our sympathies lie. Lee's savage attack—equal in ferocity to the ones that had shattered Hooker, Pope and Burnside—made Grant, who had whittled while the battle raged, tremble in his tent in its aftermath, but it did not deter him from his purpose.[4] Grant tells us that his army cheered when he pointed it south toward Spotsylvania instead of north across the Rappahannock (the way his predecessors Hooker and Burnside had gone after their initiation under Bobby Lee's fire), but there is no record of its cheering after Cold Harbor (II, 210). Yet— cheering or not—Grant's army kept up such pressure in effort after effort to flank Lee's army that Lee, his maneuverability increasingly lost, had to submit to the siege of Petersburg. Although he fought brilliantly and exacted a horrible toll, he could never regain the offensive against the man who, his soldiers said, "didn't scare worth a damn."

At Appomattox, though Lee said that he would rather die a thousand deaths than surrender, he nonetheless surrendered—precisely to avoid the thousands of deaths that *he* could not die. The fine thing about his surrender was that it was unconditional; thus, it was not abject. Grant laid down the conditions, and they were generous. If it seems one of the noblest moments in American history, it is because

---

4. Shelby Foote's account is the most detailed and vivid. See Foote, *The Civil War,* III, 184–86.

both men were noble in the moment. For Lee, the poignancy was the loss itself. But there was poignancy as well in Grant's generosity—for he gave away his nobility. He could never be so noble again. Yet he did not throw it away; he *gave* it away. Left with that nobility—his own, coupled with that which Grant had obscurely granted him—Lee rode away from Appomattox on Traveller, the wonderful horse with the wonderful name. The road of his career went not to the presidency of his nation, as had that of his model, Washington, but to the presidency of a ravaged and all but ruined Washington College in Lexington, Virginia. Although he thought of writing about the war, he did not. He lacked the records, and more important, he lacked the life. The war, which had been his life, was truly over. What was left was not to be a life of writing but of silence on the subject, a composure of submission, humility, duty, and above all simplicity—a model so restrained and severe as to be a monument of education for the life of defeated young men returning into a victorious Union. And so Lee, like Lincoln before him, died into immortality—idealized in the South and forgiven in the North, as Lincoln was idealized in the North and more and more forgiven in the South. Of the three, Grant alone realized the full material benefits of victory and went on to be president of his nation, only to find in that success a wilderness of failure, until at last, in the throes of bankruptcy and the sickness that would kill him—cancer of the throat (no doubt brought on by all the cigars he smoked)—he wrote his memoirs.

All this is prologue to consideration of those memoirs and the man in them who is my subject. But memoirs, as much as war, are both a form and act of life. Walter Benjamin, in an essay on the writer Nikolai Leskov, has some fine observations about the nature of a man writing at the point of death. He observes that after World War I the very idea of narration or storytelling has declined.

> With the [First] World War a process began to become apparent which has not halted since then. Was it not noticeable at the end of the war that men returned grown silent—not richer, but poorer in communicable experience? What ten years later was poured out in the flood of war books was anything but experience that goes from mouth to mouth. And there was nothing remarkable about that. For never has experience been contradicted more thoroughly than strategic experience by tactical warfare, economic experience by inflation, bodily experience by mechanical warfare, moral experience by those in power. A genera-

tion that had gone to school on a horse-drawn streetcar now stood under the open sky in a countryside in which nothing remained unchanged but the clouds, and beneath these clouds, in a field of force of destructive torrents and explosions, was the tiny, fragile human body.

Later in the essay, Benjamin points out how death, which had once been the source of man's authority, is steadily sequestered from the living in sanatoriums or hospitals—and today we could add, in nursing homes.

It is, however, characteristic that not only a man's knowledge or wisdom, but above all his real life—and this is the stuff that stories are made of—first assumes transmissible form at the moment of his death. Just as a sequence of images is set in motion inside a man as his life comes to an end—unfolding the views of himself under which he has encountered himself without being aware of it—suddenly in his expressions and looks the unforgettable emerges and imparts to everything that concerned him that authority which even the poorest wretch in dying possesses for the living around him. This authority is at the very source of the story.[5]

To be sure, Benjamin is thinking in terms of story and fiction rather than autobiography, but his remarks on what the First World War did to narrative—or rather on the relation between the emotional devastation wrought in that war and the disappearance of narrative in the modern world—might well be applied to our Civil War. Gertrude Stein was surely right in seeing that America, far from being the world's newest nation, was actually the oldest, for the precise reason that in its Civil War it was the first nation to enter the modern world. It is not merely that the Civil War marked the introduction of mechanized war on the grand scale, that it heralded vast troop movements by railroads, that it signaled the beginning of aerial observation by means of balloons, that it ushered in the rifled guns and breech-loading carbines, that it marked the appearance of ironclads, harbor mines, and submarines in naval warfare, that it initiated fully developed trench warfare, that it introduced the telegraph as the common means of communication, and that it perfected mass killing to the point of institutionalizing the body count. Beyond all these innovations, the war was the most wholly *written* war that had ever oc-

5. Walter Benjamin, *Illuminations* (New York, 1968), 84, 94.

curred. Not only were official records written by officers after each engagement—and ultimately published in 128 volumes by the U.S. government—but reporters were constantly in the field, covering the war.

For example, Charles A. Dana of the New York *Tribune* accompanied Grant on numerous occasions. And illustrators such as Winslow Homer and Alfred Waud were on hand. In addition, there were the photographers, of whom Brady is merely the best known. He not only waited in Washington for famous people to come to him, he also went into the field in search of them; thus, he was in Richmond, to photograph Lee three days after Appomattox before the light of battle in his eyes had faded. The ten-volume photographic history of the Civil War, published in 1911, in addition to being the first photographic war history of such scope, remains a classic. And of course there were the memoirs—hordes of them—by prominent officers as well as soldiers in the ranks.

Today we are likely to think that memoirs are autobiography, since they are so classed in libraries. But the term *autobiography* is of relatively recent origin; there was no such word until the end of the eighteenth century. Thus what is today called Benjamin Franklin's *autobiography* was called by Franklin *memoirs,* indicating that it was an account of his public or external life. The term used for a chronicle of one's inner life was, following St. Augustine, *confession.* Yet the emerging term *autobiography* had, by the end of the nineteenth century, so completely carried the field that it came to stand for both the inner and outer lives of personal narrative. Significantly, the term first appeared when *self* was displacing *soul* as the term to designate the individual life—the same historical moment when the American and French revolutions, freeing the individual as a potent political energy, established nations that, more and more separated from God, were themselves to become a religion. In our own national life the Civil War signals that moment when the religious sensibility, already cast adrift in the constitutional separation of church from state, was violently attracted from the church into the political arena. Thus, Lincoln himself seems always to be a kind of Christ figure as president, and his death on an April Friday in 1865 is connected in our minds to that other Friday that we cannot quite separate ourselves from. His Emancipation Proclamation, rededicating Jefferson's Declaration in the poetic cadences of religious rhetoric, has inevitably come to stand in the American mind as the primary document of our national religion.

Grant, however, was not Lincoln. He called the account of his life a memoir, not an autobiography, and he remains, on the whole, stolidly secular in that account. Yet his *Memoirs* are not exclusively about his public life, beginning as they do with his early "private" life, pursuing his life as a soldier first in the Mexican War and then in his Civil War campaigns, and concluding with a chapter defining what he believes that war meant in the life of his nation. Insofar as his book begins at the beginning of his life and follows his rise from obscurity into prominence, it is an autobiography; insofar as it refuses to deal extensively or intensively with his inner life, it is a memoir (in the old sense of the term). It is clear almost from the beginning, and remains clear to the end, that Grant saw his life in terms of his military and not his political career. Thus, his memoirs are in effect military memoirs, and as such, they relate him to Caesar and Napoleon. Although Napoleon did not live to publish his memoirs, on St. Helena he dictated much of his life to four members of his staff (Bertrand, Las Cases, Gourgaud, and de Montholon). Like Caesar, he spoke of himself in the third person, knowing that this usage at once related him to the preeminent military figure of the classic world and reflected his imperial identity as a separate force in history.

Grant does not, of course, speak of himself in the third person. He was, in the first place, not an emperor but a general and president. Moreover, he was an American and he wanted to remain a simple separate self, to use Whitman's formulation, and at the same time be a representative of the American possibility in the manner of Franklin, rising from obscurity to prominence. There is, for all the inevitability of that first-person pronominal "I" to designate the self, a severe problem for anyone who writes about himself in the first person. Although everyone uses the pronoun in the confident assurance that it refers to the ineffable and singular self, there remains the relentless fact of language, all but forcing everyone to resort to the selfsame signifier. If we are writing about our inner, emotional selves—if, let us say, we are truly unknown and are attempting, in the act of writing, to make ourselves known, whether to ourselves or to an intimate or impersonal audience—then we have to intensify our individuality by dramatizing or lyricizing or explaining our lives in such a way as to inscribe by the very act of writing our lives imperishably upon the page, lives that, but for the writing, would remain unrecorded and unknown. Thus, the life itself, in such a case, depends on the writing.

If such an act of writing puts immense pressure on the writer to secure his signature in autobiographical discourse, he nonetheless enjoys the freedom of his material, since there is no large referential record against which his writing can be tested.

With a writer like Grant, the situation is vastly different. His life had taken shape publicly; indeed, his life, by the time he came to write it, had already been *written* by history. And so he already had a vast record to deal with. Although that record had made him known and interesting, thus ensuring an audience for what would seem to be at last *the* authentic record of a life, the outlines and substance of which were widely known, he nonetheless faced a profound problem. Beyond making good his own account—setting the record straight, introducing material that only he could know, marshaling his evidence into coherent sequential narrative—Grant, if he were truly to succeed, had to repossess or reclaim his life from history. Otherwise, why write it? Why not, like Lee, somehow assent to history in the faith that the life, as existing in the public and historic records, would itself be the deed of gift to posterity?

The moment we come to the motive of writing one's own life, we all but touch the heart of autobiography. I do not wish, in probing the sources of the form, to slight the baser motives in such writing acts, particularly the acts of famous people. We can see, in the memoirs of Eisenhower, Truman, Nixon, and Carter, the strong commercial motive—so strong that it sometimes ensures failure in the very marketplace it is too much designed for. And certainly the commercial motive was as strong in Grant as in any of the recent presidential memoirists I have named. He had, as William McFeely has emphasized in his fine biography, come to the idea of writing his memoirs as a means of financially recovering from the questionable and disastrous speculative investments he had made—investments sufficiently disastrous and questionable to tarnish, if not taint, his already damaged reputation.[6] Indeed, the only way Grant could avoid the taint was to maintain an innocence so profound as to make him seem almost stupid. If the innocence shielded him from culpability in the political and financial world he had entered after Appomattox, it seemed all the more to expose his naked desire for power and money.

Grant was of course fortunate in having Mark Twain as his pub-

6. William McFeely, *Grant: A Biography* (New York, 1981), 493–99.

lisher, not only because he got the most liberal terms of royalty any writer could expect but also because in Mark Twain he encountered a writer equally interested in the commerce of authorship. It was Mark Twain, after all, who had written to Olivia Langdon Clemens that he would not touch a subject "if there wasn't money in it." Much as genteel writers and later academic critics might deplore the outright materialism of such an author, few could deny that Mark Twain was every inch a writer. Beyond that, Grant had found in Mark Twain a kindred spirit—a westerner who, in the world of writing, had determined to command a vast audience in much the same way that Grant had commanded a mighty army. After hearing Mark Twain lecture in Boston, William Dean Howells observed that he had held his audience in the palm of his hand and tickled it. Then, too, Mark Twain, who had felt the full sting leveled at him by literary Boston after his irreverent performance at the Whittier birthday dinner in 1877, was already making the myth of himself as the Confederate soldier who, having had the sagacity to resign—as he humorously referred to his desertion—from the Confederate army in 1861 because Grant was pursuing him in Missouri, nonetheless had the power of humor to reduce his erstwhile nemesis to helpless laughter at the reunion of the Grand Army of the Republic in Chicago in 1879. At that reunion, where speaker after speaker toasted the celebrities on the platform— Grant, Sherman, Sheridan, and others—Mark Twain had watched the imperturbably deadpan Grant sitting unmoved, with one leg across the other, while speaker upon speaker shook the house with eloquence. As the last speaker, Mark Twain chose as his subject "the babies" and observed that it was humbling to think that all people, even the heroic Grant, had once been babies. He went on to imagine Grant in his cradle, fifty-six years earlier, utterly devoted to the immensely serious strategy of trying to get his big toe in his mouth, and he ended by claiming that few in the audience could doubt that he had succeeded. I have always thought that the humor of the remark had much to do with Grant's posture on the platform—the head possibly leaning forward toward the one leg across the other, in profound concentration on the foot. In any event, the toast, which had the same irreverent audacity of the Whittier fiasco and no doubt produced in the assembled throng a corresponding anxiety as Mark Twain worked through those drawling pauses in leading up to his snapper, brought the house down, and Grant with it—at least in Mark Twain's triumphant account to Howells.[7] There was, no doubt, something particularly gratifying for Mark Twain in recounting his success to Howells. Like Grant, who had also come from Ohio, Howells had sufficiently succeeded in the genteel literary community of Boston to show undue embarrassment in the wake of the Whittier affair.

If Clemens, as Confederate veteran, had enjoyed his triumph over Grant upon the Chicago stage, he enjoyed even more his role of rescuing him from the menace of bankruptcy—and rescuing him in the role of *publisher,* thereby making Grant a writer under Mark Twain's protection rather then the general who had menaced him in the distant past. To see such possibilities is not at all to demean the relationship between the two but to begin to appreciate it. It was, after all, a happy and productive relationship and had a happy conclusion, at least in the financial sense. The Webster Publishing Company, of which Twain was senior partner, paid Julia Dent Grant a single royalty check of $200,000, the largest such check in the nineteenth century.[8] And so Grant's last sustained act of life left his heirs fully solvent.

So much for the financial motive. If that motive seems negative in terms of what we like to think of as *literary* purpose, it is at least irrelevant in terms of the literary value of the book—though we can say that Mark Twain's faith in the commercial value of the *Memoirs* prompted him to see that the book was produced in handsome style. There are, however, other negative motives that bear upon a critical valuation of the book itself. There is always a suspicion on the part of a sophisticated reader about an autobiographer's willingness or ability to tell the truth of his life. Hence the belief that either vanity, fear, repression, or downright suppression of evidence will disable the autobiographer, making his account unreliable. That is why we wait for the biographer to give us the "real" truth of the life. Nor can we exempt Grant's account from such a charge.

He makes no mention of mutely accepting the registrar's error at West Point that changed his name from Hiram Ulysses Grant to Ulysses Simpson Grant, surely one of the crucial facts of his life. Nor does he tell about his drinking, an accusation that was brought against

7. Henry Nash Smith and William Gibson (eds.), *Mark Twain–Howells Letters* (2 vols., Cambridge, Mass., 1960), I, 278–81.
8. McFeely, *Grant,* 501.

him throughout his career. After Vicksburg he went on a binge, riding hell for leather through and over tents and campfires on a horse named Kangaroo, but you may be sure that he does not regale us with that episode in his *Memoirs*. Nor does he tell of the drinking he must have done in San Francisco before the war, when, apparently in despair in the loneliness of being far from home at a military outpost in a country of speculators, gamblers, and derelicts, he may have felt doomed to join the failures who were the casualties of a society dreaming of striking it rich. To know those hidden "facts" is to want to read between the lines of Grant's steadfast, prosaic account of this losing campaign in the Far West that led him to resign from the army and led to further defeats as a farmer, as a candidate for public office in St. Louis, and finally to total retreat into his brother's leather goods store in Galena, Illinois (not far from Hannibal, Missouri, where Samuel Clemens had gotten his start, and on the same great river where the same Clemens was even then a pilot). Nor is there any mention of the night after the battle of the Wilderness, when Grant threw himself so violently on his tent cot that Horace Porter could never forget it.

Then, too, there are distortions. On the matter of Shiloh, Grant is singularly circumspect in accounting for the surprise attack he faced from Albert Sidney Johnston, though it is possible to see through the circumspection to something having gone awry on that first day of the battle. And concerning Iuka, Grant puts heavy stress on the way the wind blew the noise of battle away from him—in order to explain his failure to know that a battle was being fought in the vicinity of his responsibility. And in describing the Chattanooga campaign, Grant evades the fact that Sherman, his favorite commander, was held in check by Pat Cleburne, while Thomas, for whom Grant had carefully engineered a subordinate role, took Missionary Ridge. Indeed, anyone who wished to explore just how Grant *always* depreciates Thomas might have a field day of research.

Could it be that Grant, ever eager to promote himself and his favorites, Sherman and Sheridan, might have been concerned, to the point of anxiety, about Thomas' having come so grandly to the fore in the eyes of the nation after his brilliant action at Chickamauga? To the very end of the *Memoirs,* Grant consistently depreciates Thomas on grounds that he delayed giving battle, and he can do little more than grudgingly acknowledge the completeness with which Thomas finally routed Hood's army. As for Bobby Lee, Grant is hardly magnanimous prior to his account of Appomattox. A reader of the *Memoirs* would do well to check Freeman's *R. E. Lee* as a corrective to Grant's version of all the battles leading to the Confederate surrender, though a reader of Freeman would be equally bereft of an objective view of that year-long campaign if he had not read Grant's *Memoirs* with extreme care. And a reader of Grant, K. P. Williams, Bruce Catton, Allan Nevins, and even Shelby Foote's masterful and definitive narrative of the war is left with Lee's profound silence on the subject—a silence that grows all the more powerful the deeper one plunges into the memoirs of Longstreet, Hood, E. P. Alexander, Jubal Early, Sherman, Horace Porter, and Sheridan—to touch but the surface of this sea of narratives.

To insist on Grant's self-protection, or whatever one wishes to call it, may seem to some a disparagement of his account. How far that is from my intention I can hardly say. I simply wish that I was deep enough into this subject to point to a hundred more examples of such evasion, or even self-serving, by way of launching an initial attack on Grant that would bring fully to the fore the solidity, the stubborn, straight-ahead narrative with which Grant completed his life. Although the *Memoirs* may seem to those who contemplate Grant's life from the biographical perspective the partial life it so surely is, for me it is the complete, which is to say the essential, life of U. S. Grant. And I have no doubt that the biographical subtext, no matter how much it is completed down the years, until the last of a thousand discrepancies is shown between it and Grant's text, will all the more validate the authority of the *Memoirs*.

What is that authority that I see and foresee? First of all, it comes from Grant's having reclaimed authority over his life by the act of authorship. Never mind that even his authorship *was* contested soon after the appearance of the *Memoirs,* contentions having been made that either Adam Badeau or Mark Twain ghosted the book. One has but to look at the work of Badeau, a skillful writer, or that of Mark Twain, a great and inimitable writer, to see the folly of such claims. The point is that Grant, in the presence of death, and writing almost to the point of death itself, literally completed his life. In that sense he "took" his life, for there is always a suicidal impulse in the act of autobiography, whether the writer knows it or not. If he writes well, he ends his life. It is no wonder that Henry Adams, writing to Henry

James after completing his *Education* (in which he had converted himself into the third person), advised James to take his own life before a biographer had the chance to take it.

To begin to see the task that faced Grant in writing his life—beyond the sheer act of will required to execute his life before death executed him—one has to imagine the difficulties and complications surrounding him. First of all, as I have said, his life had already been written, and more than that, his campaigns had already been criticized by other memoirists. He himself had joined the fray of conflicting accounts in *Battles and Leaders of the Civil War,* published by *Century* magazine. So there he was, faced by the remorseless enemy, Death, that he knew was waiting directly ahead of him, and flanked by conflicting accounts of leading participants in the war—some of praise, others of blame, some Union and some Confederate—all claiming the authority of experience. Then, too, there was the essential failure of the "success" of his life after Appomattox, which led him to squander not only the ample remuneration that he had been given by a grateful nation but also the honor he had so justly won. All this and so much more constituted the remorseless divisions of the enemy. For Grant, like every true military figure, not only had enemies, he *required* them.

Now how to write his way directly into this conflict, without complaining about the enemy and without getting committed to justifying himself? There was the problem, sufficient to tax the ablest writer. There would have been every enticement to evade it by being fulsome in praise of others or overmodest in evaluation of himself as a means of disarming both friends and foes. And think for a moment of a much larger invitation—to simplify, in an utterly false way, by reducing the topography of this battle into smooth terrain, as if the battle of the writer were not a wilderness of contradictions into which the very current of narrative had to run and, somehow, run through—as Grant's life had run, all but unconsciously forward, its great ambition not so much concealed as coordinated and literally embodied in the disarming figure of the man who walked as if he were slightly pitched forward.

The more conscious Grant was about these divisions of the enemy, the more likely he was to do what other memoirists did: explain, justify, complain, insist, brag, sentimentalize, and reveal. Yet to have no explanation, no justification, no criticism, no sentiment, no morality, no pride, and no revelation was indeed to have nothing. And you may be sure that in the *Memoirs* there is explanation, justification, criticism of the most telling kind, sentiment, moral vision, calm pride of achievement, and a great deal of revelation. But the point is that all these aspects of mental existence are subordinated to the command of a forward-moving narrative.

That narrative is—and the point seems to me crucial—much more conventional than original in conception. Even so, the convention, which begins with the lineal descent of parentage on both sides of the family, eventuating in the birth of the subject, has already divided Grant into the two "I's" that constitute every first-person autobiography. There is the generating "I" of the writer, all but concealed to the reader, and the conceived "I," who seems to the reader, and even to the writer, submerged in the convention, the subject of the book, though that "I" is really the object for the writer—the object being drawn along the utterly conventional line of chronology to the present consciousness generating it. The generating consciousness of the writer can try to be at one with what it believes to have been the emotions of the past self, or it can be detached and extremely objective about the past self. Grant's narrative runs conventionally between these extremes.

The past self that Grant presents in his narrative, which is to say the boy and young man with which his book begins, is also profoundly conventional. He is, in other words, primarily a *general* boy and young man. This does not mean that he is ordinary, nor does it mean that no particular life is presented. There are fine details. There is the boy who loves horses—yet the love is never presented poetically, or what we might want to call "imaginatively." Horse is a horse is a horse, as Gertrude Stein would say (who, incidentally, wrote acutely about U. S. Grant). But horses are present all through Grant's *Memoirs,* and that presence is a kind of solid and pervasive fact about the life of the man in his book. Here it is nice to remember that almost the only time Lee waxed poetic in his letters is about the incomparable Traveller. Grant is not poetic, but he asserts his early interest in horses and then, incidentally, reveals his growing competence in managing them at the same time that he shows their recalcitrant and potentially dangerous energy. Then there is trading in horses, in which Grant presents himself the dupe, since he tells the old trader at the outset how much his father has allowed him to pay for the horse in question. But if he is the fool of the trade, he nonetheless gets the horse he wants.

This is a fine bit of dry humor—very dry—and it is related to the kind of humor that Henry Adams observed in remembering Grant's witticism: "The best way to kill a bad law is to execute it." Adams knew that in Mark Twain's writing, the remark would have been hilarious, but in the voice of Grant the president, the remark was, if not devastating, at least disconcerting in the extreme. In the *Memoirs* the humor is somehow winning in that it reveals Grant's awareness of his victimization (he goes on to observe how his folly made him the laughingstock in the town), and yet there is the confidence of the generating memoirist who has survived the ridicule to become famous. Grant can thoroughly afford to expose his youthful naïveté. Although he never asserts his mature confidence, it is implicit in his account; at the same time, and again implicitly, Grant reveals both affection and a trace of empathy for the shame-faced young trader. He can still feel the old wound in the humorous effect of revealing it. His account of having been tricked and subsequently ridiculed is not unlike Franklin's anecdote of being laughed at by his future wife upon his entry into Philadelphia—except that Grant has no such direct and neat revenge as Franklin had in marrying Deborah Read. He has instead, lying ahead in his narrative, all the strategies of a commander to scout out and waylay his foe with feints, probes, flanking movements, and frontal assaults that merely mask the larger design of getting at the enemy's rear. Yet Grant never betrays consciousness of the connection between that early and these later deceptions; if he did, the whole narrative would be different.

Grant, in a similar incident, tells of having worn his West Point uniform proudly on returning to his hometown, only to be jeered for being a "sojer." How much that simple episode is related to his having appeared at Appomattox seemingly out of uniform! Yet, here again, no consciousness of the connection is registered. Indeed, throughout the narrative, Grant shows himself as having appeared sufficiently nondescript as to be unrecognized for what he was. He can from time to time talk with a soldier, even a rebel soldier; he can pause to discuss the war with an ardent secessionist; he can at once devastate a loyal Confederate woman in Virginia with the news that Sherman has taken Atlanta and, almost in the same breath, offer her the courteous consideration of the power of his rank—and not (it is well to discriminate) the rank of his power. For Grant's power is obscurely separate from his rank or his uniform. He is not in uniform so much as he *is* uniform; he is not a general, he *is* general, in the deepest meaning of the word.

Those early humorous anecdotes of the horse and the uniform could provide a reader who watched horses and uniforms throughout the book with an elaborate tissue of connection. Thus, there are the horses Grant bought and later lost in the Mexican War—and he was again laughed at by his superiors for his failure to maintain possession of his worthless horseflesh. There is the horse he rode desperately through crossfire at street intersections in Monterey to get more ammunition. And though there may not be the account of the drunken ride on Kangaroo, there are the two times he was injured in falls from horses. Finally, there is the incident at Shiloh, in which Grant was surprised by the enemy while riding with Generals McPherson and Buell. All three generals fled—Buell losing his hat on the ride. In a sentence that could well stand for the laconic humor that shadows the simplicity of his style, Grant remarks, "He did not stop to pick it up." In the headlong flight, Grant's scabbard was hit and broken, and "McPherson's horse was panting as if ready to drop. On examination it was found that a ball had struck him forward of the flank just back of the saddle, and had gone entirely through. In a few minutes the poor beast dropped dead; he had given no sign of the injury until we came to a stop." (I, 353–54). He completes the paragraph with the summary facts, followed by a feeling: "There were three of us: one had lost a horse, killed; one a hat, and one a sword-scabbard. All were thankful that it was no worse" (I, 354).

This is an example of the conclusiveness of Grant's style: summary assertion of the facts accompanied by laconic observation about the feeling. That dead horse, in the middle of things, would have to stand for all the dead horses in the war, yet Grant neither insists upon the synecdoche nor elaborates elsewhere on the screams of wounded horses during battles nor the stench of dead ones afterward. Instead, there is only this kind of episode in the steady sequence of incidents and events.

In light of all the horses that appear in the narrative, there is something deeply touching about Grant's acknowledgment of the poor beast's having spent its dying life getting McPherson off the field, and particularly so when one considers that McPherson would be killed on horseback before Atlanta. Grant briefly acknowledges the event much later in the *Memoirs:* "It was during this battle that McPherson, while passing from one column to another, was instantly killed. In his death the army lost one of its ablest, purest, and best generals" (II, 169). Such a passage provides a fine bridge from the simplicity and humor of the book to its simplicity and restraint. Grant never goes extensively into the interior tensions of battle, nor does he make elaborate nods to the sentiments of praise, morality, or patriotism. Yet in that one word *purest,* by which he characterizes McPherson, we see the compression of true generalization.

Only in sporadic and widely isolated sentences does Grant reveal his anxiety. He recalls it in the Mexican War, when he led his first charge. He says that, though filled with fear, he lacked the moral courage to retreat. He mentions this same response in describing his approach to the enemy in Missouri. Leading his small contingent and fearing to ascend a hill he believes to hide the enemy on its farther side, yet lacking the moral courage to retreat, he goes over the crest, to discover that the enemy has retreated. From that experience, he says, he emerged with the knowledge that the enemy is always as afraid of you as you are of him, a knowledge profound enough to become a truth that carried him through all his subsequent battles. Grant's conception that forward movement into battle results from the absence of the moral courage to retreat is, to say the least, arresting. Following Henry Adams, we could say that in Mark Twain— who shared and expressed the same vision in relation to writing—the paradox is critically fascinating. But in Grant, the general and writer whose whole life moved, and is moving, forward with the ordered purpose of destroying the enemy, the laconic observation that the determination to destroy the enemy arises from the lack or absence of the *moral* courage to retreat is a paradox sufficient—the longer we brood upon it—to appall. Grant, of course, does not brood upon it but simply goes forward in his narrative, as he had gone forward in war, toward the execution of his purpose. Here again he discloses this enormous fact of life without allowing the consciousness of the fact to condition the consciousness of his narrative or distract him from pushing on. A lesser writer would have converted such consciousness into emotional emphasis upon the anguish and horror of life at war.

But here again Grant, though he reveals such anguish, never allows the revelation to distract him from his narrative. After the battle of

Belmont, his first major encounter with the enemy in the Civil War, he tells of throwing himself on a cot, only to leap up again (such a textual moment will have to stand for his failure to disclose his behavior at the end of the first day in the Wilderness). And he has this to say of the night after the first day at Shiloh.

> During the night rain fell in torrents and our troops were exposed to the storm without shelter. I made my headquarters under a tree a few hundred yards back from the river bank. My ankle was so much swollen from the fall of my horse the Friday night preceding, and the bruise was so painful, that I could get no rest. The drenching rain would have precluded the possibility of sleep without this additional cause. Some time after midnight, growing restive under the storm and the continuous pain, I moved back to the log house under the bank. This had been taken as a hospital, and all night wounded men were being brought in, their wounds dressed, a leg or an arm amputated as the case might require, and everything being done to save life or alleviate suffering. The sight was more unendurable than encountering the enemy's fire, and I returned to my tree in the rain. (I, 349)

Brief as it is, this passage is unusually long for its kind in the *Memoirs*. Grant customarily spends but a sentence (and even these sentences are rare) to indicate the immense strain of battle and responsibility he undoubtedly lived with constantly for four years. Thus he writes, in almost a phrase, of his immense relief in finally getting his troops on the east bank of the Mississippi below Vicksburg after months of failure and frustration. And he remarks the enormous anxiety he felt, as late as Petersburg, about the possibility of Lee's escaping and eluding the iron grip Grant had put round him. Finally, he mentions his terrible headache on the morning of April 9, 1865, only to have it immediately cured upon receipt of Lee's letter agreeing to discuss terms of surrender.

Then there is Grant's description of meeting Lee in the McLean house later that same day:

> What General Lee's feelings were I do not know. As he was a man of much dignity, with an impassible face, it was impossible to say whether he felt inwardly glad that the end had finally come, or felt sad over the result, and was too manly to show it. Whatever his feelings, they were entirely concealed from my observation; but my own feelings, which had been quite jubilant on the receipt of his letter, were sad and depressed. I felt like anything rather than rejoicing at the downfall

of a foe who had fought so long and valiantly, and had suffered so much for a cause, though that cause was, I believe, one of the worst for which a people ever fought, and one for which there was the least excuse. I do not question, however, the sincerity of the great mass of those who were opposed to us. (II, 489–90)

Both Grant's restraint and his truth are evident in every line. There is the truth of his not knowing what Lee felt and the restraint to refuse to imagine it; there is the truth, or at least firm confidence, of his knowing what *he* felt and the restraint to refuse to embellish it. Even in his evaluation of Lee's lost cause, Grant carefully interpolates the fact that it is his *belief* and not necessarily the ineffable moral truth.

If the laconic humor, simplicity, and restraint of Grant's style at once qualify and define the clarity of the *Memoirs,* they do not reveal Grant's heart. There is always a two-front war that he sees himself having fought, and that he fights again in the act of writing his book. From the moment his narrative enters the Civil War, Grant sees himself faced not merely by the Confederates in his front but harassed by enemies from the rear, in the persons of rival generals. He presents himself, of course, as a modest, relatively unassuming, and certainly unpretentious man, somehow swept forward into fame by vast forces beyond his control. As a reader, I have no doubt that he was such a man. His steady, straightforward prose, with its essential clarity, its slight laconic edge, and its fine simplicity of plainness—so different from Lee's style with its equal simplicity, but a simplicity of humility—serves to allay any doubt about Grant's sincerity or accuracy of self-portrayal.

Yet there is Grant's ambition, and anyone who thinks it was not a vaulting ambition would be foolish indeed. After all, here is a man who has been commanding general of one of the largest armies in history, then president of the United States for two terms (who sought with all his might a third term and almost succeeded), presenting himself as a modest person thrust forward into destiny and history. Early in the book he gives fine portraits of Zachary Taylor and Winfield Scott, portraits that clearly foreshadow the contrast between himself and Lee. Taylor is capable, casual, and politically unambitious, according to Grant—a man who sits his horse with both legs on the same side and who eschews pomp and military formality. Scott, on the other hand, is immaculately dressed, politically ambitious, and very conscious of his own worth. Both are, in Grant's eyes, fine generals. Yet it was the unassuming and politically unambitious Taylor who, like Grant later, became president; Scott did not. Grant would like to think that Taylor's modest informality, representative of the life of democracy, was the transparency through which the common people could recognize his merits and lift him to the presidency. And Grant clearly, and in all probability sincerely, believed that his elevation to the presidency came not from personal ambition but from a similar recognition on the part of the people.

Yet Grant's whole narrative runs counter to such passivity. Once Grant enters the Civil War, he immediately finds his real enemy to be Henry Halleck. To be sure, there is evidence, both in the *Memoirs* and elsewhere, that Halleck pointedly depreciated Grant, particularly in the early part of the war. But in making the conflict emphatically present in his narrative, Grant conceals from the reader (and, I think, from himself) just what it was that Halleck feared, or possibly saw, in Grant. Let us allow him Halleck's ambition that led him to be general-in-chief in Washington. The point is that Grant uses Halleck in his own narrative—Halleck being happily (happily at least for Grant) dead—to mask from himself his own ambition. Besides Halleck there was McClernand, whom Grant sees as a politician-general pursuing the possibility of the White House. Now, twenty and more years later, Grant the writer, who has occupied the White House for eight long years, devotes himself to steadily exposing McClernand's ambition and potential insubordination. Grant all but makes it brutally explicit that, in Sherman and McPherson, he found allies sufficient to enable him to thwart, and ultimately rout, McClernand (it is worth remembering that McClernand was a Democrat). Let me be clear. I am not doubting Grant's estimate of McClernand, but emphasizing how he uses his two-front war as a representation of the force that thrusts him forward to the very presidency he would have us believe they coveted. This immense contradiction is not some concealed motive in the book; it is always all but on the surface of the narrative. It shows how the effective soldier-politician in a democracy shields himself from his own ambition by finding and attacking that ambition in his rivals.

The events of the war, cast in the deliberate sequence with which Grant narrates them, are the external force that preoccupied him in his march to power and fully occupy him as a writer, displacing the political life that lies between him and the lived conflict in which and through which he emerged as a recognizable and relentless military and political force. In recounting that life, Grant was, at the threshold of death, once more in touch with that fugitive part of himself that was, though fighting to be known, still unknown. His determination was thus undetermined. He was back in the field of force where his own acts were, on a terrain of vast contingency, still completing him.

It is no surprise that contingency is everywhere in the narrative. Grant sees it dominating the accounts of other memoirists. Thus, he excoriates William Preston Johnston's Confederate account of Shiloh, on the ground that it is one big *if*.

> *Ifs* defeated the Confederates at Shiloh. There is little doubt that we would have been disgracefully beaten *if* all the shells and bullets fired by us had passed harmlessly over the enemy and *if* all of theirs had taken effect. Commanding generals are liable to be killed during engagements; and the fact that when he was shot Johnston was leading a brigade to induce it to make a charge which had been repeatedly ordered, is evidence that there was neither the universal demoralization on our side nor the unbounded confidence on theirs which has been claimed. (I, 363)

Yet by the end of Grant's account of the battle, he, too, has been lured into the realm of the hypothetical, contending that if Halleck had let him proceed after the victory at Shiloh, all would have been different.

His entire narrative is fairly studded with similar resorts to *if*'s: if it had not rained, if Halleck had not dissolved his command, if the victory at Donelson had been quickly followed up, if Anderson had not made his all-night march into Spotsylvania (barely beating the Federals to the crossroads), if Butler and W. F. Smith had made a swifter march upon Petersburg, if the northern press had not devoted itself to praising Lee, if G. K. Warren could have been persuaded to move, if Siegel had shown more initiative in the Valley. These *if*'s, all through the narrative, are the hypothetical defenses Grant to the last throws up as he pushes his narrative forward, toward what is at once the end of the war and the end of his life. They are nothing less than the wilderness thicket with which Grant flanks his forward progress. They tell us not only about the life of a general but about life in general, reminding us of the fragile man Benjamin imagined after World War I and reminding us, as well, of Grant's fragility throughout his life.

There still remains the forward progress of the narrative, a progress that is the very soul of Grant the writer. As Grant moves toward his end, he increases the incidence of the battle orders and letters he wrote at the time. These orders, dispatches, and letters show how great a writer he was long before he wrote his memoirs. At their best, battle orders are not merely the prediction of the future but the making of it. That is why Grant is careful to quote his own orders. Here again, he is in the utter convention of the memoir, but Grant's battle orders, such as the one he wrote to Buckner at Donelson, defined not only the end of that brief campaign, and not only "Unconditional Surrender Grant," but the end of the war—though that end would be three desperate and frightful years later. To see how frightful things had become, one has but to read the order Grant sent to Halleck (which he duly includes in his narrative): "I am sending General Sheridan for temporary duty whilst the enemy is being expelled from the border. Unless General Hunter is in the field in person, I want Sheridan put in command of all the troops in the field, with instruction to put himself south of the enemy and follow him to the death" (II, 317–18). And Grant includes the dispatch he received from Abraham Lincoln, referring directly to that battle order: "This, I think, is exactly right, as to how our forces should move. But please look over the despatches you may have received from here, even since you made that order, and discover, if you can, that there is any idea in the head of any one here of 'putting our army *south* of the enemy,' or of 'following him to the *death*' in any direction. I repeat to you it will neither be done nor attempted unless you watch it every day, and hour, and force it" (II, 318).

Here his order to Halleck comes back upon him, and him alone, to take full responsibility to see that Early is followed to the death. Here is the full implication of having determined upon unconditional surrender far back at Donelson. Moreover, it comes at a time when Grant can see the possibility of the total defeat and annihilation of his enemy. If Lincoln, fully committed to his support, urges him on to the annihilation, it is Grant who, having originated the strategy, will have to pursue it personally to realization. No wonder that, as Grant faced Appomattox and Lee's ravaged army, he dreaded the annihilation that he had commissioned himself, and had been commissioned, to inflict. No wonder he had that terrible headache on the morning of April 9, when he waited through Lee's refusal to submit at once; no wonder his headache was annihilated upon receipt of Lee's letter of willing-

ness to discuss terms for "the surrender of this army." Spared by Lee
from the responsibility of taking the full consequences of the strategy
he had laid down, no wonder that he could be magnanimous.

Yet he *was* magnanimous—as magnanimous as he had been courageous in bearing the responsibility of his commission. And he is
courageous in his *Memoirs*—courageous in executing them. There is
a passage near the end of the book that seems to me to define Grant the
writer. Asked by Lee at Appomattox to write out the terms of surrender, Grant describes how he faced his task: "When I put pen to
paper I did not know the first word that I should make use of in writing
the terms. I only knew what was in my mind, and I wished to express
it clearly, so that there could be no mistaking it" (II, 492).

Here is a writer who has a force—note that he does not call it an
idea; it is merely a *what,* it is in his mind, and he knows it. The words
follow or are consequent to that energy, and they will express it
clearly if it is clear in the first place, and Grant is sure that it is. Thus,
writing not only has order, it *is* an order, in the dynamic meaning of
that word. It may be secondary to the clear energy behind it, but it is
primary and directive to all who read it. Grant's *Memoirs* have that
clarity.

Autobiography and Washington

In the event that my title is misleading, let me say at the outset that Washington is neither the city, which cannot write; nor George, who wrote no autobiography; but Booker T., who did. Although I shall deal at some length with *Up from Slavery,* a book that seems to me well worth attention, I am using it as a pretext for remarks on autobiography so that those remarks will in turn serve as a pretext.

A discussion of *Up from Slavery* would hardly have been a subject for a literary essay thirty years ago. The civil rights movement, though profoundly present in the whole course of the nation's history since the advent of the abolitionists, had not seized the foreground of the nation's life, and autobiography, though an important presence in American literature, had not been accessible through the poetics of the New Criticism. Thus, if the national culture was in no position to deal with the autobiography of a *black* man, the literary culture was in no position to deal with the *autobiography* of a black man. The national culture would have, at that time, seen *Up from Slavery* as the life of a famous Negro; the literary culture would have seen it not as literature but as a document in the history of Negro culture. In each instance the book would have occupied space in a realm distinctly subordinate to the culture estimating its value. Moreover, these determinations of cultural value, whether in national or literary terms, would have been rendered largely out of ignorance of the life and form of Booker T. Washington's book. Ignorance, if we do not wish to raise a moral tirade against it (and I do not), can be seen as the dark side of social as well as aesthetic power. This dark side is not to be confused with our unconsciousness, for we know about it—sometimes we know *all* about it—just as we know about the dark side of the moon. We even entertain a moral and an intellectual determination to approve as well as to discover this darker realm. But morality and intelligence, as they often assert themselves, are no more than mere wishes for experience. They are wishes to approve and wishes to know, prompted by our confident and liberal place in the sun. When we experience the dark side of our life—that is to say, when we suffer the materialization of our wishes—then the very categories that had possessed form *because* of our ignorance become so dissolved and disintegrated that we no longer know what is good or what is beautiful. It was no doubt ever thus, this trial of existence that, as Robert Frost so wisely said, is the spirit's courage to risk substantiation.

We have in the past thirty-five years of the civil rights movement (the school desegregation decision, the military occupation of Little Rock and later of Oxford, Mississippi, the Selma march, the Civil Rights Voting Act, the summer riots, the emergence of George Wallace, and the embattled resistance to busing in northern cities) experienced the materialization and even the demoralization of our national desires. Conservative literary and social critics may be able to say, "I told you so." But they have been saying it for so long that we know the desire to say it is an addiction. Disillusioned liberals may say, "If only we had known." But that is a tiresome lament. Liberals still shielding themselves from the glaring present may say, "We were ignorant then, but now we know." But that is a self-congratulation too weak to bear responsibility. As humanitarian desires materialize into political reality, idealism departs from politics.

Similarly, the institutionalization of the New Criticism in the academy has materialized in thousands and thousands of interpretations of the "major" writers, until a newer criticism tries to be born. Jonathan Culler has gone so far as to pray for a literary criticism that will be against interpretation, because, he contends, interpretative criticism has all but ruined the study of literature. He and a whole school of newer critics have imported a French criticism that, by demystifying and deconstructing the new critical autonomous text, seeks to establish a relation between and among works of literature, thereby reconstructing a literary history that the unique interpretations of the New Criticism presumably took away. This newer criticism, coming to us in texts that make the most elliptical style of R. P. Blackmur seem like a blessed clearing in the memory, aspires to raise itself to the primary status of the literature that it defines. That literature will essentially be the same old "great" tradition but stripped of its privileged status by virtue of the critic's claim to make both himself and the long-suffering reader equal to it.

Meanwhile "political" criticism—criticism that refuses to abandon the social and political content of literature—has sought to equalize the literary field not by raising the status of criticism but by lifting "minority" literature into a competing position for academic study. Hence we now have college courses in folk literature, popular literature, proletarian literature, Native American literature, and, most of all, women's literature and black literature. Such proliferation often dismays critics of American literature who, suddenly feeling old-fashioned, find themselves ruefully lamenting such thematic upsurges, forgetting that American literature was, as a course of study, no more than a minority literature itself when it was first institutionalized. It has no superior theoretical claims as a subject over black or women's or any other literature in English. Having no native language to sustain its identity, it has only a powerful national culture to support its claims.

Be that as it may, the present critical scene presents a division in which theoretical criticism is democratizing the relationship among author, critic, and reader, all the time shoring up the fiction of the "major" writer. The advocates of minority literature, on the other hand, are attempting to democratize the subject of literature itself. In this democratized field, increasing attention has been focused on autobiography. It has, we might say, risen, gaining the eye of theoretical as well as thematic criticism. I am in no way prepared to give a theory of autobiography any more than I am able to offer a thematics of black autobiography. All I shall do is to touch upon the actual movement in recent literature itself toward autobiography, offer some rudimentary reflections on autobiography, and try to give some sense of what I see in Booker T. Washington's *Up from Slavery*—a book that would have been surrendered by the old New Critics to the status of a document for social historians, that would probably lack sufficient textual identity or energy to be worth deconstructing by the newer theoreticians, and that would strike proponents of minority literature as a gross presence to be scornfully dismissed or gotten around.

If we look back at the decade of the fifties, there are five books that certainly reflect, and possibly promise, the changes we now so confidently feel have happened. There was first of all James Baldwin's *Notes of a Native Son* (1955), a series of essays linked in such a way as to come to the threshold of a narrative autobiography; there was Ginsberg's *Howl* (1956), which, departing both culturally and formally from the poetry represented by Eliot, Stevens, and Frost, attempted to recover a declamatory voice after the manner of Whitman; there was Kerouac's *On the Road* (1957), a novel in which the narrator, though fictively named, greatly reduced the space between author and persona; there was Lowell's *Life Studies* (1959), which intruded a fragmentary prose "family background" between the sequence of his poems; and there was Mailer's *Advertisements for Myself* (1959), an anthology construed as an autobiographical text.

Lowell and Mailer seem to me particularly significant in this incipient autobiographical configuration. They were both strongly established writers—strong enough to have made their marks as poet and novelist respectively and established enough to make their decisive shift in form a significant aesthetic gesture against the closure of poetic and novelistic structure championed by literary criticism. Moreover, they both persisted in this open form, and though each continued to see himself as poet and novelist respectively, each nonetheless continued to pursue autobiographical form, as if this more direct presentation of a "life self" were a publication of individual dissent.

If the five books I have mentioned represent a movement of literature in the fifties to break out and down toward a freer form of autobiography, there was a corresponding movement in the sixties from the nonliterary world to rise up toward autobiography. The book that best embodies that movement and that I think is in many ways the most important book of the decade is *The Autobiography of Malcolm X* (1965). It is the effort of a "nonwriter" to rise from a minority and nonliterary culture into the form of autobiography. If, in other words, the literary world went toward autobiography for freedom from form, Malcolm X emerged from the political world to seek freedom in the form of autobiography. That is a major point—it may be the strongest point that I can make in this essay—for it indicates the true relativity of the form, which stands directly between the realm of literature and the realm of society. Relative to the aesthetic world of form, autobiography stands as a kind of freedom at the same time that it is a lower order of writing; relative to the nonliterary society, autobiography stands as a threshold to freedom in form.

There is no better way to see this whole problem than to remember that Malcolm X did not even write his autobiography. To a resident of the literary or academic world, such a fact poses a problem. How, after all, can an author be a writer unless he writes for himself? That question is not quite as easy to answer as it is to ask. To begin with, God is considered by Christians to be the author of the universe and the Bible along with it, yet he did not write the Bible but presumably spoke it through the mouths and eyes of his prophets. It is not only the first book, but is, as low churchmen rightly say, the Good Book. That does not make all other books bad; they just are not as good as it is. In the world of secular literature, all is changed. Well, not quite all, since we now know that Homer is probably the fiction of a literary and author-centered culture. And we cannot be absolutely sure that our beloved Shakespeare is not a fiction too. Nathaniel Hawthorne took a perverse delight in Delia Bacon's brave attempt to claim Sir Francis Bacon as the author of Shakespeare's plays, and it is still possible to goad Shakespeareans into indignation by questioning Shakespeare's authorial identity. Beyond that there is the issue of the Muse—the divine inspiration to which the very best authors have attributed their works. We may know that the muse did not whisper *Paradise Lost* into Milton's ear in the early hours of the morning, but we had better not know it too well.

Even so, an autobiography not written by the autobiographer seems a contradiction in terms. We have, it is true, a whole host of "as told to" autobiographies just as we have a host of ghostwritten autobiographies. The "as told to" autobiography presupposes a person who cannot write talking his life to a person who can. *All God's Dangers: The Autobiography of Nate Shaw* is such a work, though Theodore Rosengarten, the writer and "listener," substituted the fictional name of Nate Shaw for the historical Ned Cobb. The ghostwritten autobiography presupposes a life written by a professional writer for a person who "has" a life and presumably could even write it but who secures the professional writer to give it "finish."

The *Autobiography of Malcolm X* falls interestingly between these two categories. Malcolm could write: he wrote speeches as well as spoke them; he scribbled notes for Alex Haley, who was writing the life Malcolm was dying into; and according to Haley he kept a diary from which he thought he might make his own book if he lived. But he did not live; indeed his whole autobiography increasingly moves toward, and is motivated by, the death he is to die. For Malcolm the narrative of life more and more becomes the book he will not live to see; for Alex Haley the narrative leads toward the death Malcolm must die in order for him to finish it. Thus, it is an "as told to" autobiography not because Malcolm cannot write but because he lacks the time, in every sense of the word, to write it. But it is also a ghostwritten autobiography in that Haley is *finishing* Malcolm's life in every sense of that word. No wonder the two men "spooked" each other, as Haley says of their first meeting.

If from a literary point of view Malcolm's life is less than literature, since it is not even written by the author, from an actual point of view it is the narrative of a self in the process of dying into the form of a book. This fact, so much a part of both the form and substance of the book, brings us squarely back to autobiography as a point midway between the higher form of literature (or the form of high literature) and the more rudimentary form of life that literature is always seeking. It was Emerson's impatience with the bookishness and refinement of literature that made him both long for and envision a progress of literature that would eventuate in autobiography.

Yet this borderline form is fraught with peril, as Emerson must have known. It is at once the easiest and most difficult act to attempt or to contemplate. We know absolutely what an autobiography is at the same time that we know nothing about what it absolutely is. It is the only literary genre (if it is a genre and if there are genres!) that we can take for granted. We believe that we live, just as we believe that we have selves if not souls. If myth can be defined as the fiction in which we helplessly believe, then the fiction of our own life is the one fiction from which we cannot escape. Structuralists may give us models of thought, but one of those models will be real; game theorists may give us games upon games, but there is one game that is not a game; philosophers of language and literature may give us theories of fiction, but there is one fiction that they do not believe is a fiction. When they say "I," they cannot believe that that erect pronoun refers to a fiction, unless they are prepared to say that they are writing first-person novels.

This is a two-headed issue. For those enamored of the common-sense belief in the reality of their own lives, there is the irony that the "I" that they use to refer to themselves is the linguistic convention used by all individuals in English Christendom to refer to themselves. That is why autobiography, of all literary forms, is probably the most conventional. For all his confidence in his revolutionary identity, Malcolm X casts his life in the most conventional form, the "story" of his life. Truly literary authors, such as Henry James, Mark Twain, Yeats, and Mary McCarthy, on the other hand, struggle against the convention even as they write their autobiographies. It is almost amusing to watch Henry James, who deeply believed that his art was his life, avoid at all cost covering the part of his life that he had converted into art. He knew with all his imagination that such coverage would have involved him in a project less imaginative than the dreariest memoir of a statesman; hence he spent two volumes elaborating the life that he lived before becoming a writer. Autobiography, for the writer, has to be the form for discovering the experience not already written about; that is what it becomes for Rousseau, Thoreau, Adams, Mark Twain, and James.

For the "nonwriter" or naïve autobiographer, it is much more likely to be the waiting mold into which he can empty the experience he confidently believes that he has had. He could, and seems to me does, contemplate the autobiographical act with much more equanimity than the literary author could muster. U. S. Grant, for example, who has the strong illusion that his life has been formed in a world of decision and action, undertakes his memoirs in the spirit of someone who is ordering his life. Having entered history by making it, he has the assurance that his life is *there*. The words he calls upon will be, if anything, less recalcitrant than the brigades and regiments he once commanded. Believing almost completely in the priority of his life, he has little doubt that the language into which he moves can be made to refer to it. Words are the inertial signifiers that can fix the energy of experience into record. The motive for such stabilization is nothing less than the knowledge that the life is over and that death is at hand. For such a writer autobiography exists as memoir, a final setting of the life in order. Anticipating the natural act of death awaiting him, the writer fixes himself in words in a metaphorical suicide sufficiently repressed for him to be unconscious of the metaphor. The knowledge that death is coming or that he has fully "made his name" all but frees him from the feeling that he is taking his life.

To have said so much about the unconsciousness of the naïve autobiographer may imply that there is no consciousness of what is metaphorically happening as the life is put into words. Yet even Grant is aware, as he recounts his victorious campaign over his old enemy Bobby Lee, that he is involved in a losing campaign with death, the enemy confronting him at the end of the battlefield of his memoirs.

The very fact that language is in rhetorical relation to the reference of the life being recounted gives urgency to the writer's wish to finish his life before it finishes him. Sure of approaching death, as Grant was, or sure that life is over in his retirement from it, as many another memoirist is, the writer can be sure of his fixed rhetorical position in relation to the life. That gives finality to the memoir, making of it an epitaph even as it unfolds. If the writer is not sure, then the point of view becomes increasingly less fixed.

What all this comes down to is that the convention of autobiography, for the literary as well as the naïve autobiographer, presupposes a complete life or the completing of a life. It involves the writer in some form of ending or envisioning an end to a narrative that he helplessly wants to be equal to his life. Insofar as the narrative is equal to the life, it cannot be finished without death, either actual or metaphorical. The autobiographer can, like Franklin, begin and intermittently work on a narrative pursuit of the life that runs ahead of it; or like Richard Henry Dana, he can record an autobiographical segment of his life; or like Thoreau, he can establish a metaphorical strategy of making a single year stand for a whole life; or like Henry Adams, he can openly commit metaphorical suicide by casting his life into a third-person historical narrative. All such autobiographers retain the illusion that some life is left them, either in front of the writing if they are catching up to the present, or after it if they pursue a strategy of metaphorical closure.

Yet even metaphorical closure is not without dangers. Dana, for example, so deeply identified himself in *Two Years Before the Mast* that the legal and political career to which he committed himself after writing it could never seem more than a failure, a loss of life. If Dana succeeded too well before the public, Thoreau's symbolic closure failed, and he withdrew into his journals, preferring to keep his life in a box about the size of a coffin for posterity to unearth and resurrect. Adams, by facing the suicide head on, was condemned to live out a life that he called posthumous. To be sure, this death involved in the language and form of autobiography is metaphorical and, instead of inducing a complacent dream of autobiography as death, should put us in a dialectical position to see autobiography as an attempt at rebirth, an effort to elude the death in life as well as the death after life. Augustine comes immediately to mind: he ends the old life in order to set a seal on the new one, his conversion being the action that guarantees a vision of the God who makes a time-transcending memory possible.

To consider *The Autobiography of Malcolm X* in this light is to see that, just as Malcolm is struggling to elude the pursuing Muslims in actual life, he is trying to elude the form that Alex Haley's narrative is fixing upon him. The religion of Elijah Muhammad is the fixed point of view from which Malcolm imagines the form and direction of his life as he and Haley begin their collaboration. But as Malcolm experiences his second conversion in Mecca, the Black Muslims become his imminent executioners for his betrayal of faith. Similarly, Haley's narrative is thrown into a new relationship, for it, too, is pursuing his life from the point of view Haley has taken from him and is at the threshold of being his metaphoric murderer. It is interesting in this connection that, once Malcolm experienced his Mecca conversion, he was, according to Haley, so uncertain about Haley's narrative that he covered the margins with penciled suggestions. Alarmed at Malcolm's profound impulse toward revision, Haley never allowed him to see any more of the narrative unless he was present. Increasingly conscious that he will not live to see the end of "his" book, Malcolm ultimately surrenders his reservations and allows Haley's narrative to stand. That surrender releases Malcolm's autobiography into Haley's biographical epilogue.

Although Haley's biographical presence is an actual fact in this epilogue, it should remind us that there is a biographer implicitly present in every autobiographical consciousness. If we can say that autobiographical form possesses a strong element of metaphorical suicide, we should also be able to say that biographical form possesses an equally strong element of metaphorical murder. The autobiographer is, I think, much more likely to see the metaphorical implications than the biographer, who is locked in the powerful illusion that he is giving "life" to his subject, even as he directs the narrative toward the subject's historical death. This illusion of resurrection, sustained by the protective emotion of devotional re-creation, by the protective facts of objective history, and by the protective aim of interpretative significance, all but suppresses the sinister aspects of the biographical enterprise. The autobiographer, however, alert to the death he is to die in life as well as in form, is likely to settle on the hope that he can end his life, emerging as the biographer, who, having successfully killed the dead self, possesses the secret life of a

fugitive killer! Louis Renza sees that the entire writing act of autobiography phenomenologically creates a private and inaccessible text
for the autobiographer—an unwritten past that every word of writing
both secures and creates dialectically parallel to the published text.
This phenomenological creation on the part of the writer corresponds
to the phenomenological distrust on the part of every reader of every
autobiography.[1]

All these are but reflections by the way. Autobiographers may scoff
at them; biographers almost certainly will. Yet they seem to me to
have their origin in common sense rather than in a wish to probe the
psychological "depth" of autobiographical act and motive. They are
intended, as I noted at the outset, to be a pretext rather than a prepara-
tion for or an introduction to *Up from Slavery*. That work is much
more than they are or can be. A view of it should make possible a
conclusion that goes beyond them.

Up from Slavery is a resistant text. The autobiography of a prominent
public figure, it almost affronts the literary critic with the bleak inertia
of its prose. Its content is equally resistant—its didacticism, its self-
gratulation, its facts, and its policies are all but in front of its form.
Thus, cultural historians will see it as representative of a time that
they hope history has transcended; black militants will see it as the
record of an Uncle Tom who made his way at the expense of his
people; white liberals will see it in a light much the same but weaker.
Representatives of all these constituencies would inevitably choose
W. E. B. Du Bois' *Souls of Black Folk* (1903) as a stronger piece of
writing. Du Bois' eloquence and poetic presentation would satisfy the
literary critic; his scholarship would please the historian; his intellectual and moral grasp of the racial questions would gratify the cultural
critic. Yet the cultural fact to remember is that Du Bois knew how
powerful Booker T. Washington was, and in powerfully risking a
counterview to Washington's life and vision, he initiated a dialectic
upon the racial question that has no more been settled than the racial
question itself has been settled.

More important for my immediate purposes than the actual contro-

---

1. Louis A. Renza, "The Veto of the Imagination: A Theory of Autobiography," in
James Olney (ed.), *Autobiography: Essays Theoretical and Critical* (Princeton, 1980), 269–
95.

versy between two black views of the racial question is the resistance
that Washington's text raises against my own reflections on autobiography. It is not, first of all, Washington's only autobiography. A
year before he published it, he had published *The Story of My Life and
Work* (1900). It is not uncommon for an autobiographer to write two
versions of his life. Du Bois was to write at least three in his long life;
so did Sherwood Anderson; so did Frederick Douglass. Edward Gibbon never could settle on a version of his life, and he left behind six
manuscript versions of his memoirs. If Gibbon's multiversion manu-
scripts indicate an unwillingness to stabilize (and thereby finish) his
life in a text—here he would be similar to Wordsworth, who kept *The
Prelude* from publication for forty-five years, revising it throughout
his long, dying poetic life—Du Bois, Anderson, and Douglass would
in their triply published versions be recasting their lives in order to
render each prior version less final. Although such strategies allow
the writer a chance for revision, each succeeding effort throws more
and more into doubt his capacity for any secure point of view. The
insecurity may keep him alive, but it diminishes the finality of each
life that he writes.

Even here Washington is different. He wrote neither of his lives
alone. Instead he supervised them, something in the manner of an
overseer. *The Story of My Life and Work* was, as Louis Harlan points
out in his biography of Washington, actually written by Edgar Webber, a black journalist whom Washington brought to Tuskegee in 1897
largely for the purpose of assisting him in his life story. But Washington was so busy and so exhausted that he took his first vacation, a
trip to Europe, and did not oversee the final chapters of the manuscript. Webber on his part proved inadequate to the task, making
many errors and resorting to the short-cut methods of padding the
book with schedules, letters, and copies of speeches, which are in
reality substitution for the text rather than fulfillments or extensions
of it. Published by J. L. Nichols and Company, a subscription house
of Naperville, Illinois, which catered to a black audience, the book
was so full of typographical errors that Washington fired Webber and
in subsequent editions removed his picture from the photographs in
the book.

Even before Webber had finished the book, Washington was, according to Harlan, already planning another book, this time for the
regular rather than the subscription trade; this time he got a white

journalist, Max Thrasher from St. Johnsbury, Vermont, to help him with the project. This time, too, Washington supervised the work every inch of the way, leaving Thrasher practically no freedom. He dictated to Thrasher on trains, took Thrasher's notes and in turn wrote his own draft of the autobiography, letting Thrasher check the manuscript. I have on occasion heard scholars of black studies point gloatingly to Thrasher's presence in the project as evidence of Washington's having been a captive to the white mind. It would actually be difficult to imagine a more reduced role than Thrasher was forced to play; even to call him a ghost, as Harlan does, is to use the term loosely.[2] He seems much more like a slave to Washington's narrative. That fact, concealed from the text, provides both a starting point and an index for scrutinizing the life story that Washington ordered for himself.

That story is, as everyone knows, one of the great success stories of American history. Washington tells in the simplest, most straightforward terms of his rise from slavery to a position as leader of his people. He begins his life as a slave in Franklin County, Virginia, is taken by his mother to Malden, West Virginia, after the slaves are freed, works first in the salt mines and then in the coal mines near Malden, but does manage to go to school. From that meager beginning he determines to go to Hampton Institute in Virginia, where he makes a sufficient impression on General Samuel Armstrong, head of the school, to be recommended to go to Alabama "to take charge of what was to be a normal school for the coloured people in the little town of Tuskegee in that state."[3] By dint of hard work, ceaseless diplomacy with the white population of Macon County, and unremitting perseverance in the face of ignorance, poverty, inertia, and doubt, he builds Tuskegee from nothing but the dilapidated outbuildings of a ruined plantation into Tuskegee Normal and Industrial Institute. Money for the school comes primarily from white northern philanthropists; students come from the black population of the United States, though largely from the South; survival comes from Washington's carefully orchestrated interdependence between Tuske-

---

2. On Washington's autobiographical efforts see Louis R. Harlan, *Booker T. Washington: The Making of a Black Leader, 1856–1901* (New York, 1972), 243–48.

3. Booker T. Washington, *Up from Slavery*, in John Hope Franklin (ed.), in *Three Negro Classics* (New York, 1965), 85. All subsequent citations are from this edition and will be given in the text.

gee and the dominant southern whites. The climax of Washington's career, as he narrates it, is his speech at the Atlanta Exposition in 1895. That speech not only represents the achievement of an ex-slave addressing a largely white southern audience; it also marks Booker T. Washington's emergence as a national leader of his people.

That is the barest outline of Washington's story—or the story he chooses to tell. The way he tells it is simple and unadorned. His prose is reduced to an almost impoverished simplicity; metaphor is sparse; eloquence is all but absent; there is neither richness of texture nor complication of consciousness; even the simplicity never condenses into the energy of compression but retains an air of immobility being put into slow and steady motion. Although Washington was a successful public speaker and although the Atlanta speech (which he quotes in full in his text) shows oratorical flourish and declamatory urgency, the narrative throughout is characterized by what can best be called almost pure inertia.

In calling Washington's style purely inertial, I mean that he writes as if language were matter rather than energy. The words are things that, added one to another, do not record so much as they build the narrative life upon the line that the structure of his life has taken. Thus, the events that Washington recounts are not so much dramatized as deadened into matter with which to make the narrative. They are being set steadily in place by the narrator, as if he were constructing the model of his life. The pain, fear, anguish, self-doubt, and anxiety that attended Washington's life are there, of course, but they are muted into the very matter of the narrative. This tendency to treat language as material causes Washington's narrative consciousness to seem literally housed in his narrative. If Washington is moving the blocks of his life into position, they seem to rest in place by their own weight.

That solid stability is one aspect of Washington's inertial style. But there is also motion—for Washington is moving his material into place. Yet here again he seems to be following the course of his life rather than directing it. The relatively strict chronology of autobiographical convention to which he adheres provides the form that draws him along. If he drove himself to make his actual life—and he explicitly indicates that he did—his belief in the existence of that life gives him the powerful illusion that it has created him as the narrator of it. This combination of conventional form and self-belief conveys

the strong sense that Washington is pursuing the slow and steady
motion of his life.

His use of chronological convention to order his life is but a reflection of his capacity to use time to make his life into a book just as he
had used it to make his life as a man. His belief in the weight of his life
puts all his language into a rhetorical rather than a dramatic or imaginary relation to that life. The solid reality to which his language refers
now exists for language to use. If it was the result of desire, ambition,
and fierce determination, it now becomes the matter from which
Washington will read higher laws. Here again Washington's book is
conventional, embracing as it does the moral and exemplary fatalities
of autobiography. The exemplary autobiography is the secularized
version of the Christian confessional form. The confessional form
(with the exception of the revolutionary Rousseau!) denigrates the
man by relating his conversion into God; the exemplary form converts godlike achievement into a model for man to follow. The one
portrays the fallen child attaining to the spirit of the Father; the other
becomes the model father to provide principles for the children. The
one seeks goodness as truth, the other goodness as conduct. Franklin's *Autobiography* is a classic example of the exemplary convention, and Washington is clearly Franklin's descendant. Having
achieved success, he publishes his life as an example of the virtues he
believes that he practiced in gaining the high ground from which he
writes.

If Franklin is almost disarmingly simple in his exemplary narrative, Washington is dismayingly simple in his. Franklin enunciates
principles with sufficient ease to disclose the possibility that he lacks
principle altogether; he can thus reveal an implicit amusement in his
life of himself. Washington clings almost desperately to his virtues.
What for Franklin is policy becomes gospel for Washington. Keeping his life under much stricter control than that of Franklin, Washington is constrained to reiterate his smaller number of principles—
the principle of constant work, the principle of helping others to
help themselves, and the principle of building a life from the ground
up. Thus, where Franklin takes pleasure in the disclosure of his principles—he even writes the autobiography in moments of leisure—
Washington's principles are themselves his only pleasure. He hardly
knows how to play. If Franklin's very mode of himself is a gift that
he easily bequeaths to posterity, Washington's life is all but asking

for the reader's charity—as if he were waiting in the parlor for one more contribution.

Then one must confront Washington's idea of education. It is as single-minded as his adherence to the Protestant work ethic—and as unpopular to critics of his life and work. Believing that education for people on the bottom of society has to begin at the bottom, Washington wants the body and hands cleaned and disciplined before he cultivates the head. Foreign languages and even books themselves have little benefit in his eyes unless students are able to command a trade. He championed industrial education, particularly in his autobiography, as a means of teaching his people how to work. This philosophy of education, reiterated throughout the book, galled blacks in Washington's own time, and it galls them all the more in our time when they can see, just as white readers can see, that this was a means of placating whites. Washington was assuring them, in effect, that Tuskegee graduates would know how to work more than they would know how to think.

These aspects of Washington's narrative make it singularly unprepossessing for both the literary and the cultural critic. They are there, and I could not wish them away even if I would. Yet a reader willing to encounter the book and give it a degree of consciousness—Washington's book, like his life philosophy, is going to ask for something—has a chance for revelations in Washington's inertial narrative.

First of all, there is the fact that Washington was born in *Franklin* County, Virginia. That inertial fact reveals its energy once we think of the book in relation to Franklin's autobiography. He is born a slave, but does not know his father, who is said to be a white man. Thus, he has white blood from an unknown father. When he goes to Malden he has no name—but names himself Booker Washington, in a schoolroom. For all his matter-of-factness Washington does note that one of the advantages of having been a slave was his freedom to name himself. He even mentions other slaves taking names such as John S. Lincoln. But he chose Washington; at the time he did it, he was no doubt attempting to follow a pattern he saw others pursuing. Yet in light of all that he was to do, the early act is charged with significance—a significance that Washington never stresses because he does not need to. George Washington was, after all, a Virginian who owned slaves yet was the Father of His Country. Booker Washington is also a Virginian who has been a slave and has an unknown white father. In naming himself he lays claim to the white blood in him and relates himself to the Father of His Country. He himself clearly sees his original naming of himself as a promise of being a father to his people.

As for Washington's actual call to his vocation, here is what he says about it.

> One day, while working in the coal mine, I happened to overhear two miners talking about a great school for coloured people somewhere in Virginia. That was the first time I had ever heard anything about any kind of school or college that was more pretentious than the little coloured school in our town.
>
> In the darkness of the mine I noiselessly crept as close as I could to the two other men who were talking. I heard one tell the other that not only was the school established for the members of my race, but that opportunities were provided by which poor but worthy students could work out all or part of the cost of board, and at the same time be taught some trade or industry.
>
> As they were describing the school, it seemed to me that it must be the greatest place on earth, and not even Heaven presented more attractions for me at that time than did the Hampton Normal and Agricultural Institute in Virginia, about which these two men were talking. I resolved at once to go to that school, although I had no idea where it was, or how I was going to reach it. I remembered only that I was on fire constantly with one ambition, and that was to go to Hampton. (51)

That quotation stands out in my context much more than it does in Washington's text. I have seen students read right through it, numbed by the patient plod of Washington's inertial style. Yet it is Washington's *calling,* as he makes unmistakably clear. The whole episode may be a fiction; certainly the two men conversing were unaware of Washington's secret presence. In any event here is a *black boy in a coal mine* hearing his life's direction named, and any wish to call it a fiction seems to me merely a weak theoretical formulation in the face of Washington's capacity, from the established ground he has come to hold, to *make the facts of his life*. If his identity as ex-slave gave him the freedom to name himself and make that name a fact, his achievement as founder of Tuskegee gives him the freedom to make the fact of his call. He even shows that he is creating the fact when he intrudes the full name of Hampton, which the two men could hardly have named. When we consider that it is a coal mine, that he is black, that both he and the coal possess implicit or inertial energy, we begin to see both the act and style of *Up from Slavery*. The inertia of the style produces the effect of an indeterminate consciousness on the part of Washington, the autobiographer. If I say that he intended the significance that I see, both the style and the skeptical readers reading it almost smile in my face, implicitly accusing me of trying to make a "symbol" of that passage. And of course the accusation is to a large extent right. That is why I am willing to leave it as a made or earned fact—inertial in its existence until it is put into relation to a consciousness prepared to invest it with dynamic energy. If the coal mine incident set Washington's mind on fire with ambition, it should at least warm the reader's consciousness.

Such a consciousness, once attracted to that inertia, feels the whole possibility of Washington's life about to come to life; relationships start up like rabbits from a blackberry patch. It was Henry Adams, after all, who in his dynamic *Education* determined to measure the line of force of American history in terms of coal production. And it is coal that to this very moment holds the inertial energy of all the weight of geological ages pressing down upon it to create the potential fire of civilization. Set against Henry Adams' autobiography of a failed education, Washington's calling to a successful education strikes sparks. Yet the very critic who would write a book on Henry Adams' art would likely smile indulgently at the comparison.

But let that go. The point is that coal is in the earth. It is the earth into which Booker T. Washington's life is driven and out of which it stands. In his slave cabin, which had no wooden floors, he tells us, there had been a hole where sweet potatoes were kept. When he comes up out of the coal mine to go to Hampton Institute, he makes his way to Richmond, where, without enough money to get a meal or a room, he sleeps under a board sidewalk on the ground. Although beneath the pedestrians, he is yet on the earth. And when he ultimately goes to Tuskegee, the first thing he does is to acquire land on which to build his school from the ground up. He helps clear the fields of this farm—it is actually a ruined plantation—that his school is to occupy. The first building takes the place of the burned-down ruin of the original plantation house; he and his students "dig out the earth" where the foundations are to be laid. Washington is proud that the cornerstone is grounded in the great "black belt" of the South; he

knows, and says, that the black belt refers both to the dark soil of the
Deep South and to the dark people who live there. All this is the
ground of Washington's world—the ground where slavery had existed and the ground in which he is determined to found his school.
Both his act of life and his vision of education are rooted in this land.

The purchase and possession of the land are the very base of
Washington's whole program of education. It is there that Washington means to teach his people that freedom means freedom to
labor, not freedom from labor. As Washington sees the time he has
lived through, he regrets that the trades and skills that were taught in
slavery have been denigrated by a vision of education as an escape
from labor. School for Washington means being able to build a
school, to acquire land and clear it, to make bricks and lay them, to
get lumber and measure it, to build beds and make mattresses for
them, to grow food on the acquired land and cook it. His own transition from an unlettered to a lettered society is scarcely ever defined in
the books that he has read. It has instead involved learning to clean a
room, as Mrs. Ruffner had taught him to do. That background enabled him to pass the examination for entry to Hampton, which was
cleaning a classroom. He had to learn how to sleep between sheets,
how to wear clothes, how to eat a balanced diet; he knows that these
acts cannot be taken for granted in teaching blacks in the unreconstructed South. Yankee women, Mrs. Ruffner of Charleston and
Mary Mackie of Hampton, have taught him these rudimentary but
utterly essential lessons, and Washington clings to such discipline as
if it were a lifeline. He teaches the "gospel of the toothbrush" at
Tuskegee, as if the toothbrush were a synecdoche for civilization.
Keeping clean is not a ritual but a rule, a discipline that Washington
enforces with a master hand. Traveling through the South, where
there are often no bathing facilities, Washington makes his way to
nature, to bathe in streams. When one sees all this, it is possible to be
condescending; it is also possible to see that Washington has discovered the root meaning of the name he has chosen. No wonder,
with such a name, he criticizes the city of Washington, where black
women have lost the skills of washing clothes. Such an emphasis on
these aspects of education may make, and has made, readers lament
this educator's bare mention of books. Again it is well to remember
that his name is *Booker*. If the cleanliness is contained in his last
name, the books are contained in his first. He knows books—he says

that he likes biography and dislikes fiction; he claims to have read everything written about Abraham Lincoln. But he does not emphasize his bookishness. He does not have to, since he is making and ordering his own book, a fact that a reader should not be blind to. His strategy does well enough, particularly when compared with the books that presidents of Harvard, Yale, and Dartmouth have written.

All this is not to praise Washington's vision of education but to see that vision. His discipline is the measure of the rudimentary struggle to gain the ground on which education can be founded. That ground is in the South, under the political sway of whites who, having been dispossessed of their slave world, have nonetheless ridden out Reconstruction to regain their damaged dominion. Washington is placating them. He has to; to do otherwise would be to abandon his school or go north to relocate it. His whole theory of education can justifiably be viewed as a promise to southern whites that Tuskegee graduates will not have big ideas. But it cannot justifiably be seen as simply that. The desperate order of the skilled hand, the toothbrush, the clean body, and the clean school is a great hope rooted in a great fear.

We might want to say that the hope represses the fear, but that simply is not true. Fear is everywhere present in Washington's narrative. When he was a slave boy bringing food home late from the mill, he feared that he would be caught in the dark and have his ears cut off by deserting soldiers. On the way to West Virginia with his mother and brothers, the family spent the night in an abandoned house, only to be frightened away by a black snake. Even when he names himself, he is in anxiety at not having a name as the teacher begins to call the roll. There is fear present in being "called" in the coal mine; thus, he noiselessly creeps to hear the two men talking. He is glad to be called to be a teacher—partly out of fear of being called to be a preacher. He is afraid of the whites around Tuskegee and afraid of the whites in the North from whom he has to beg money, but most of all he is afraid of the psychological space he occupies between the two hostile camps. The space and the fear are almost one and the same thing. Riding on a train in Alabama, he is trapped into eating with two northern white liberal ladies, and he suffers the anxiety of knowing the hostility his presence in the dining car may provoke.[4]

4. Cultural as well as intertextual critics might wish to reflect on the relation of this scene to that in Richard Wright's *Native Son,* in which the liberal whites, Jan and Mary, insist that Bigger Thomas take them to a black restaurant in Chicago.

This fear never diminishes with Washington's success; if anything, it increases—not in intensity, since the inertial style precludes emotional crescendo, but in presence. For as Washington gains recognition, he is more and more exposed. Beyond fearing lack of money for Tuskegee from the North or resistance to the school from the South, he has to fear how his action as a public figure will be interpreted by his conflicting constituencies. In preparing to speak at Atlanta, he faces fear on every hand—fear of what southern whites may say, fear of whether he will hurt his school, fear of the visiting northern whites, and fear of the speaking act itself. That fear is, to be sure, a rhetorical background for the success of the speech, but it is also one of the great facts in Washington's book. He discusses his profound fear of public speaking—the fear that some single member of the audience may walk out, the performer's fear of going on stage, the gnawing anxiety of eating a multicourse dinner with the knowledge of having to give an after-dinner speech. When he at last takes his first vacation—the trip to Europe—he fears the luxuries, the dinners, the society, and the possible misunderstandings the Tuskegee community may have about his absence. As he ends the book, he is very much on the defensive. He knows that Du Bois and hundreds of northern blacks are raising their voices in criticism; he knows that the Tuskegee teachers and students are restive; it seems to me that he profoundly knows that his own success is being accompanied by mounting victories of anti-Negro legislation; and for all his success and all his placation he knows about lynching and raises one last plea against it. He ends his book with an account of his triumphant welcome in Richmond, the capital of his native state; yet anyone sensitive to the narrative will feel Washington's anxious wonder whether he may have been as secure under the sidewalk as he is on top of it.

In citing this fear in the book, I am once again forced to distort the nature of its presence. The inertial style cannot and does not express it dramatically but contains it constantly. That, it seems to me, is the mastery of the inertial style. To speak of Washington's mastery may again provoke a smile. But my point in using the word is that Washington is a master. His whole book is devoted to coming up *from* slavery, not up against it. Slavery is the deep ground of his experience; to reject it totally would remove all possibility of becoming a master of the self—and self-mastery is what much of Washington's

book is about. It is the iron discipline that he pursues, and it is
the basis on which he builds a school and is its master. He becomes
the master speaker who aspires to total control of his audience; the
description of that control he leaves to white reporters, whose
description of his galvanizing presence he almost self-servingly enters in the text.

It would be easy to misconstrue the figure of Washington as master.
By converting it into a metaphor, I could jump on the bandwagon
with Washington's innumerable critics and say that Washington is
playing the role of white master on the old plantation, getting along
with the white society of former masters, and making his students the
same old black laborers on the new Tuskegee plantation. I have heard
it said, and I cannot quite unsay it. For Washington is deeply related to
the old white world. He is a slave son of an unknown white father
from that world, and even George Washington, the white father of
freedom whom Washington "adopts" once he is free, did own
slaves—a paradox that Henry Adams contemplated with almost paralyzed dismay.

The fact remains, however, that Booker Taliaferro Washington, if
not all black, defines himself as black, not white. He determines to
remain in a society that will aggressively see him as black. If the
name he takes is white and the civilization that he is set on acquiring
for himself and for his people is white, these are to be acquisitions,
not being; they are property, not identity. They constitute a self to be
moved and built, both in Washington's life and in his book. If it is
possible to say that this model self is white, I think it equally possible
to say that the white model of self is Washington's very slave. It is
simply, fiercely reduced in its outlines, kept rigidly in line, and controlled with an iron discipline. It has enormous dynamic energy that
can only be implicitly seen.

The inertial style makes Washington seem like an old man rather
than a relatively young man. He was at most forty-five when it was
published; he was only twenty-five when he went to Tuskegee. It is
hard to believe, this youth so given over to age, this drive that moves
so slowly. Yet it is just this slow and steady movement that is the black
being of Washington—the being that he retained for himself, yet
represents for his people. He does not create the motion; it has been
created by the force that ended slavery. It is slow, but it is relentless: it

is both a force and a fact—the emotion of identity and the motion of history—that cannot be stopped. Since it is everywhere present, it cannot be revealed.

To have said so much may not prove that *Up from Slavery* is literature. I certainly cannot prove it so to anyone disposed to exclude it from the shelf of our "major" works of art. I do believe that it is a wonderful parallel text to Henry Adams' *Education,* just as I believe that it is a remarkable counterpart to Du Bois' *The Souls of Black Folk.* Du Bois' style is at once intellectual and poetic, yet what gives his book its dynamic power is his full awareness that it is just this style that has cut him off from the souls of his people; his imagination and his achievement are to direct the very language that has taken him away from those souls—and is taking him away with every sentence he writes—across the gulf of his separation to reach behind the veil.

That soul that Du Bois so poetically seeks to recover is what Washington has retained all the time. In discussing his practice as a public speaker, he observes that, for all the rules of speaking one can master, "none of these can take the place of *soul* in an address" (161). But that is a statement, not a revelation. There is a passage that touches closer to the inertial heart. Describing his anxiety as he eats the fine dinner after which he is to give a speech, he writes:

I rarely take part in one of these long dinners that I do not wish that I could put myself back in the little cabin where I was a slave boy, and again go through the experience there—one that I shall never forget—of getting molasses to eat once a week from the "big house." Our usual diet on the plantation was corn bread and pork, but on Sunday morning my mother was permitted to bring down a little molasses from the "big house" for her three children, and when it was received how I did wish that every day was Sunday! I would get my tin plate and hold it up for the sweet morsel, but I would always shut my eyes while the molasses was being poured out into the plate, with the hope that when I opened them I would be surprised at how much I had got. When I opened my eyes I would tip the plate in one direction and another, so as to make the molasses spread all over it, and in the full belief that there would be more of it and that it would last longer if I spread it out in this way. So strong are my childish impressions of those Sunday morning feasts that it would be pretty hard for any one to convince me that there is not more molasses on a plate when it is spread all over the plate than when it occupies a little corner—if there is a corner in a plate. At any rate, I have never believed in "cornering" syrup. My share of the syrup was usually about two tablespoonfuls, and the two spoonfuls of molasses were much more enjoyable to me than is a fourteen-course dinner after which I am to speak. (162)

Think of the teachers of college English who could show Washington how to improve that passage. They could show him how, by reducing the number of words and by cutting out the repetition, he could eliminate the slightly awkward manner of his description. Yet that awkwardness seems to me Washington's very hold on the experience. It is the slow but desperate possession of a bare something that the fear of speaking has enabled him to take hold of. How little is there, yet how much: the present anxiety, the wish for the lost past that nonetheless *cannot* be forgotten, and then the memory itself—with its expectation, its anxiety (in the tightly closed eyes), its habitual disappointment (implicitly revealed in the effort to make the small amount bigger), and then the molasses, caused to move by the moving plate that the child moves, then moving in slow inertial expansion.

That passage may not be greatly moving in its effect, but it is slowly moving. The memory has not been enhanced, but it cannot be forgotten. Max Thrasher could no doubt have enhanced it, but he took Washington's dictation. It was not Washington who died after the book was done (he survived for fourteen years); it was Thrasher. He died of peritonitis at Tuskegee in 1903.

LEARNING THROUGH IGNORANCE:
THE EDUCATION OF HENRY ADAMS

The Education of Henry Adams remains a neglected book in American literature. It has always attracted attention of the highest quality. The books and essays on Henry Adams are nearly always good, from the initial responses of T. S. Eliot and Ezra Pound through the fine work of R. P. Blackmur, William Jordy, J. C. Levenson, John Conder, Vern Wagner, Melvin Friedman, Earl Harbert, and finally Ernest Samuels in his definitive three-volume biography. The editions of Adams' letters by Worthington C. Ford and Harold Cater are excellent, and Ernest Samuels' edition of the *Education,* available in paperback, should be in the library of every educated citizen.

Yet the *Education* continues to be relatively unknown to students of literature—and even to students of American literature. Think of the students who know more than one work of Hawthorne, Melville, Henry James, Hemingway, or Faulkner, yet who have never read Adams. Of course all those writers are novelists, and everyone knows how completely the novel has come to dominate the literary curriculum. Teachers who once would have taught courses devoted only to fiction now teach—or rather do not teach—courses in nonfiction. Yet even in the realm of nonfiction, Adams remains much more obscure than Franklin, Emerson, or Thoreau. Other prose writers have suffered decline. Mill, Newman, Macaulay, and Carlyle have almost disappeared from the curriculum in the face of the novel's onslaught. But Adams is different. The *Education* was never in the curriculum. In period anthologies it was represented by the invariable choice of "The Dynamo and the Virgin"; there Adams ended.

The neglect is not the result of a plot—or if it is, Adams himself may have been the first conspirator. Not only did he efface himself in his book, but he published the book privately in his own lifetime; when it was published after his death, he had taken pains to write a depreciative and deprecatory preface bearing the signature of his friend and former student Henry Cabot Lodge. The response to that 1918 publication of the *Education,* far from being negative, was sensitively and intelligently positive. The book was recognized for what it was—a remarkable achievement. If it has not penetrated the literary curriculum, it has nonetheless taken its place as an American classic in the minds of all who know it. If those minds are not legion, they have possessed enough force to keep it alive for the educated if not for education. Only in the schools can it be said to have failed.

Possibly the schools may take it up at last. It is, after all, an American book, and American literature has had sufficient impact in departments of English (where would the study of English literature be but for its subsidization by students of American literature since the early years of the Great Depression?) to provide a ground for its support. More important is the current rage for interdisciplinary courses, and if ever there existed a genuinely interdisciplinary book, it is the *Education*. Finally there are signs that recent literary criticism, seeking to break up the generic categories institutionalized by the academic success of the New Critics, may succeed in weakening the novel's stronghold upon literary study. The signs of generic dissolution, though not appreciably significant in course offerings, are obvious in the contemporary critical emphasis on autobiography. Although almost completely neglected by the New Critics, autobiography has become a focal point for widely varying contemporary approaches: for critics seeking literature of sociological, psychological, and historical reference; for critics pursuing a more democratized definition of literature; and for critics contending for the ultimate absence or presence of linguistic signification. James Olney has acutely seen that if the lyric poem was the literary form on which the New Criticism was based, autobiography provides the literary model for much contemporary critical theory.

The Education of Henry Adams should thrive in this changed educational and critical scene. For those readers truly interested in interdisciplinary subjects, it affords a vision in which science, history, art, and literature are brilliantly integrated. At the same time, it challenges the most acute literary theorist with its literary form. All this does not assure it a place in either an interdisciplinary or a literary curriculum. The *Education* is a long, demanding work, and what follows is but an introductory hint of its identity and vision.

First of all, *The Education of Henry Adams* is written by Henry Adams, which means that a reader—an American reader—is thrust simultaneously outward into the reality of American history and in-

ward to the issue of autobiographical reference. Henry Steele Com-
mager, writing on Adams as an American historian, contends that
the most important fact about Adams as historian is that he was an
Adams—was in fact the great descendant of one of the founding
fathers and was therefore a cardinal embodiment of American history. He *was* history even as he wrote history. His nine-volume history of the United States in the administrations of Jefferson and
Madison is by almost all counts the finest history written by an
American. In method and focus it signals the triumph of history as
science; in manner and theme it bears comparison with Gibbon's
Decline and Fall and thus exemplifies history as art.

Yet, if the most remarkable thing about Henry Adams as historian
is that he was an Adams, it is even more remarkable that Adams as an
artist was an Adams. John Adams, consumed with his wartime duties
as minister to Paris, had written home:

> I could fill volumes with descriptions of temples and palaces, paint-
> ings, sculptures, tapestry, porcelain, etc., etc., etc.; if I could have
> time; but I could not do this without neglecting my duty. The science of
> government is my duty to study, more than all the other sciences; the
> arts of legislation and administration and negotiation ought to take the
> place of, indeed to exclude, all other arts. I must study politics and war
> that my sons may have liberty to study mathematics and philosophy.
> My sons ought to study mathematics and philosophy, geography, natu-
> ral history and naval architecture in order to give their children a right
> to study painting, poetry, music, architecture, statuary, tapestry, and
> porcelain.[1]

Although John Adams turned out to be wrong by one generation in
his prophetic aim, his great-grandson nonetheless made the aim a
prophecy. He not only was a student of all the items in his great-
grandfather's list, but was himself an artist of the highest order in his
two great books, *Mont Saint Michel and Chartres* and *The Education
of Henry Adams*. He had been an artist in his long history of the
United States, but the history had dominated and finally enthralled
him until it had ended his life as historian. Approaching seventy, he
set about once more not to leave history but to end it—and not merely
the history he had inherited but all history, his own included—in art.

1. Charles Francis Adams (ed.), *Familiar Letters of John Adams and His Wife Abigail
Adams* (New York, 1876), 381.

The work he envisioned would not and could not be art for art's sake and thus an end in itself; it would not and could not be the precious luxury that John Adams' official duties forced him to defer. It would, and had to be, an end of himself in art, which would in turn be the education of future generations. To make one's art a life study for others meant that Adams had to convert himself into a student; to make an end of himself in history, he had to complete his life; and to make an end of himself in art meant that he had to convert himself into form and thus become a still life—which is to say a silent life, a fixed life, and yet a life still—not merely a life of motion but one in motion. If that was not the task Adams as autobiographer set himself, it was nonetheless the life he accomplished as an artist.

The task Adams actually set himself as a writer is plainly set forth in Chapter 29 of the *Education:*

> Eight or ten years of study had led Adams to think he might use the century 1150–1250, expressed in Amiens Cathedral and the works of Thomas Aquinas, as the unit from which he might measure motion down to his own time, without assuming anything as true or untrue, except relation. The movement might be studied at once in philosophy and mechanics. Setting himself to the task, he began a volume which he mentally knew as "Mont Saint Michel and Chartres: A Study of Thirteenth Century Unity." From that point he proposed to fix a position for himself, which he could label: "The Education of Henry Adams: A Study of Twentieth-Century Multiplicity." With the help of these two points of relation, he hoped to project his lines forward and backward indefinitely, subject to correction from anyone who should know better. Thereupon, he sailed for home.[2]

There in a nutshell is the conception of Adams' still life of himself. It significantly ends the chapter entitled "The Abyss of Ignorance."

This is the conception of Adams' autobiography, not the order of his life. As Ernest Samuels points out in the third volume of his biography of Adams and again in his notes to his edition of the *Education,* there is no evidence that Adams actually planned the two works in such a fashion. When he wrote these words, he had already completed *Mont Saint Michel and Chartres.* But what would be distortion from the biographical point of view is the very essence of

---

2. Ernest Samuels (ed.), *The Education of Henry Adams* (New York, 1973), 435. All subsequent citations are from this edition and will be given in the text.

truth in the autobiographical act of consciousness. For even as Adams asserts his *conception* late in the book—he had actually quoted the conception in his own preface to the book, which followed the "Editor's Preface" he had written for Lodge's signature—he immediately casts his consciousness outside the *Education,* putting it between two books—one devoted to unity, the other to multiplicity. Thus, *relation,* which would move chronologically in a narrative of one's life, is made dynamic alternation, as the lines run forward and backward from one book to the other.

Although Adams' dynamic conception of education moves the two books away from chronological relation and into an instantaneous gravitational field of relation, the fact that the lines of force move forward and backward rather than from side to side indicates that temporal sequence is not lost. Unity is clearly the first term in the sequence both in order of time and in order of text, yet it just as clearly eventuates in multiplicity. Adams had put the issue clearly in the first chapter of the *Education:* "From cradle to grave this problem of running order through chaos, direction through space, discipline through freedom, unity through multiplicity, has always been, and must always be, the task of education, as it is the moral of religion, philosophy, science, art, politics, and economy; but a boy's will is his life, and he dies when it is broken, as the colt dies in harness, taking a new nature in becoming tame" (12).

The child begins in unity as if his will were, as Longfellow had written, the wind's will. He is one with the will of nature, and the education that breaks his will, causing him to take on a new nature, is the working out of the very multiplicity of natures to find a new unity. At another point Adams puts the matter precisely: "Truly the animal that is to be trained to unity must be caught young. Unity is vision; it must have been part of the process of learning to see. The older the mind, the older its complexities, and the further it looks, the more it sees, until even the stars resolve themselves into multiples; yet the child will always see but one" (398–99).

If the two books may be thought of at the same time, they cannot quite be read, or written about, at the same time. Thought is somehow an energy different from words: it runs ahead of them as projection or lags behind as reflection. An account of *Mont Saint Michel and Chartres* throws light upon Adams' autobiographical enterprise.

Instead of recovering Wordsworthian childhood and the will that had not been broken, Adams the historian went back to fix a point of unity in history that could be placed in relation to the multiplicity of his own time. He knew that he could not reconstruct that moment after the method of Leopold von Ranke, revealing history as it had "actually" happened. Instead he portrayed himself as a tourist uncle taking nieces into the medieval world through the art that had survived. Yet he knew that his pilgrimage was not with the will of a Catholic but with the imagination of Wordsworth.

> The man who wanders into the twelfth century is lost, unless he can grow prematurely young.
>
> One can do it, as one can play with children. Wordsworth, whose practical sense equalled his intuitive genius, carefully limited us to "a season of calm weather," which is certainly best; but granting a fair frame of mind, one can still "have sight of that immortal sea" which brought us hither from the twelfth century; one can even travel thither and see the children sporting on the shore. Our sense is partially atrophied from disuse, but it is still alive, at least in old people, who alone, as a class, have the time to be young.[3]

Yet the tourist uncle with his nieces is not a romantic poet nor a Sir Walter Scott nor a Boston brahmin medievalist, but an American historian who emerges from the portals of his cathedrals not with unity but with multiplicity.

He has two churches—Mont Saint Michel, the masculine church, and Chartres, the church of the Virgin. Mont Saint Michel is itself two churches, one built over the other as the Gothic mounts the Romanesque (which had itself mounted the mountain). So is Chartres, containing as it does three centuries between old and new towers. In that space he had set out to discover the precarious equilibrium between the old tower of the Virgin and the new tower, which he associates with St. Thomas Aquinas. For all his interest in the immediacy of art, it is the immediacy of history that Adams seeks. The immediacy of art is in the resistant stones and glass and structure of the cathedral; the immediacy of history is in the space between the old and new towers, between the true Romanesque arch and the broken Gothic arch. Romanesque art could conceal its bracing in its walls,

3. Henry Adams, *Mont Saint Michel and Chartres,* in Henry Adams, *Novels, Mont Saint Michel, The Education,* ed. Ernest and Jayne Samuels (New York, 1983), 343–44.

but its height requires perpetual broadening of its base. Breaking the arch made possible unlimited aspiration in height but required external buttresses. The aspiration toward God the Father was then made possible by devotion to the Virgin Mother. She is at once the motive and the beauty for the builders, ordering them (in Adams' vision of cathedral structure) to build and decorate her temple in precise relation to her infallible taste. The power and gravity of this divine aesthetic gives back, or drops down, upon her devotees the irrational love and mercy that the rational judgment of the Father helplessly withholds—helplessly, because the Judge is at once logical and masculine.

In Adams' tourist feeling, the Virgin is the unity toward which and in which her petitioners and pilgrims aspired. There had been at first the cross with man crucified upon it; then the cruciform of the church itself; then the church, male and militant, yet simple in its warlike strength even as it lifted itself upward into the broken Gothic arch and single spire at Mont Saint Michel and expressed itself in the poetry of *The Song of Roland;* then Chartres, with its magnificently simple old spire, its massive portal, its great blue window for the Virgin—this the church radiant, the church of love, in which man could be a child at the mercy of the Virgin—and its poetry embodied in *The Romance of the Rose;* and then the second tower, taller than the first and beautiful, too, but this time masculine, as Adams' consciousness discovering itself in the space between the towers begins to generate the historical sequence between old and new tower. If the old tower belongs to the Virgin, the new one belongs to Aquinas, whose *Summa* was the external buttressing required by the vaulting imagination of the broken arch. The *Summa* was, after all, the visible logic that the Prince of Schoolmen erected to buttress the vault of faith. Thomas had conquered the mystics with reason, and his church finally put woman back in her place. For a long moment she had embodied the unity of a unified faith; the precarious poise of the Gothic cathedral was proof in art that the unity had existed. The father could only make man a Son. But the mother could make him a child—and in the radiant light of the Virgin the child could again "see but one."

Thomas sought in logic to get back to the Father, the first cause, the prime mover. Adams insists that Thomas' mover is a prime motor, and he further insists that Thomas, in accounting for individual identity, brought the soul down from heaven to find its form in earth. This

meeting of a particular soul in a particular body was, in Thomas'
view, part of God's continuous act of creating the world. It meant for
the church that St. Thomas was at the threshold of pantheism, since
matter was elevated to the status of helping to individuate the soul; it
meant for Adams, who was not a churchman but a historian, that
Thomas was at the threshold of science, since he was bringing the
primal energy from heaven to earth. In the sequence of force it was
but a step from Thomas to Bacon, who, instead of evolving the
universe from a thought, determined to evolve thought from the
universe. Matter thus became the charge of mind.

This sequence is not fully evident in *Mont Saint Michel;* if it were,
Adams would have been inertly trapped in a sequence of books rather
than dynamically pursuing a sequence of force. In the relation between the books the sequence of force discloses itself. Seen through
the *Education, Mont Saint Michel* becomes Adams' act of entering
the past through the portal of art. He goes in as a tourist, to be
converted into neither a Wordsworthian poet and child of nature nor a
brahmin Episcopalian yearning to be a medieval Catholic, and
emerges as a historian of force. Thus, his romance with the Virgin
ends with an account of St. Thomas' masculine and logical triumph
over the church of the Virgin. The new tower thus stands taller than
the old; it is the reassertion of masculine logic and judgment over
feminine love and grace. The relation between the two forces was the
energy embodied in the transition Gothic; it was the power at the
intersection of nave and transept, where the heavenly axis of Virgin
and God the Father crossed the earthly axis of Pierre de Dreux and
Blanche of Castille. Or, even better, it was the volatile space between
the two towers, where the Virgin's love and Thomas' logic are held in
the contradiction of asymmetrical tension.

Seen in this light, the image of the two towers of Chartres has sufficient meaning to generate a metaphor for *The Education of Henry
Adams* and *Mont Saint Michel and Chartres.* The two books are
analogous to the two towers: they are the artistic structure Adams
leaves behind him. *Mont Saint Michel* is, of course, the old tower—
simpler in its exterior structure, romantic and poetic in its tone,
dominantly feminine in both its subject and its sensibility. The *Education* is the later larger structure—elaborate in style and logic, masculine in subject and aim. It is about Henry Adams, and its avowed

purpose is "to fit young men, in universities or elsewhere, to be men of the world, equipped for any emergency" (xxx). Beyond that, it is an American book, about not an American Adam but an American Adams. Anyone who reads it with *Mont Saint Michel* in mind knows that St. Michael, standing atop his Norman church, looked into the Atlantic, where the Norman descendants of William the Conqueror were to make their way via England to the shores of America. But Adams goes much further in emphasizing the masculine identity of America. He knows to the marrow of his New England bones the Puritan denial of Mariolatry, and thus he knows how powerfully the Puritan version of the Church Militant asserted the masculine God. More than that, he knows how the American Enlightenment that conquered the Puritan theocracy—or secularized it—was a combination of the republican spirit and scientific spirit of the founding fathers. Thus, if Henry Adams, the descendant of John Adams, felt New England Puritanism in his blood, Henry Adams, the historian of Jeffersonian democracy, knew that Franklin and Jefferson were scientists and that America was the ground where science would thrive.

Yet this figure of the two books as Adams' cathedral structure is perforce metaphor because structure is itself spatial whereas Adams' form is necessarily linear. Adams' interest is itself linear—in history and time and motion. His whole recognition of Chartres lies in making it move intellectually just as its stillness moves him emotionally. That alternation is the reciprocal movement of emotion and thought, of art and history. He thus determines to define the space between the two towers in terms of the religious, sexual, scientific, and political force informing the invisible temporal sequence between them.

His task in *Mont Saint Michel* had been to convert the enduring art of the cathedral into historical force; his task in the *Education* was to convert the history of his own life and times into art. Both of his "towers" would be history, just as the towers of Chartres "were" religion. He knew that the primary barrier separating him from the world of Chartres was the force that had overcome or "converted" God into science and revelation into secular history. That sequence began with the medieval period, in which man and woman—Mont Saint Michel and Chartres—were poised in precarious equilibrium; it ran from the old tower through St. Thomas Aquinas' new tower to Columbus' discovery of America and the Protestant Reformation; it was accelerated by Bacon's attraction to Nature and reached its first great period in the triumph of the Enlightenment and the Declaration of Independence. Yet, even as the American nation was being declared, the industrial revolution was taking full shape in the form of James Watt's steam engine and the formulation of Adam Smith's free-enterprise capitalism. Adams' historical research and writing had already led him to see that America was to be the scientific nation, and in the *Education* he made unmistakably clear how the United States was, by the end of the nineteenth century, overtaking England in the production of coal.

Adams realizes that at the beginning of the twentieth century he is confronted by a transitional moment possessing the magnitude of that which evoked Chartres cathedral. Then the attraction of woman drew man's imagination into the radiant generation of a cathedral and in effect converted the masculine God of judgment and thought into a God of love and mercy. Although Aquinas' theological synthesis regained masculine dominion, it started the process by which God was brought down toward nature. Adams saw his own time of conceiving and writing the *Education* (1905–1907) as the moment when the matter of nature, which had become the mass of the mechanical era, was being fully and finally converted into the electrical energy of the twentieth century. He knew that the process had been accelerating throughout the nineteenth century, as mechanical power was steadily and relentlessly converted into electrical power. Thus, Faraday's primitive dynamo of 1831 had, by the end of the century, become the means of converting steam power into the electric power and light to run subways, lift elevators (and thus raise skyscrapers), and illuminate whole cities. Watching the dynamo at the Paris Exposition in 1900, Adams felt its power grasp his imagination.

> As he grew accustomed to the great gallery of machines, he began to feel the forty-foot dynamos as a moral force, much as the early Christians felt the Cross. . . . Before the end, one began to pray to [the dynamo]; inherited instinct taught the natural expression of man before silent and infinite force. . . .
>
> Between the dynamo in the gallery of machines and the engine-house outside, the break of continuity amounted to abysmal fracture for a historian's objects. No more relation could he discover between the steam and the electric current than between the Cross and the cathedral. The forces were interchangeable if not reversible, but he could see only an absolute *fiat* in electricity as in faith. (380–81)

He senses in this enormous electromotive and electromagnetic force the attraction upon his mind of a force equal to the Virgin of Chartres.

She had actually come between God and man to generate the cathedral of the Gothic transition. Largely pushed aside by the early church fathers, she emerged to radiate her own energy. Embodying the inertial reproductive motion of the race, she became the grace and beauty of the church in a moment of art and power.

Looking at his own time, Adams knows that it is the dynamo that has the power: it is the attraction as well as the attractive force. Moreover, as he sees history, the dynamo is literally attracting Russia and the East from what he sees as their racial inertia into the Western orbit of science and technology. Even more important, it is attracting woman from her orbit of reproduction and the family into equality with the male. Adams sees this dynamic breakdown of racial and sexual inertia as a part of the vast acceleration concentrated in and represented by America. The Declaration of Independence, the very sum and crystallization of Enlightenment political theory, had asserted by creative fiat the equality of all men, and in so doing it had opened up a new magnetic field of force. In such a field the individual, who had been mere matter, gained political power at the same time he faced infinite replication into political *mass*. Adams, looking back on the intrusion of America into the history of nations, could see not only how this political field was related to the religious, scientific, and sexual fields but also how inevitably America was to dominate the twentieth century. Not for nothing had he occupied his post of observation at Lafayette Square in the beautiful house that Henry Hobson Richardson (his Harvard classmate) had designed for him. Whereas his friend Henry James was, in Adams' words, teaching "the world to read a volume for the pleasure of seeing the lights of his burning glass turned on alternate sides of the same figure," Adams was determined to define and chart the direction of the force that he felt had excluded him from occupying the office held by his great-grandfather and grandfather. James had devoted his imaginative powers to a central intelligence that could freely discover the plot always on the point of enclosing that intelligence. Adams sought to survey, measure, volatilize, and even direct the force and motion of the history that had cast him aside and left him behind.

We come at last to the form of the *Education,* the "new tower." I have sketched the substantive relation between the two books because it is a difficult sequence, because it is so often neglected, and above all because the more it is articulated as substance, the more it becomes inertially sequential, thereby violating or contradicting the dynamic sequence that Adams both sought and achieved. Seeing Adams' "ideas" related in historical sequence, as if time were a cause rather than a measure of motion, is to lapse into the very history Adams knew, or hoped, was dead. It was the history that his own cathedral structure meant to kill. To see Adams' "idea" die into inertia even as it is articulated is to see history as dead relation. But it is also to face the necessity of Adams' form, which, juxtaposed against his matter, converts history into a relation of energy.

There is probably no better figure for the movement of Adams' thought in the *Education* than Faraday's primitive dynamo. The great eleventh edition of the *Britannica* describes it: "On the 28th of October 1831 Faraday mounted a copper disk so that it could be rotated edgewise between the poles of a permanent horseshoe magnet. When so rotated, it cut the lines of flux which passed transversely through its lower half and by means of rubbing contacts, one on its periphery and the other on its spindle, the circuit was closed through a galvanometer, which indicated the passage of a continuous current as long as the disk was rotated." If we remember how Adams imaginatively cast his conception of his project *between* his two books, the analogy becomes clear. The two books are the poles, and the conception is itself the dynamic intrusion cutting across the lines of force to generate its own continuous narrative current. By just such means Adams converted the stream of history into a charged current.

The dynamo is not the only figure from the world of science and technology that provides an analogy for Adams' form. There is also geodetic triangulation from the world of surveying. We should remember that Clarence King, who with John Hay formed the triangular friendship that Adams used to "measure" the success and failure of his life, headed the survey of the fortieth parallel. The aim of geodetic triangulation is to achieve a survey of the earth's surface that takes into account the curvature of the earth. To take it into account, points have to be made or located on the landscape sufficiently high to lengthen the primary baseline of spatial measurement. Geodetic triangulation is much more possible in mountains than in plains, since a larger area may be taken in by virtue of the higher points. King's surveying team pioneered in strategies to work from mountain peaks as a means of accelerating the area survey.

If we think of both the dynamo and geodetic triangulation as figures related to Adams' form, we can tentatively suggest possibilities for grounding his form in history. The dynamo and geodetic surveying give us, in a literal sense, the constituents of a magnetic field: the dynamo conducts the current, and geodetic triangulation provides the most accurate measurement of the spatial area. In historical vision the magnetic field becomes a metaphor, but a metaphor instantly related to Adams' ambition, which was to make his study of history scientific and make metaphor promise method. He would have seen that the word *field,* for example, was itself both an embodiment and reflection of the force of thought transforming agricultural space into intellectual discipline. Looking from the field of history, he would have seen that the fields of nature were literally being transformed into the electromagnetic fields of science. He was determined to draw energy from these scientific fields back into the field of history by using scientific method to measure the sequence of thought that had led from one "field" to another.

To get this far is to see how the two books must be put in a polar relation with each other and must at the same time be tall enough "moments" in the historical field to make possible a large or significant triangulation. What remains is to see what Adams did in the *Education* itself, the work that would try to *be* the vision of history it conceived.

The signal fact of form in Adams' "new tower" is his decision to cast himself into history. To accomplish that, he converts the "I" of conventional and inert autobiography into the third person. This decision comprises two momentous achievements. First, it explicitly acknowledges the necessary division of self implicitly involved in the autobiographical act. Anyone who gives significant thought to autobiography comes to know that the first person of autobiographical narrative is by no means identical with the consciousness of the writer but is instead an utterly conventional signifier into which the "experience" of the author is serially and "historically" poured. Yet, develop this "self" as the author will, he cannot bring it to the moment of consciousness that conceives it. It is thus a "dead" self, hopelessly unable to reach the "life" that generates it.

But Adams' third-person strategy accomplished much more than dealing decisively with a generic difficulty in autobiography. His manner of dividing himself enabled him to realize his matter. By converting himself into the third person, he at once made himself the central matter of the nineteenth-century history in which he had lived. Yet the consciousness of the young Henry Adams is much more than mere matter: it is a unit of force being acted on by the much larger forces of history. These forces act not so much by crushing (though they can do that) as by attracting the unit Henry Adams. But the largest force in the book is the historical consciousness of the author who has conceived of "himself" as the unit of force and is attracting Adams through history to what is at once his end and origin. This consciousness is literally *generating* the forces of history that attract and determine the life of the young Adams, and it is regenerating Adams himself as a *student*.

This regeneration produces another division, a division of irony. The young Adams should have been drawn to success, since his family more than prepared the way to political power. But the mind that has converted the young Adams into a unit of force and made of him a student is constantly generating the historical currents that whelmed him and all his family line. Thus, the very family securities that should guarantee success become the inertial liabilities that make him fall behind the movement of history. Having inherited from his forebears an eighteenth-century mind, he is in no way prepared to encounter the forces of the nineteenth century. All his knowledge must be converted into ignorance so that the generative conceptual consciousness can *educate* the unit Henry Adams, who, because he was born too late, never caught up with the history of the nineteenth century. The book forces this issue into view almost at once and reiterates it all along the way: "He and his eighteenth-century, troglodytic Boston were suddenly cut apart—separated forever—in act if not in sentiment, by the opening of the Boston and Albany Railroad; the appearance of the first Cunard steamers in the bay, and the telegraphic messages which carried from Baltimore to Washington the news that Henry Clay and James K. Polk were nominated for the Presidency. This was in May, 1844; he was six years old; his new world was ready for use, and only fragments of the old met his eyes" (5).

Not only does this passage state a theme that will be repeated and developed, but its style lets us see just how the book articulates at every moment its conception. Just as the figure of Henry Adams is separated from the consciousness that generates it, so is the figure of

Henry Adams being *divided* from the forces that make up his world. He is declared by the absolute fiat of this assertive style to be separated *forever* from his native city by virtue of the intrusion of the forces that define and constitute nineteenth-century progress. Thus the steam engines, on one hand, are already accelerating the westward movement of the nation, and the steamships, on the other, are drawing it more swiftly toward the Europe from which it had tried to separate itself. Finally the telegraph instantaneously informs Washington that two westerners have been nominated for the presidency. The style deliberately yet extravagantly asserts this complete and final separation.

Through such conceptual and stylistic division the narrative consciousness gains power, giving decision to individual sentences and, much more important, creating a gap in both thought and style, a gap that is closed by the energy that continuously leaps back across the breach and forms a negative relation between Henry Adams and his time. A strong element of irony inheres in this negative relation. We are getting Henry Adams defined as a failure in about the brightest and most intelligent style we shall ever read. The aggression of this irony is two-edged. First, in addition to exposing Adams as a failure, it exposes the failure of his society and his century. Second, it makes us wince, for if this intelligence has failed, who of us shall escape whipping? Even so, this irony remains a secondary constituent to the actual truth of the negative relation.

The fact, or rather the history, is that Adams has failed. And his life must be continually generated as a failure by the narrative. Having begun, as he says, with some of the best cards of the century, he has failed to achieve power and responsibility. His emotional relation to that failure could be one of contempt for the less-educated masses who have more and more gained the vote, disdain for the newly rich tycoons who have seized the power, self-pity at being rejected by men less capable than he, visionary melancholy at the decline of history away from the purity and integrity of his own forebears. Not only could his emotional relation toward both his failure and his history have something of this cast—it does profoundly. This cast of mind is precisely what is attracted by the Virgin.

But we are being given the education of Henry Adams, not his emotional history. And so the narration subjects its third person to the forces of history, not merely exposing but exaggerating his unpreparedness, his failure, and, above all, his ignorance of the forces attracting or repelling him. Just as he could not, at the age of six, realize that steam and telegraph had cut Boston off from his eighteenth-century mind, neither can Harvard prepare him for life; nor can study in Germany prepare him for the law, which is about to be violently changed by civil war in America; nor can his indignation at the treason of the South prepare him for the treason of Charles Sumner against his father; nor will his experience as private secretary to his father in England during the Civil War prepare him for returning to the victorious Union he and his father had patiently and precariously served; nor does his study of Darwin's theory of evolution prepare him to face Grant in the White House.

This exposed and failing and ignorant Henry Adams is by no means an absolute dunce; he studies, works, offers his services to his government, offers his journalistic criticism to expose fraud in public office, only to end up as a professor of medieval history at Harvard and editor of the *North American Review*. Never mind that Adams was "really" a remarkable professor and an able editor. In terms of education he was out of his own historical time, out of touch with a significant audience (neither the general public nor General Grant read or cared about the *North American Review*), and out of society ("several score of the best educated, most agreeable, and personally the most sociable people in America united in Cambridge to make a social desert that would have starved a polar bear"). We may say, and Adams will gleefully show us in almost the next moment, that if Cambridge society was a desert, the society of Washington, where he is soon to return, was little better than Neanderthal. And we may remember that English society—which had passed for high society—had been catastrophically boring. Such deprecations in no way cancel out one another, nor do they invalidate Adams' contention of his own failure. As appreciators of Adams' art or as believers in higher education, we may conclude that Harvard society either then or today is superior to Washington society or that being a professor at Harvard has its own power and rewards—rewards superior to the kind of vulgar power possessed by politicians, businessmen, or, for that matter, deans. Adams would understand such a valuation, yet would instantly see that it merely confirmed the hopeless inertia of so-called education. Adams would perfectly understand why Henry Kissinger instantly left Harvard to become Richard Nixon's (yes, even Nixon's) adviser. Why is it, he might ask and in a real way does ask throughout the book, that people committed to education so often foolishly lament their powerlessness to influence society or fatuously claim that they are influential? Such responses are themselves the index to the colossal failure of education in a democracy.

This whole record of his failure, culminating with his appointment as professor at Harvard, constitutes the first twenty chapters of the thirty-five chapters of the *Education*. Significantly, the twentieth chapter is entitled "Failure." It ends with Adams meeting Clarence King at Estes Park and realizing how King's scientific education stands him on a pinnacle of success as tall as the mountains from which he heroically conducts his triangulations. At precisely this point there is a break or gap in the *Education*. On the other side of that gap, twenty years later, Adams resumes his narrative. He does not say why the gap exists, though he refers to the history he has written, and he sums up the lives of his two friends—Hay (who has written the life of Lincoln) and King (who has retired from government to seek his fortune). But we infer from the gap itself that there must be a huge reason for the twenty-year blank or lesion in a continuous record.

To know Adams' biography is to know the reason almost too well. His wife of thirteen years, Marian Hooper Adams, killed herself in 1885. Such a fact may be known too well because its very volatility may, for the knower, annihilate other reasons. Yet it is so hugely there that, like a magnet, it has immense attraction. Biographers, or critics of biographical disposition, are helplessly drawn into that space (though they are likely to think of it as a hole) and call it (if they are of novelistic bent) a dark room (since Marian Adams was an amateur photographer and took her life by drinking potassium cyanide). But we shall remain in autobiography, reading as much as we can from Adams' form and theme. What we can see in the form is that Adams' book breaks in two at this point, thus showing in its visible sequence the principle of division multiplying before our eyes. If we take the two books with the conception cast between them as our master trope and the two towers of Chartres with the conception of history being discovered between them as the theme of the earlier book (the old tower), then we can begin to see and interpret the possibilities of the actual formal division in the *Education*.

This book is not only about education but is *The Education,* and this twenty-year gap demands or at least asks to be filled. In a word—

and a word crucial to Adams' form and theme—it does *attract* us, and attracts us especially if we are ignorant. If we convert the ignorance of those missing years into the knowledge of Marian Adams' suicide, then we have begun, but only begun, the dynamic interpretation of the book. By putting the suicide of the wife (and all the years of marriage) in the space between the parts (which are interestingly asymmetrical like the towers of Chartres), we see or might see an instantaneous relationship to the form of the book that is attracting the unit of force, Henry Adams, through the nineteenth century to his end. Unlike conventional autobiography, this one, though it may have a gap in the middle, has an end in which Henry Adams, who is likened to that other student Hamlet, is ended: "There it ended! Shakespeare himself could use no more than the commonplace to express what is incapable of expression. 'The rest is silence!' The few familiar words, among the simplest in the language, conveying an idea trite beyond rivalry, served Shakespeare, and, as yet, no one has said more" (504).

These sentences begin the last paragraph of the book and refer first to John Hay's death and then to Adams' departure from his book. Hay has died the death of Hamlet the hero, at the height of his power, "in full fame, at home and abroad universally regretted, and wielding his power to the last" (504). With King dead three years before, Adams dismisses himself: "It was time to go. The three friends had begun life together; and the last of the three had no motive—no attraction— to carry it on after the others had gone" (505). Adams is here the suicidal Hamlet, the one who could not be the king his ancestors expected him to be and could not avenge them by killing the usurper. He was doomed, this Adams-Hamlet, to be the melancholy observer of the White House of his fathers. But here the analogy breaks down. For Adams, unlike Hamlet, is actually ending his life, and in this sense he is carrying out the truth of his form at the same time he "matches" or marries his wife's suicide, which the student-reader has had to put into the twenty-year gap. To me it would not be amiss to be attracted back to the Hamlet analogy and wonder whether Adams had not driven Marian Adams to the madness of suicide as Hamlet had done to Ophelia.

Yet that way madness surely lies. It is better and harder and more rewarding to come back to the book's great form—back to the *Education*—and see dynamically, as Adams, not dying historically, dies into his conception. The last chapter is unforgettably entitled "Nunc Age." That last word, which in English connotes slowing down to a stop, is dynamic in Latin. We are thus at the true threshold of the still life we saw at the beginning. To be there is to see that Adams' "suicide" is a match for, or marriage to, the knowledge of suicide with which we "historical" and "biographical" readers fill the gap to the right of center in the book. More important, the book as figurative suicide is the object of art matching the great Saint-Gaudens sculpture that Adams commissioned to mark his wife's grave. Any reader who thinks I am being fanciful should remember what Adams wrote to Henry James: "The volume is a mere shield of protection in the grave. I advise you to take your own life in the same way in order to prevent biographers from taking it in theirs."

Even so I *am* being figurative. The book is not and cannot be an actual suicide despite Adams' contention that his subsequent life as a writer would be posthumous. The book is an education—and an education in the sequence of thought. And so instead of looking for the death of the wife that is *not* there in the text—though all the more present by virtue of its absence—we need to look for the death of the woman that is unforgettably in the text: the death of Adams' sister, Louisa Adams Kuhn, of lockjaw, at the Bagni di Lucca, in 1870:

> One had heard and read a great deal about death, and even seen a little of it, and knew by heart the thousand commonplaces of religion and poetry which seemed to deaden one's senses and veil the horror. Society being immortal, could put on immortality at will. Adams being mortal, felt only the mortality. Death took features altogether new to him, in these rich and sensuous surroundings. Nature enjoyed it, played with it, the horror added to her charm, she liked the torture, and smothered her victim with caresses. Never had one seen her so winning. The hot Italian summer brooded outside, over the market-place and the picturesque peasants, and, in the singular color of the Tuscan atmosphere, the hills and vineyards of the Apennines seemed bursting with midsummer blood. The sickroom itself glowed with the Italian joy of life; friends filled it; no harsh northern lights pierced the soft shadows; even the dying woman shared the sense of the Italian summer, the soft, velvet air, the humor, the courage, the sensual fullness of Nature and man. She faced death, as women mostly do, bravely and even gaily, racked slowly to unconsciousness, but yielding only to violence, as a soldier sabred in battle. For many thousands of years, on

these hills and plains, Nature had gone on sabering men and women
with the same air of sensual pleasure. (287–88)

The location, the intensity, the structure, and the beauty of this remarkable passage are vital to understanding the book. The passage
appears in the nineteenth chapter, "Chaos." The intensity is sustained as the passage moves through a crescendo of accelerating
divisions and polarities. First, the immortality of society is set against
the mortality of the individual (and here we see how the unity of the
unit Henry Adams is registered by the formality of the pronoun *one*);
then the masculinity of Society and Henry Adams is set against the
femininity of Mother Nature caressing and killing her victim Louisa
Adams. Thus the pain and anguish of death are converted into a kind
of pleasure and beauty and sensuality, but imaginatively converted to
Nature's pleasure as a means of emotionally heightening the pain and
anguish felt by both spectator and victim. Yet just as there is always
the visible move toward polarized division in Adams' style, there has
already been a prior conceptual thrust toward unity. Thus, the account
of Louisa's approaching death, though it moves extravagantly into
what we might call emotional response, is nonetheless generated by a
consciousness that has already converted emotion into an aspect of
mind. For all his divisions, Adams' vision remains one of mind: that
is what life as education *must* be converted into. It is precisely this
unity that Adams achieved in his initial act of dividing the generative
consciousness (the "I") from the third-person "subject" of the book.
That third person can take the pronoun *one* as its substitute, the *one*
that begins the passage.

But the paragraph immediately following this "sensual" description shows the full violence of what is happening at this critical
moment in the book.

Impressions like these are not reasoned or catalogued in the mind; they
are felt as part of violent emotion; and the mind that feels them is a
different one from that which reasons; it is thought of a different power
and a different person. The first serious consciousness of Nature's
gesture—her attitude towards life—took form then as a phantasm, a
nightmare, an insanity of force. For the first time, the stage-scenery of
the senses collapsed; the human mind felt itself stripped naked, vibrating in a void of shapeless energies, with resistless mass, colliding,
crushing, wasting, and destroying what these same energies had cre-

ated and labored from eternity to perfect. Society became fantastic, a vision of pantomime with a mechanical motion; and its so-called thought merged in the mere sense of life, and pleasure in the sense. The usual anodynes of social medicine became evident artifice. Stoicism was perhaps the best; religion was the most human; but the idea that any personal deity could find pleasure or profit in torturing a poor woman, by accident, with a fiendish cruelty known to man only in perverted and insane temperaments, could not be held for a moment. For pure blasphemy, it made pure atheism a comfort. God might be, as the Church said, a Substance, but He could not be a Person. (288–89)

What becomes fully clear in this passage is that the mind of Henry Adams splits as it feels the force, the attraction, of his sister's death. There are two minds—the mind that feels and the mind that reasons. Once that split occurs, there is chaos, but there is also energy, for, as Adams says at another point, "Chaos breeds energy where order breeds habit" (249). The force of the unified mind splitting could well stand for the volatile or dynamic principle of the book, the point at which style, action, and theme coalesce with full force. It is hardly a leap to see the true sequence that Adams has in mind. There would first be Adam, a unity; then there would be Adams, a multiplicity. The very name of the subject (and that name is played with from time to time throughout the book) holds the dynamic potentiality of the conception that Adams articulates in his preface. Finally, there would be the atom, the single unit of force into which Adams converts himself. Having wrought such a conversion, the autobiographical consciousness then attracts this atom through all the forces it can generate. Adams thus remains an atom and becomes an atom—the available energy of the historian as artist in the act of converting his life history into a model of history as science. Thus, from the emotion (or the mind that feels) Adams leaps (or is he attracted?) like an electrical spark across the gap of negative energy figured forth in that twenty-year parenthetical blank. If Poe had believed that the great subject for poetry in the nineteenth century was the death of a beautiful woman, Adams converts the death of a beautiful woman (whether it be his sister or his "own" Marian) into the anguished energy that will hurt him into thought.

That is why, in terms of the book, the *mind* that feels visualizes nature as chaotic energy before the mind that reasons can attempt a synthesis of multiplicity into unity. That is Adams' particular conversion of Rousseau's autobiographical assertion "I felt before I thought." By projecting the self as a unity of thought, Adams is able to split the mind or atom with the force of feeling converting thought into motion. Thus, just before the book "splits" apart, the mind has split into a mind that reasons and a mind that feels. The first response Adams makes to that split of mind is to find himself accepting the professorship of medieval history at Harvard. He is, in his own weakened state, attracted to the inertial form of institutional education. When he "resumes" life in 1892, he begins it from the point of the shrouded sculpture that Saint-Gaudens made to mark Marian Adams' grave.

Watching visitors to the monument pause before the mystery of art, Adams takes up his life again almost as if he were beside himself. I do not mean that the prose or style changes in this second part of the book any more than I mean that Adams was not beside himself in the first part. The very notion of being beside oneself strikes me as a fine equation for this book, which is so close to schizophrenic self-division, yet is itself the vision of life being concentrated into the attraction of thought. Even the two parts of the book are side by side. For all that, however, the second part is set against the first, and the mind that reasons attempts a synthesis that will comprehend the supersensual forces that it envisions science discovering. Unmoored from purpose after completing his long history, Adams is a drifter and a wanderer, attracted primarily to world's fairs: to Chicago in 1893, to Paris in 1900, and to St. Louis in 1904. It is at the Chicago fair that he first sees the dynamo, a symbol sufficiently powerful to make his last conversion. St. Augustine's conversion had come when he denied his old self and assented to God: he denied not by willing but by assenting or being willing, which is to say yielding utterly and miraculously to God. He was not "saved" so much as he was made visionary enough to ask what memory was, what time was, what Genesis was, and how to read the word of God in the beginning. Adams cannot be converted to God, who was all but annihilated when the mind split. Instead Adams brings the split mind—the mind that feels and the mind that reasons—into polar relation at the beginning of the twentieth century by juxtaposing two symbols: the Dynamo and the Virgin. It is extremely important to see the sequence. The Dynamo comes first. In the inert "progress" of history the Virgin came first, just as the thirteenth century preceded the twentieth. But it is the consciousness of the Dynamo that generates the Virgin in this book, just as it is the consciousness of Henry Adams the author that generates Henry Adams the unit of force. The Dynamo is the organization of the vertiginous energy Adams had seen nature convert herself into when his sister had died. And the Virgin is the energy of the medieval world that Adams contends he had inertly professed at Harvard. Juxtaposed in abrupt relation to each other, the Dynamo and the Virgin are symbols at once powerful and polar enough to generate a dynamic theory of history and a law of acceleration to measure the movement of thought.

The dynamic theory and the law of acceleration are the constituents of Adams' intellectual vision. I have already given the roughest, most inertial outline of the sequence that Adams saw running from Chartres to twentieth-century America. I am too ignorant in science to follow Adams' effort to convert history into science. It is material for another essay that I shall probably never write. Yet it is possible to sketch aspects of the conversion. Adams realized that science and technology, the forces defining the nineteenth century, had constantly accelerated. Positioning his consciousness precisely at 1905, he generated sufficient intellectual force to *attract* the unit Henry Adams from birth to "suicide"—which is to say arbitrary dismissal at a fixed moment. In order to dismiss this unit of force, Adams (who is always both the old and the young Adams) is determined to discover a "science" of history sufficient to envision the future. His vision is often dismissed by both scientists and historians; yet he saw the dynamo itself as both force and symbol that was attracting and would attract Russia (the inertia of race) and woman (the inertia of sex) into the orbit of America. Between 1838 and 1905 America had grown from a provincial nation into a world power strong enough to make the treaty after the Russo-Japanese War. Seeing the twentieth century as the American century (with all that America meant), he charted, or attempted to chart, the force of American attraction. If I am too ignorant to pursue every meaning of his chart through the formulas of science, I think I dimly see Adams' meaning of dynamic—as opposed to inertial—education. Inertial education—the education of the schools—is always trying to eliminate ignorance, whereas dynamic education is forever seeking to find it, as if it were raw material, the *matter* that education is to convert into energy. Education is, in this view, hid behind ignorance, and there is no way to go but straight through all the ignorance one can see to find it. To do that is to begin to see the dynamics not only of nature and nations and history but also of language and beauty and form. It is to see the broken arches of the Gothic transition become the *arcs* of electricity leaping across a world broken in halves; it is to see the incredible meaning of that word *race,* which at one and the same time is the utterly inertial race of man and the utterly dynamic race of man. Adams does not pun weakly on such a word; he thinks bravely and strongly about the whole concept. It is to read enormous force back into the word *attraction* and at the same time enhance the aesthetic element in that word. Thus, Adams makes attraction simultaneously designate magnetic force and worldly beauty. Written for men of the world, his book possesses throughout the great virtues of the Augustan and the genteel tradition. It is, in two words, an utterly attractive and an utterly worldly book—dealing in beauty *and* in power, in art *and* in science. To finish it is to feel something of the finish, the polish, the attraction of a man of the world, and so to be educated in the fine old sense of the word. And it is to touch the power, the speed, the direction, and the very course of the world that Einstein formulated in the year 1905, and thus to feel the ignorance and the mystery and the knowledge— yes, the knowledge—of all we do not know yet still believe we may accelerate our minds to discover.

The Memoirs of Henry James:
Self-Interest as Autobiography

————⟨∞⟩————

I have remarked elsewhere that the convention of autobiography offers descent from form into "life" for the professional writer at the same time it offers ascent from life into form for the "amateur" writer. Of course I know there is no way for the artist to leave his form any more than there is a way for the man of action to leave his life— save by the broad though difficult avenue of death. And of course I also know that the medium—or shall we say the current?—of autobiography is language, and so amateurs as well as artists are condemned to that current the moment they embark upon writing their lives. Still and all, the artist of language—the student, if not the master, of forms—perforce views the great, gaping convention of autobiography as an opportunity for experiment, a chance to expose the very rigidity of the convention to the pressure of craft, artifice, and experiment, whereas the man of action views it as the sturdy convention for chronicling his life. The one writer would follow Henry James's contention to H. G. Wells that art makes life; the other would, with a naïveté far exceeding that of Wells, believe that life made art.

Because James is, by the whole conscious devotion of his life to art, the consummate artist, I have always wanted to pursue his autobiography. For a writer of James's particular and very conscious identity, autobiography presented a particular problem. After all, James's whole creative project rested on the premise that his art *was* his life, and after completing his prefaces for and revisions of the works he selected for the magisterial New York Edition of his works, he had, perhaps more than he could afford to know, completed his life and could have, following his friend Henry Adams, contended that whatever life remained to him would be posthumous. But James was not Henry Adams. As long as the artist in him remained alive, that active, creative principle would make life. Since that principle was insatiable, he turned, after the death of his brother William James, to the task—or the pleasure—of making the unlived life, which is to say the life before he became an artist, into the life of art.

Thus, in a very proper sense, not merely for James but for the critic of James's autobiography, James's fiction *is* his life, and if it is, why is it not, properly speaking, the true autobiography? I don't wish to say that it is not, yet James—by whom I mean the author of the novels—would be most resistant to such a critical contention or strategy for the simple reason that his art, his truest life, was cast or rather made by the novel, the term as well as the form that made the life. And if James was sure of anything, he—who was so sure of many things—was sure that the novel was *not* autobiography. He could see, and all his truest life was bent on seeing, that if the novels were seen as autobiography, then the critic would perforce become the biographer—which is to say the critic would become Leon Edel, writing a magisterial biography to translate the novels, which make the life, into the life that expressed itself through the novels.

That is not all. James did not merely accept conventions; he believed in them. And genres *were* conventions, which is to say that they were at once the social forms and categories of written experience. Thus, there were conventions of literature—there were poems, plays, travel books, essays, and prose fiction—and in prose fiction there were short stories, novellas, and novels. These forms constituted not so much the socialization as the society of literature. They were the ground or the inheritance of the writer, an inheritance that the writer was not to defy but to take possession of. And James saw himself as having taken possession of the novel and, in that possession, as having lifted it from the status of bourgeois or middle-class art into high art. Such elevation gave the novel classic form, in effect finished it, which is to say gave it the full finish of consciousness and living design.

To see so much is to begin to see the meaning of the action, the form, and even the title of James's New York Edition. The fiction James chose for inclusion in the edition was preponderantly international in scope, and the considerable amount of fiction that was not international was exclusively European in setting and repeatedly dealt with the life of art and artists. Thus, James excluded from the New York Edition such estimable works as *The Bostonians* and *Washington Square,* indicating that, inclusive as the twenty-four volumes of the New York Edition clearly were, they nonetheless represented, on the part of their author, an act of deliberate choice in relation to the entire body of his work. Moreover, the terms of the international theme are fairly clear, involving as they do the American in Europe. The American, leaving an essentially formless, unfurnished world from which he had accumulated—whether through inheritance, enterprise, or speculation—sufficient monetary wealth, embarks for Europe, the embodiment of history, social forms, and finished society. This American spirit—innocent, morally confident, intelligent, and essentially good-natured as it rides on the money it has inherited, made, or won—returns to Europe to experience the world from which it had originally separated itself. The European spirit, seeing the American and recognizing the wealth, the good nature, and the innocence of social forms, nonetheless holds hard to the conventions, the society, the discriminations and time of life against the inrushing, returning spirit. The inrush and the resistance to it constitute the romance of the James international novel—a romance usually built on a melodramatic substructure. But James's scene of Europe, with its forms, its exclusions, its discriminations, its art, its history, comprises not only the setting but the layered world of manners that literally socializes or, we might say, realizes, the melodrama of the idealistic American's quest for love in the darkened world of experience. James's resolution of the international theme may seem to many irresolute, since the American spirit encounters in the face of European form sufficient resistance to discover that its impulse toward freedom and possibility had more possessiveness at its root than its outsetting consciousness has taken into account. Similarly, the European counterpart discovers that its receptiveness to the impulse toward renewal is nonetheless bounded by form and authority that have become increasingly rigid and conventional in the face of a determination to be free. Put another way, the American spirit finds, in going to the romance of Europe, that it is at the threshold of wanting possession of its old home, thereby losing the America of free good nature that had originally drawn it forth from Europe, whereas the European spirit is always threatened with the suffocating realization of why it had never left Europe in the first place.

In the resistance of the relationship, James as writer tends to relinquish authorial omniscience in favor of the point of view of the questing American. That point of view, beginning from innocence and freedom of impulse with the confident moral assurance that accompanies such illusory spiritual well-being, confronts in the resistant form and scene of Europe a disillusionment that the point of view can only overcome by allowing its intelligence to displace the moral rigidity with an acquisition of impressions. Such displacement and such acquisition are at once the readiness and the responsibility of the American hero or heroine. The relation between America and Europe is thus not realized in the opposition or even the reconciliation of the melodramatic substructure, but by a conversion of the conflict into growth of awareness and realization of the limits of the originally innocent, abstract spirit.

I realize that this summary—an extreme abstraction of James's authorizing themes and action—may seem like a constructed strait-jacket to impose on whatever I shall say about the autobiography. But James *was* a writer who had, through the most heroic and devoted concentration, lived his life through the form of his writing, and with the completion of *The Golden Bowl,* he had consciously completed his long fictional life in the international novel.

It is significant, I think, that upon completing *The Golden Bowl,* he returned to America, after a more than twenty-year residence in England, to devote himself to facing what he was to call "the American Scene." Indeed, it would be possible to say that the most significant works he completed after *The Golden Bowl* were, with the impressive exception of "The Jolly Corner," not only nonfictional but also prominently autobiographical. First, there was *The American Scene,* in which James faced the bare and, to him, often barren scene from which he had launched his fictional American expeditionary force into Europe. Then there was the New York Edition of his work, which he not only selected and revised but for which he also provided prefaces. In addition to affording an occasion for the artist to review, criticize, and define the nature of fictive art, the prefaces put James directly in touch with the memory—which is to say the experience— of creating those works. As he repeatedly announced, he was, in describing the way the separate fictions took seed in his mind, "remounting the stream of composition." Finally, there were the three relatively direct autobiographical works—*A Small Boy and Others, Notes of a Son and Brother,* and the posthumous fragment *The Middle Years*—in which James, ostensibly setting out to provide a memoir of his recently dead brother, William James, all but immediately displaced the declared subject with his remembered—or is it his creating?—consciousness of himself as a small boy experiencing his relations to his family and his world.

If we look at *The American Scene,* the prefaces to the New York
Edition, and the relatively direct autobiography, certain salient facts
come to the fore. First of all, these works are decisively in James's
late style, the style that represents the height of Jamesian elaboration
and refinement, the style in which objects are circumlocuted or displaced with emotional states, a style not so much involved as interpolated—the interpolations extending and multiplying a process of
qualification. This continuous process of qualification puts the quality of persons or things prior to their objective reality; it also puts
consciousness prior to action to such an extent that consciousness
itself becomes the action. Surveying the upper-class world of James,
a world of leisure, refinement, and possessions, we are truly seeing
what Huck Finn would have called the Quality. For James, this quality
consists essentially of taste achieved through intelligent discrimination. Quality is, in other words, the end process of aestheticizing
experience.

The basic model for the process is the world of capitalism in which
James had his being, a world of trade, greed, aggression, and ac-
quisitiveness that qualified taste can only deplore as vulgar. A great
part of James's genius lay in his capacity to commit himself to an
aesthetic world of high art and exclusive society that would yet disclose through a highly wrought and elaborated style the primitive,
ruthless, and vulgar activities that were not repressed so much as
discreetly—oh, *so* discreetly!—operating in the very sanctuary of
aesthetic contemplation. The very terms that James employs for defining the aestheticism he seeks disclose how conscious he is of this
capitalistic base of operations. There is, for example, the idea of
moral principle, which James constantly imagines as resting on a
moneyed base—true principal. Similarly, the freedom to imagine—
or at least the freedom to realize projects of the imagination—requires a free inheritance, as in the instance of Isabel Archer, or a free
spirit of enterprise to "make" money, as in the instance of Christopher Newman, or freedom of speculation to win money, as in the
instance of Adam Verver. Money is thus the minted material refinement of nature at the base of the American's *good* nature. It provides
the ground for the investment of that good nature into the aesthetic
operation—the action of *appreciating* the objects, landscapes, persons, and places of Europe. Such appreciation requires time and takes
money. Thus, history and society on one hand are forms and conven-

tions that are the resulting accumulations of time; on the other, they are the embodiment of experience, their very existence being a seal of their capacity to endure through time. These are the properties of the Old World that actively generate an accompanying system of manners or propriety to protect as well as sustain them.

Such a world is at once exclusive and powerful, which is to say possessed and attractive—attractive enough to excite acquisitive desire on the part of an outsider with means. Vulgar use of those means is mere purchase, seizure of the object without being possessed by it. Desire invested through time, resistance, and risk brings acquisition not of the object but of consciousness of the object, so that the object (whether it be a thing or a person or a place) literally comes to life with its experience, its endurance, its genuinely appreciated value. Here is true appreciation, an exchange resulting in added value, an acquisition of consciousness superior to conscience, since conscience rests too easily on original principle and has a correspondingly fixed and exclusive vision of goodness. The aestheticizing of capitalism is thus toward acquisition not of money or things but of consciousness, the very act of which will be the *interest* of life and the novel. For the artist, whose act is imagination and invention, the form of the invention is the novel—which is at once an art "object" that yet has life within it both waiting and yearning for the investing consciousness of the reader to meet and bring out. The final result of this aestheticism is to convert the original principle of freedom and good nature into growth of consciousness that takes generous account of others and at the same time discovers the implications of its own actions. Such a consciousness comprises the generosity, the responsibility, and the beauty of action. This aestheticizing of conscience into consciousness, of realism and romance into a very particular act of impressionism, of art into life, of still life into life still—this was the James novel as act of life; this was the finished form and the achieved style that James brought from Europe to America as the monumental New York Edition.

If *The American Scene* was his strongest attempt to confront America with that style, his autobiographical effort was to reinvest that style and consciousness into his own relatively unconscious life *before* he became an artist. Thus, in *A Small Boy and Others* he literally lavishes the finished style on his relatively impoverished American life before art. His Small Boy is envisioned as the delicate, sensitive, dawdling, and gaping consciousness—a consciousness literally over-wrought with the finished style of the achieved life. It is just here that I think grave problems emerge for James, problems that had initially and all but fatally emerged in *The American Scene*. In his interna-tional novels, largely abjuring American landscape, James had played his American character of good fortune and good nature against the European scene of culture and genuine social experience—a true dialectic situation providing the ground for an extended dramatic action and, in James's repeated returns to the situation, an ever-emerging style of increasing refinement.

But when James brought the achieved style of *The American Scene* and his autobiography to what he wanted to believe was the simplicity of his and America's past, the style lacked sufficient ground to justify itself. Rather than emerging out of a conflicting relation, it is more and more applied to the American scene and the American past. Now the late James style has always been subject to charges of snobbery, obfuscation, and overripe mannerism, but in *The Golden Bowl* it achieves a clear reflection of sensitive characters responding to one another. The tightness of the plot holds the complicated language in fine suspension. But in *The American Scene,* when James attempts to use it as an instrument of cultural analysis, it tends to caress what is familiar and reject what seems foreign. What seems foreign is simply all but the whole of America that had grown up in James's twenty-year absence. Where there was once simplicity of community there is now the simplicity of violent energy sending up skyscrapers; where was once good old inherited money, there is now the vulgar acquisition and accumulation of mere trade. Not that James is not aware of his problem. Casting himself as restless analyst, he from time to time has the architecture or the streets or the throngs, of which the cultivation of his style has to disapprove, talk back to him in comic dialogue. Sensitive and intelligent about America, James sees that the cult of the common man reduces the individual's power for discrimination; he on occasion sharply selects polarizing details that raise haunting questions. Thus, in Philadelphia he finds himself setting the prison famous for first putting criminals in solitary cells against the ideal architecture and ideal of Independence Hall that had housed the pos-sibility of individual rights.

Yet the cumulative effect of *The American Scene* is more disap-pointing, tending toward retreat from difficulty rather than persistent encounter with it. To be sure, the analyst's intelligence recognizes in the very lack of discrimination and loss of "beauty," consequent upon American insensitivity to history, an energy of rising expectation to be seen in the parents' confident belief in children and the children's belief in themselves. Yet the consciousness of the restless analyst—his determination to see the possibilities of that energy—is prone to stop precisely at the point of the raised question, choosing to move comfortably, even complacently, to another place in the itinerary.

This movement is nowhere more evident than in the Newport chapter. Faced with the huge mansions of the newly rich that have come to dominate the Newport scene, James can only verbally caress the old remembered Newport in which he spent such happy times. In the old Newport there was a "circle," to use James's figure for the exclusionary principle that, he feels, was not based on the principle of mere money but on a broader culture, sufficiently European in quality and discrimination to be detached and isolated from the essentially barren and egalitarian impulses of an America that, even in the old days of a finer simplicity, threatened it. True culture in James's terminology is synonymous with leisure, and in the old days the leisure could be purchased with a minimum of means—say the *interest* that the James family enjoyed from the bequest of the redoubtable Billy James of Albany, who had amassed a fortune of three million dollars at his death in 1832, which was parceled out in twelve partitions to his heirs. As one of those heirs, the elder Henry James determined, as far as we can say, to live as freely as he could on his interest, content to let principle rest free from business. Not that such interest, and the freedom it provided, was not itself a principle of enormous value. And not that the fortunes that produced the vulgarization of Newport after the Civil War did not represent a decline of the culture James nostalgically holds so dear. Yet James, for all that he casts himself in the role of the restless analyst, does not try to analyze the space, or the time, between the new money and the old. That time was, of course, the Civil War itself, the precise time that the James family returned from years in Europe to Newport at the outbreak of hostilities.

Of course, in *The American Scene,* as the very title suggests, James is not dealing, or would like to think he is not dealing, with history. He can thus contend that he is looking at the present face of a nation that can do no better than name its towns Jackson, New Hampshire,

or Jacksonville, Florida. Why such a name is deplorable and why the
old name, Radley's, of the Adelphi Hotel in Liverpool is charming,
James never makes clear, remaining supremely and, I like to think,
comically content on dismaying us with the arbitrary evaluations
available to the genuinely cultured traveler.[1] I cannot help somewhat
liking these abrupt sallies of cultural authority with their power to
anger readers holding to a democratic ethos and to discomfit those
committed to an upward cultural mobility.

Yet the fact remains that James is dealing with history when, seeing
the present Newport, he can only fall back upon the past. Beyond
that, the moral attitudes James perforce has to exploit in relation to the
Civil War are of course northern, which is to say, whether in 1904 or
1865, American. Thus, when James revisits Cambridge and sees the
eclectic and jumbled architecture of the expanding and confident
Harvard of 1904, though he regrets the loss of the old simple Harvard
(in which he had attended law school during the Civil War), he
nonetheless finds Memorial Hall, erected to commemorate the northern sons of Harvard who had died in the war, a hushed and almost
sacred place. Similarly, he finds Saint-Gaudens' bronze relief of
Robert Shaw leading his Negro regiment, unveiled in 1897, a monumental achievement precisely by virtue of its capacity to evoke personal memories of a heroism devoted to an ideal cause that James
shows no sign of disapproving. Yet the heroism and the cause that
James approves are surely related, and related economically, to the
displacement of the fine old Newport society by the vulgar new one.
James, in giving himself up to the extravagances of metaphor afforded by the late style, likens Newport to a delicate and secluded
haunt that "had simply lain there like a little, bare, white, open hand,
with slightly-parted fingers for the observer with a presumed sense for
hands to take or leave. The observer with a real sense never failed to
pay this image the tribute of quite tenderly grasping the hand, and
even of raising it, delicately, to his lips; having no less, at the same
time, the instinct of not shaking it too hard, and that above all of never
putting it to any rough work."[2] Extending the analogy for two or three
pages, James proceeds indulgently to approve the remembered New-

1. James's dislike of the names in all probability arises from a long-standing abhorrence
of Andrew Jackson, the figure who at once heralded and embodied the threat to inherited
wealth, culture, and privilege.

2. Henry James, *The American Scene,* ed. Leon Edel (Bloomington, 1968), 210.

port scene and the society that had a sufficient aesthetic sense of the place to build nothing more than modest "cottages" to escape the summer heat of cities. Such modest structures had the good taste not to dominate or obscure the scene; rather they harmonized with it in just the way to keep the place a small white hand.

The extended analogy of the hand is precisely what displaces the process of change that has overtaken Newport. Sustaining that image involves James in retrospectively and courteously kissing the hand that was, at the consummation of which he retreats from what he calls the white elephants—the huge vulgar houses—that have intruded themselves upon the tasteful scale of Old Newport. This violent intrusion is not, of course, to be attributed solely to the Civil War and its consequent release of capitalistic energy; yet clearly it is related— and the violence of this history was going on at precisely the time of James's evocative kiss of the delicate hand of the past. Here again, I am not requiring James to have dealt with the history—the process— of the white hand being displaced by white elephants, but pointing out how the elaboration of the aesthetic style circumvents that space with a transfiguring image.

Such circumvention is at the very heart of James's mobility in America, exposing a motive of retreat in his relatively arbitrary itinerary. Departing from Newport, he enters Boston, where once again deplorable urban energy has risen, not merely to crowd out but literally to tear down the houses and structures of his personal past in the same way that New York energy has demolished the house in which he was born. From Boston he pursues his itinerary south to Philadelphia, Baltimore, and Washington, where, in the monosyllabic utterance of the Washington Monument and the polished public buildings, he faces the architectural constitution of "the brazen face of history and . . . the printless pavements of the State."[3]

This is the America of the present state, from which the restless analyst, though he cannot deny its power, nonetheless recoils. But his recoil leads him directly to Richmond, and here he sees the specter of the ruin upon whose demise the printless pavements were built. Yet here again, James eschews the relation of that ruin to the power and energy he finds so disconcerting. All that he can see is the futility of a region having recourse only to the worthless relics of its past, relics

3. *Ibid.*, 364.

that, in their very poverty, merely affirm the hopelessness and lostness of the cause that has left such unappreciable articles for posterity. In arriving at the judgment, James, though he does not advance it in moral terms, is clearly relying on the moral capital of the war against slavery. Conversing with a southerner who is living on the approval of the deeds of his countrymen who fought the hated Yankees, James indulgently allows him the romance of his memories and his contention that he would like to fight the Yankees again, yet cannot forbear observing that the very impotence of the contention might be but an index of the violence such a man might do to a Negro.

That is not all. Looking at the pathetic unreality of the Confederate museums, James reflects that the real aesthetic force of the past would surely reside in the battlefields. Yet he does not go to the battlefields; he does not even regret, beyond the sentence of his observation, not going. The battlefields are, however, the *land,* and James's not going to them reflects more than the mere constrictions of his itinerary. He is not really interested in the land at any point in his visitations, since he sees land only as landscape, as cultured scene, not as agricultural life. Instead of going to land to contemplate its power—whether on a battlefield or in a cornfield—James goes instead to what he calls a "castle of enchantment" in North Carolina—actually the great Vanderbilt monstrosity of a chateau above Asheville—before going on to Charleston and Florida. The circumlocution of a style that can call the Vanderbilt mansion a castle of enchantment (James actually deplored it, and I like to think that the attack of gout he suffered there was a punishment for having taken shelter in such a white elephant) is surely related to his evasion of the land, which, he concludes, is simply flat, vast, and vacant. The reader who recognizes how the late style effaces nature almost as much as it displaces history will begin to see that the fierce process by which land becomes scene, nature becomes culture, and money becomes beauty is what is largely left out of James's encounter with and rejection of the American Scene.

This missing struggle James must have wanted to come to terms with once he undertook his account of his unlived life in his autobiographies. There are two key points, one in each of the two completed volumes, that reveal his wish. One is the nightmare—the dream of the Louvre—in *A Small Boy and Others;* the other is the account of the obscure wound suffered at the time of the Civil War in *Notes of a Son and Brother.* It strikes me as far from accidental that these two incidents have constantly struck appreciators of Henry James as the primary narrative capital of James's autobiography.

Both incidents constitute "negative" revelations in otherwise largely positive and approving accounts of his past. For in both books James, lavishing his late style upon his unlived life, clearly intended to provide a varnish or finish that would give his fresh portrait of his early years something of the fine tone of an old portrait. The portrait in each volume was, of course, quite new, since James, even in remembering the past, was freshly painting it. And just as James at the outset of his career concealed his youth by adapting, in his earliest book reviews, the style of a confident, authoritative, experienced, and mature critic, so in his age he brought to the painting of his youth a style of the utmost urbanity characterized by the ultimate refinement of taste. He says at the outset of *A Small Boy and Others*—a volume to be devoted to memorializing the life of the recently dead William James—that it was to "memory" that his "appeal" to the past had to be made in order to "recover anything like the full treasure of the scattered, wasted circumstances" and so "live over the spent experience itself, so deep and rich and rare." There would be, he says, "sadder and sorer intensities even with whatever poorer and thinner passages, after the manner of everyone's experience," which would cause him

> to find discrimination among the parts of my subject again and again difficult—so inseparably and beautifully they seemed to hang together and the comprehensive case to decline mutilation or refuse to be treated otherwise than handsomely. This meant that aspects began to multiply and images to swarm, so far at least as they showed, to appreciation, as true terms and happy values; and that I might positively and exceedingly rejoice in my relation to most of them, using it for all that, as the phrase is, it should be worth. To knock at the door of the past was in a word to see it open to me quite wide—to see the world within begin to "compose" with a grace of its own round the primary figure, see it people itself vividly and insistently. Such then is the circle of my commemoration and so much these free and copious notes a labour of love and loyalty.[4]

I quote the passage at such length in order to show the presence and

---

4. Henry James, *Autobiography,* ed. F. W. Dupee (Princeton, 1968), 3–4. All subsequent citations are from this edition and will be given in the text.

intention of James's style. It is accomplished style, easily and socially elaborating itself through a confident and articulate expansiveness and abundance equal to the abundant treasures it is already receiving from its knock on the door of the past. It is thus a recovery of the treasures that are the wasted or spent experience that the recovering memory—working through the rich, mature style—will bring together in an accumulated unity that will in turn all but conceal the fragmentation into which their spentness has scattered them. The terms of the style, as Richard Hocks in his discussion of the late style has pointed out, assume a decency, a world of refined social relations in which the expansion and qualification disclose that the process of consciousness is more important than any fixed position. Thus, the style immediately discloses that the process of recovering the treasures is as important as the treasures themselves (which could not even be treasures without the process), just as the process of composition is as important as the things being composed. Moreover, the tone is deeply set—the composition is one of freedom and abundance coupled with love and loyalty.

And indeed that declaration of intent prevails throughout *A Small Boy and Others*—prevails, if anything, too much. But that is not all. By the time James reaches his reference to the primary figure of the commemoration—the figure clearly and irrevocably being William James—the figure has already been thrown into dubiety by the very description of the process of commemoration. Thus, at the very outset of the volume, the figure to be commemorated is already being crowded out by the mental process of the commemorator. How quickly and how fatally this is all done. And how completely it is done is attested by the whole book itself. It is James the author in league with the gaping, dawdling, small boy he sees himself as having been—these joint components of the compositional process—who crowd out William James throughout the entire volume. Thus, William James becomes one of the Others, a presence to be sure, but seen through the glow of commemorative consciousness as an able older brother whose very confidence and competence originally threatened the small boy now being reinvested as the primary figure of commemorating autobiographical consciousness.

It is just in this larger context of the whole act of composition and commemoration that the famous nightmare scene takes on a special illumination.[5] In this nightmare, the dreamer envisions himself trapped in a room into which a threatening figure is attempting to make its way. Suddenly turning the tables, the cowering dreamer forces the door outward and drives the "awful agent, creature, or presence" down a long corridor that, in the lurid glare of thunder and lightning, is revealed to be none other than the Galerie d'Apollon of the Louvre, which the memorializing autobiographer has just been describing as the place of his nascent artistic ambition.

This "appalling and admirable" nightmare—to use the auto-biographer's terminology—has naturally inspired interpretation precisely because it is uncharacteristic in the encomiastic narrative. For F. W. Dupee it is the nightmare within the dream of the past that signals the "growth of relative moral servitude to relative moral freedom." For Leon Edel it is doubly focused, reflecting on one hand James's disclosure of his having literally displaced his brother in the realm of art, and on the other acting for the aging autobiographer, who has suffered a breakdown when the New York Edition failed, as a kind of therapeutic vision, a promise of a return of his suspended creative powers. Paul John Eakin, in a fine essay on James as auto-biographer, follows Edel's biographical interpretation but goes on to show that the nightmare, in a condensed symbolic act, discloses James's autobiographical art itself, the housing of an ambitious artistic self in a world of art. Eakin feels that the dream is a double prophecy—on one hand forecasting for the remembering auto-biographer the true future of the small boy whose consciousness he is pursuing; on the other promising for the autobiographer his own artistic triumph awaiting him in the second volume of the autobiography, the triumph over his obscure wound suffered in the Civil War.[6]

I do not wish to take issue with these interpretations. They are trials of a dramatic textual moment offering almost undecidable possibilities. Indeed, that moment is at once the most dramatic and

5. The nightmare, situated in the twenty-fifth of twenty-nine chapters, was actually dreamt much later in the autobiographer's life, but he makes it apply to the passage of life that is presently coming through the door upon which memory has knocked. The passage recounts the Small Boy's growing love of, yet inadequacy to, the art in which brother William is already advancing.

6. Dupee, introduction to James, *Autobiography,* xiii–xiv; Leon Edel, *Henry James: The Master, 1901–16* (Philadelphia, 1972), 434–36; Paul John Eakin, *Fictions in Autobiography* (Princeton, 1985), 56–125.

undecidable in the entire book. Without trying to determine the meaning of the nightmare univocally, I nonetheless think that a more negative reading might be wrought from it, though it would have to be somewhat hurled in the face of the positive reading James himself wants to give it. But then James's commitment to everything in the book *is* positive; that is both his tone and his determination. Even so, this *is* a nightmare, the only one in this consciously positive and commemorative book. Yet, significantly, we are brought to a door not altogether unlike the "door of the past" upon which the auto-biographer's memory knocked at the outset. That door opened wide. This one is being assaulted by an agent, a creature, a presence, and a terrified self within suddenly thrusts the door outward and appalls the apparition. James has throughout this rather oversweet book been presenting the small boy as timid with nothing to show. Yet here the cowering consciousness reveals aggression sufficiently frightening to terrify the "presence." Would not or could not the "presence" be a nightmare sense of the *present* autobiographer prying into the past, wishing to fondle the timid, frightened, retiring past spirit of himself, only to be routed by the true image of himself as fierce aggressor and usurper—who, whether or not he usurped William James's past place in the house of art, has certainly usurped his place in the present book? This nightmare, like Spencer Brydon's in "The Jolly Corner," surely reveals the two halves of the self in an admirable and appalling light—and in a nightmare form that the autobiographer's "labour of love and loyalty" has actually aroused rather than repressed.

I suggest such a reading not as an attempt to displace past readings but as an antidote to the positive readings that have formed an overlay on James's own largely positive reading of his hoarded treasures. Here, in the form of a true nightmare—and admirable because some-how true even as it is appalling in its figuration—a revelation breaks out of the overrich style that is somehow offending truth with its loyalty. Small wonder that, as *A Small Boy and Others* ends, there is a loss of consciousness, again similar to the loss of consciousness in "The Jolly Corner." In that story the loss of consciousness first occurs in the space between the time Spencer Brydon pursues and corners the ghost of what he would have been and his subsequent confronta-tion with the mutilated presence that stands at the front door of the loved house of his childhood; it occurs again after he has seen that overwhelming presence blocking his escape. This time the loss of consciousness occurs when James reaches a moment of crisis in Boulogne as he remembers a tutor he had there—a M. Ansiot—who was kind, sweet natured, and a representative of the *vieux temps,* but "too helpless and unaggressive, too smothered in his poor facts of person and circumstance, of overgrown time of life alone to incur with justness the harshness of classification" (235). Something in M. Ansiot's weak tutorings begins to seem sufficiently immense to the Small Boy to bring on a sickness that puts him to bed, where, alone and helpless, he feels a momentous change into "something queer" coming over him—a change so immense that in a kind of fright he tries to get up, but the "strong sick whirl of everything" about him causes him to fall into the "lapse of consciousness" that ends the volume (236). Here again, not that I insist on my interpretation, there nonetheless seems to me a relation between the sweet, unaggressive old tutor living in the dear old past—a past that was producing reflexive "three-volume bad novels"—and the act of the solitary old autobiographer knocking on the door of the past to welcome the throng of impressions that come flooding out in such sweet abundance. That abundance that "swarmed in images" turns into a swirl and loss of consciousness at the end of the book.

Be that as it may, as Hawthorne was so fond of saying, the lapse of consciousness ends the first volume with what James calls "a considerable gap." That gap is the space of discontinuity between the first and second volumes, since the autobiographer never refers back to it as he takes up his narrative again. Equally important, the form of the second volume reflects a marked discontinuity with that of the first volume. It is much more conventional in form, following as it does the life-in-letters model that sons or relatives of prominent figures were prone to adopt in memorializing their subjects at the end of the nineteenth and beginning of the twentieth centuries. Such a convention enables James to include the direct presence of the Others who could only appear as *impressions* of the richly invested consciousness of the Small Boy.

This direct presence of the Others takes the form of *texts* of letters by three members of the James family—Henry James the elder, William James, and Garth Wilkinson James, a younger brother—as well as a correspondence between a dying cousin, Mary Temple, and an "admirable friend" (actually John Chapman Gray). The commemorative text of the autobiographer is devoted to elaborately glossing these texts in an effort to register the life of the correspondents, all of whom are dead at the time of his writing. The letters, vividly possessed of enough life in and of themselves, justify the autobiographer's ruminations, and so the "past" in the form of these life-giving texts has sufficient body to feed the autobiographical consciousness that fleshes out its own narrative of the years 1855–1870, in which James was finding his vocation. I do not use this analogy lightly, though I would want to retain an element of lightheartedness in using it. For James, in caressing the past with his labor of love and loyalty, is nonetheless pleasurably feeding on it. The letters, the visible remains of the dead, thus provide the solid body of text out of which James peoples his narrating consciousness as he struggles to convert the death of the past into the life of art.

But the texts of the dead, while they provide something of a spine for James's narrative, are by no means the only body of the work. There is the continuing narrative, in which the autobiographer pursues his "unlived" life through the years when he was all but paralyzed as to what to do with a life that, according to the old autobiographer, had nothing to show until he determined on the vocation of writing. Time after time, even in *A Small Boy,* and particularly in *Notes of a Son and Brother,* James alludes to cousins and acquaintances cut off in the bloom of life by typhoid or tuberculosis—a strain of the book culminating in the long last segment recording the death of Minny Temple.

The prime killer of that earlier time, however, was the Civil War. From the moment James knocks on the door of the past, he is not only moving toward his choice of vocation, which would be his life, but also toward the war. These two actions—the one personal, the other historic—converge as James confronts, almost at the outset of his autobiographical project, the fact that many of the friends and kinsmen of his youth are slated for death during the time James is to discover his life. There is, for example, his cousin Gus Barker, whose mother had died at his birth and whose fine military quality and authority of youth led only to stopping a Confederate bullet in 1863; there is Vernon King, who, the epitome of ideal youth and education, "laid down before Petersburg a young life of understanding and pain"; there was Cabot Russell, nephew of James Russell Lowell, who had been in Robert Shaw's regiment and had fallen at Fort Wagner. His father, searching vainly for him on the battlefield, found instead Henry's badly wounded brother Wilky and accompanied him home. Those ghostly presences, appearing unforgettably to the auto-biographer's memory, are a measure of the inevitable burden the narrative at once carries and forecasts as it makes its way toward 1861. They are intimately related to the James family either by blood or action. Thus, Cabot Russell, though not a blood relation, is a relation of the poet Lowell whom James idealizes. As brother Wilky's closest friend, he brings Wilky's own fate to the front of the narrative. Wilky, who James says was the most vivid, frank, and friendly of all the brothers and dedicated to a life of action, never did get over his wounds. Although James does not detail Wilky's essentially defeated life after the war, the incident of his being brought back north by Cabot Russell's father provides the gateway through which James, significantly in the ninth chapter of his Augustinian thirteen-chapter second volume, enters the obscure and difficult narrative of the ob-scure wound accompanying his birth as an artist.

That narrative, taking place in what had been the little, bare, white hand of Newport, constitutes the most treacherous terrain in James's autobiography. For in confronting the multitudinous death out of which his life as an artist took shape, James faced the deepest neces-sities of his narrative—the point at which what had been the private life of a campaign that failed was to be converted into the public art of a newborn life in literature that succeeded. The elaborateness of the conversion is sufficient to exceed the resources of the celebrated later style. For though the obscurity of the wound is made to order for the style, there is more convergence of forces than the style can negoti-ate. The autobiographer begins the difficult campaign by insisting that the wound occurred at the time of Fort Sumter. Biographically considered, it did not happen then, but in the fall of 1861.[7] Without wishing to take away all the biographical freedom from James, the critic of autobiography can at least see the strategy of the artist realizing the determination of the narrative. James has already set up the relation between the artist and the soldier only pages before the difficult personal campaign begins, first by referring to Wilky's war wound and then, in a preliminary diversion from rigid chronological sequence, by remarking his meeting Dickens in 1867 at the Shady Hill home of Charles Eliot Norton. In the brief moment of being

7. Leon Edel, *Henry James: The Untried Years, 1843–1870* (Philadelphia, 1953), 175.

formally introduced to that towering literary figure, James felt himself exposed to what he calls "a merciless *military* eye," as if the recognition by the senior author of the outsetting artist were being framed in terms of a military challenge (389).

Such preliminary deployments are the simplifications, even the manipulations, designed to bridge the treacherous passage of narrative James is determined to negotiate. He begins the sequence of his private civil war with his decision to enter Harvard Law School in 1862, a decision that he still has trouble accounting for. He was not interested in law, but going to Cambridge gave him retirement from the public eye and the opportunity more easily to pursue the vocation he had rather hesitantly begun to "want to want"—the vocation of being "just *literary*" (413). Reflection on the law school decision leads him back to the obscure hurt he had suffered, according to the autobiographer's calendar of events, more than a year earlier at the time of Fort Sumter. The later James style refuses to get more specific, just as it refuses to call the elder Henry James's loss of a leg anything more than an "accident" he had suffered in youth. Here is how the late James style at once encounters and screens the event.

> Jammed into the acute angle between two high fences, where the rhythmic play of my arms, in tune with that of several other pairs, but at a dire disadvantage of position, induced a rural, rusty, a quasi-extemporised old engine to work and a saving stream to flow, I had done myself, in face of a shabby conflagration, a horrid even if an obscure hurt; and what was interesting from the first was my not doubting in the least its duration—though what seemed equally clear was that I needn't as a matter of course adopt and appropriate it, so to speak, or place it for increase of interest on exhibition. The interest of it, I very presently knew, would certainly be of the greatest, would even in conditions kept as simple as I might make them become little less than absorbing. The shortest account of what was to follow for a long time after is therefore to plead that the interest never did fail. It was naturally what is called a painful one, but it consistently declined, as an influence at play, to drop for a single instant. Circumstances, by a wonderful chance, overwhelmingly favored it—*as* an interest, and inexhaustible, I mean; since I also felt in the whole enveloping tonic atmosphere a force promoting its growth. Interest, the interest of life and of death, of our national existence, of the fate of those, the vastly numerous, whom it closely concerned, the interest of the extending War, in fine, the hurrying troops, the transfigured scene, formed a

cover for every sort of intensity, made tension itself in fact con-
tagious—so that almost any tension would do, would serve for one's
share. (416–17)

There it is. The insistent repetition of that word *interest* tells us
much about how the later style both labors in the war encounter and at
the same time capitalizes upon it. The interest is, of course, primarily
self-interest. At the same time, the obscurity of the wound gives the
style the latitude of an elaborate relation of the wound not only to
private pain and family injury but to the wound the body politic of the
entire nation experienced at the time. To make the relation clear,
James tells first of going with his father to a famous Boston surgeon
after suffering more tha.1 a year from the unhealing hurt, only to be
pooh-poohed, all of which left him in an even more troubled relation
to the tides of war. For the visit complicated the troubled family
privacy of his condition by exposing it to an evaluation at once public
and professional, at the same time making the law school decision
more possible, since James could scarcely remain at home in the face
of the surgeon's clean bill of health.

What resolution could there be for this young man entering a law
school having no interest for him even as he suffered from an isolat-
ing private wound made all but imaginary by virtue of a professional
evaluation? James finds his way out of the dilemma by telling of a
visit to the war wounded at Portsmouth Grove in the late summer of
1862 and asserting that this war experience, unlike those involving
his accounts of Wilky's wound and the handsome Cabot Russell's
death that merely accentuated his own absence and isolation from
the fields of decision and action, gave him, with his highly complicated sense of inner hurt and depression, a tragic fellowship with the
mutilated, fragile, and depressed soldiers returning from the summer of their war. He goes so far as to contend that his felt sense of
community with the wounded actually anticipated Walt Whitman's
ministrations to and imaginative comprehension of the wounds of
war (424–25).

Paul John Eakin, in what is unquestionably the finest account of
James's narrative of his obscure hurt, is the first interpreter to give
sufficient weight to the Portsmouth Grove experience. Along with
James himself, he sees it as the autobiographer's resolution, in the
fullest sense of the word, to face and answer his difficult passage
through war to vocation. Fully facing the difficulties of James's ac-

count—his tortured style, his transfer of the Portsmouth Grove episode from its biographical happening in 1861 to its autobiographical location in 1862, and his general evasiveness even in efforts at precision—Eakin follows James in concluding that the experience at Portsmouth Grove successfully integrates James's sense of separation between himself and American life into the resolved unity of the life of art.[8]

Yet, granting James both the courage of his determination to face the Civil War and to recover—or is it to discover?—his choice of vocation in terms of a reexperienced, reconstructed, and refought Civil War campaign, I find an alarming treachery in James's vision of himself as the forerunner of the poet he calls "dear old Walt" on one occasion and "the good Walt" on another. For the fact is that James reviewed Whitman's *Drum Taps* for the *Nation* in 1865 and found Whitman a fraud of a poet, a poet whose blatant assertion of ego deserved the righteous judgment of a stern and war-tried people. James was young and bold when he wrote that review, surely one of the best negative reviews of Whitman ever written. Indeed, I find it much more penetrating and decisive than the old autobiographer's rather fulsome account of having anticipated "the good Walt" in feeling the wounds of the soldiers even though he did not "come armed like him with oranges and peppermints" (24–25).

When one thinks of how much more Whitman came armed with than the oranges and peppermints he so touchingly did bring to the hospitals, of how genuinely he had prepared himself in the 1855 *Leaves of Grass* to speak through the faint red roofs of the mouths of the dead, and of how, facing the amputated arms and legs at Fredericksburg, he spoke through the wounds of the body politic and wrote letters home for soldiers, southern as well as northern, who did not know how to write—when one thinks about all this, what *is* one to say of James's claimed anticipation of such an achievement? James's youthful attack on Whitman is one thing; his failure in old age, for all the complexity of the celebrated late style, to recognize the real significance of Whitman's achievement is quite another. Although James may have won his own campaign, or persuaded himself that he had won it, his victory does not result in genuine literary vision.

Nor does it result in enhanced political vision. Once out of his

---

8. Eakin, *Fictions in Autobiography,* 109–16.

passage on the war, James can do no more than make the easiest, the most utterly complacent and conventional judgments on national politics. Lincoln of course gets accolades for having a "commanding Style," with his "mould-smashing mask," whereas Andrew Johnson is merely "common," a national catastrophe, a product of a nation unable to mount the stairs where the world could be viewed from the high window of "aesthetic sense." Yet surely, if anything is sure, it was just such a high window that would have precluded a vision of Lincoln in 1861 as anything more than common. It is hardly surprising that James has nothing to say of the *living* Lincoln. Only in death does he assume the exquisite figure whose "unrelated head had itself revealed a type—as if by the very fact that what made in it for roughness of kind looked out only less than what made in it for splendid final stamp" (490–91).

Content to see the figure of Andrew Johnson as little more than a monstrosity sufficient to cause people of exquisite sensibility to express a sense of national guilt about what had been done, James shows, in 1913, no sign of having moved a jot forward from the complacent reconstruction politics of 1866. About all we can say is that though the style is rich, the vision is impoverished.[9] Small wonder that James was totally unprepared for World War I, writing that it had burst catastrophically upon the unsuspecting decent civilization in which he had lived. Small wonder, too, that, turning back to the commemorative style, he concluded his second volume with an affectionate and sensitive commentary on the brightly vivid letters of the dying Minny Temple. Small wonder, finally, that, after

9. Compare the utterly conventional vision of James with that of Henry Adams' account of meeting Johnson: "The interview was brief and consisted in the stock remark common to monarchs and valets, that the young man looked even younger than he was. The young man felt even younger than he looked. He never saw the President again, and never felt a wish to see him, for Andrew Johnson was not the sort of man whom a young reformer of thirty, with two or three foreign educations, was likely to see with enthusiasm; yet, musing over the interview as a matter of education, long years afterwards, he could not help recalling the President's figure with a distinctness that surprised him. The old-fashioned Southern Senator and Statesman sat in his chair at his desk with a look of self-esteem that had its value. None doubted. . . . The Southerner could not doubt; and self-assurance not only gave Andrew Johnson that look of a true President, but actually made him one. When Adams came to look back on it afterwards, he was surprised to realize how strong the Executive was in 1868— perhaps the strongest he was ever to see. Certainly he never again found himself so well satisfied, or so much at home." Ernest Samuels (ed.), *The Education of Henry Adams* (New York, 1973), 245–46.

beginning a third volume of autobiography that quickly degenerated into an account of meeting great authors of the dying Victorian period, he simply quit his autobiography, for he was doing no more than converting the period in which he had genuinely lived into a memorial of his death. Surely he must have known that his title for that third volume, "The Middle Years," had a chilling personal irony. Dencombe, the dying author in James's great story of the same title, yearned for a second chance enabling him to exceed what he had previously done, only to discover at the moment of death that such a vision was itself the delusion: "There never was but one. We work in the dark—we do what we can—we give what we have. Our doubt is our passion and our passion is our task. The rest is the madness of art."

James had indeed given what he had out of his doubt and his passion and his madness to make the life of art. In his autobiography he must have felt himself increasingly submerged in the illusion of the second chance in which his doubt was being stifled by belief and his criticism was being suffocated by his determination to praise. He had lived long enough. What remained for him in the terror of World War I was to try to nurse the wounded, as Whitman had done before him, and finally to reject the America that he had bravely left so long before.

SHELBY FOOTE'S *CIVIL WAR*

Shelby Foote's *The Civil War: A Narrative* is a great work of literature, surely one of the great works written in this or any other country—a work to rank with that of Thucydides, Clarendon, Gibbon, and Henry Adams. Like those writers, Foote chose a great subject, and like them, too, he proved himself equal to it. But what chance is there that this splendid achievement will be recognized and supported? It will be classified as history and, in this age of departmentalization, will remain largely outside the ken of teachers of literature and literary critics. Yet historians will not really welcome it either. Faced with the onslaught of the cliometricians, they have become more and more suspicious of narrative. Even Vann Woodward, who reviewed it for the *New York Review of Books,* rather than devoting his attention to Foote's remarkable narrative achievement, found himself lamenting the absence of narrative in contemporary historical studies. Part of Woodward's defensiveness came from his own troubled sense that Foote's concentration on battle action opened him to a charge of having neglected the political and social history of the Civil War. Then, too, there was, accompanying the debacle of Vietnam, the growth of an antiwar culture into which Foote's three volumes had to make their way. If the intensity of the antiwar movement has somewhat abated, its dominance remains essentially intact. Beyond that, Foote's three volumes come to 2,934 pages (I include his seventy-five pages of index as an indispensable part of his account).

Considering its forbidding length, considering the specialization separating history from literature, and considering, too, the general cultural recoil from war and military history, we can see that access to these volumes is all but reduced to that group of readers depressingly called Civil War buffs. But Foote's subject is the Civil War, which forever looms like a beacon upon our sense of ourselves. Southerners are prone to fight the war over again in their minds; northerners, adamantly attached to the ideals of freedom that the war guaranteed, are ready to send federal troops to Little Rock or Oxford on one more invasion of a recalcitrant and lawbreaking region.

This state of affairs serves to remind us of how central the Civil War remains as a presence defining both the American nation and the American identity. If the white southern mind too much remembers the actual military conflict in order to distract itself from the paramount issues of slavery, race, and secession, the white northern mind too much represses the actual war in its precise fixation on the moral certitudes about slavery, race, and constitutional law that were established and secured by the bloodiest and most violent war in American experience. Realizing that the white northern mind is in effect the dominant American mind, we can begin to know how deeply the war that liberated us—southerners as well as northerners—from slavery blinds us to the intimate and terrifying relationship between the justice we surely believe in and the violence that brought us that justice. The violence of our secured ideals arms us for future violence even as it makes us forget their violent origin. Yet we cannot forget that origin, and despite ourselves we long for one more written account of the Civil War, which, with its 128 volumes of official records, was from the beginning the most *written* war in history. As if that were not enough, there were also the hordes of autobiographies, letters, and diaries of participants that have continued to surface to this day. Then, hard upon the conclusion of the war, there were the arguments and recriminations generated by partisans loyal to individual commanders. Finally, there were and are the histories that will never cease to be written. At the same time, there was the yearning for the Civil War novel, an imaginative construct that would distill the reality lurking behind the facts and analysis that history could not touch. There have been hordes of these novels too, though none but *The Red Badge of Courage*, in both its compression and violent irony, discovered in the rage of color coming through the mind of a private soldier a symbolic fury equal to the chaotic conflict on the battlefield. And even here, for all its intensity, Crane's interior battle left Ernest Hemingway feeling that the narrative was a boy's long dream of war. Moreover, literary scholars in their speculations about just what battle Crane was portraying—the chief candidate has been Chancellorsville—disclose, in their wish for facts, terrain, and time, a need for history. Yet the extensive histories—the fine ones by Douglas Freeman, Bruce Catton, K. P. Williams, and Allan Nevins—with all their knowledge, their responsible reliance on sources, their discriminating reflection on problems and arguments, their summarizing hypotheses and judgments, and their immensely helpful maps, footnotes, and bibliographies—leave us with a sense of their partiality and incompleteness.

And so, coming at last to Shelby Foote's narrative from this field of past attempts as well as from the old desire for yet another account of the Civil War, we encounter what seems to me the qualities we have so long awaited in such a work—completeness and impartiality. The very title—*The Civil War: A Narrative,* as true a title as we shall meet in our lifetime—is telling in the full sense of the word. It is indeed a narrative, and the Civil War, in all the meaning of those words, is its subject. No one who reads the book will find it incomplete. I do not mean that it is complete in every detail. For example, the battle of Gauley Bridge, in what is now West Virginia—the battle in which my own grandfather was wounded—is not touched upon in this narrative, and I have no doubt that other readers who trace themselves back to a particular Civil War action will find similar omissions. And certain Civil War specialists will no doubt find their specialties insufficiently dealt with. But if we mean by completeness the full comprehension of the panoramic field of action of that war, then I have not the slightest doubt that Shelby Foote's narrative is incomparably the single most complete narrative of the war that has been or is yet to be written. His three volumes panoramically encompass the war, which is to say that they fully comprehend it from its beginning to its conclusion. To achieve this comprehension, Foote had to *see* the war, as if from above, which meant that he had to see its tremendous space from the air. It is no accident that he defines distance, whether from Washington to Richmond or Memphis to Vicksburg, in terms of airline miles even as he fully recognizes the agonizing discrepancy between such an abstract measurement and the overland distances across which the armies had to toil. Indeed, the economy of his perception, combining a modern overview of the war with an incisive recognition of the true, which is to say relative, resistance of both actual and historical terrain, is one of the chief sources of his authority as a narrator. It is truly a double view, at once characterizing his overall, swift, and mobile vision and his close-up, penetrating, and intense pursuit of individual engagement.

Then there is his impartiality. In a small note appended to the first volume, he contends that, aside from having a typically American sympathy for the underdog, he believes that, for all his being a Mississippian, he has written an impartial account of the war. His narrative is, if anything, even better than his word. Some reviewers, evidently trapped by the modest confidence of Foote's frankness in his endnotes to each volume, have observed that the pulse of his prose beats faster as he follows southern armies toward victorious exploits. Admitting that my own southern pulse might beat faster as it follows Foote's narrative before Second Manassas, Fredericksburg, and Chancellorsville, I still can see nothing but an awesome impartiality in Foote's narrative—an impartiality utterly related to its comprehensiveness of scope. One could well say that because the narrative is complete, it is never partial.

The most visible basis of the impartiality lies in Foote's balanced structure—balanced not only between North and South but between East and West. This balance is evident from the opposing portraits of Jefferson Davis and Abraham Lincoln, which constitute Foote's prologue to the conflict. Born in Kentucky log cabins within a hundred miles of each other, Davis and Lincoln moved in divergent directions—the one southwest to Mississippi, the other northwest to Springfield. For all that, and for all their differences in temperament—Davis serious, formal, and intensely principled, Lincoln humorous, relaxed, and shrewdly skeptical—they were yet western in their vision. Thus, both knew how utterly crucial the Mississippi River was to their opposing causes. Foote's vision of the two men therefore equips him both narratively and thematically for his task of achieving a balance between the eastern and western theaters of war. He balances those two arenas of action from the outset, showing just how the battle of Wilson's Creek in Missouri followed hard upon First Manassas, and how Lee's failures in western Virginia were juxtaposed to Grant's success at Fort Donelson. The very subtitles of his three volumes—*Fort Sumter to Perryville, Fredericksburg to Meridian,* and *Red River to Appomattox*—are an index to both the balance and the coverage of his narrative.

Foote's balance between North and South measures the historical conflict at the heart of the war, giving the narrative remarkably economic access to the social and political issues at stake. To be sure, he does not treat those issues as extensively as Allan Nevins does in *The War for the Union.* But Nevins' commitment to the political aspect of the struggle makes him see the war itself as a result of the political forces, whereas Foote sees the war as the essence of his narrative and is determined to make that dramatic action revolve around the men who fought it. That is why he begins with the portraits of the two men, Davis and Lincoln, who represented the warring sections. Yet anyone who concluded that Foote's paramount interest in the actual battles resulted in a military history in the manner of K. P. Williams' *Lincoln Finds a General* would be profoundly mistaken. Having portrayed Davis and Lincoln at the outset, Foote is always poised to show the reciprocal relationship between battlefield action and political skirmishing at the seats of government. He sees and tells, with remarkable acuity, how both northern armies and politicians were at war with each other as well as with the South. At pains throughout the war to reconcile the deep division within his political constituency, Lincoln was perpetually threatened by political rearguard action almost as much as he was by Lee's tattered army. Even as late as 1864, when Sherman boldly decided to move seaward from Atlanta instead of pursuing Hood's retreating army northward and westward into Tennessee, both Lincoln and Grant knew that failure of such a strategy might cost the Republicans the election.

Not only did Lincoln, in order to consolidate and maintain power, have to reconcile the opposing political factions within the North; he had to reconcile politics and principle. However much he was against slavery in principle, he had to manage affairs in such a way that principle *politically* prevailed. That prevalence was the unity he sought in order to save the Union in which he believed. However much he was against slavery, he was for Union more.

With Davis things were different. Since the Confederate constitution provided for a six-year presidential term, Davis neither faced nor had the opportunity of an election. Spared the deep division of a two-party system, he could fall back confidently on the unity of principle and could call on his nation for sacrifices necessary in war. The severity of Davis' adherence to principle kept him on the brink of self-righteousness and made him brittle in brooking differences from colleagues; at the same time, if he experienced loyalty from his subordinates, he returned it with fervor. While Lincoln was moving cagily and at times almost humbly before the ambitious and popular McClellan even as he was listening sensitively to the growing cabinet criticism of this Young Napoleon, Davis was discovering in Robert E. Lee the man who could at once lead armies yet constantly defer to his president's political authority. But if Davis had unquestioned authority of command, he was nonetheless presiding over a nation increasingly isolated and driven in on itself. Seeing its hopes of European recognition dwindle, its economy at the point of disintegrating, its armies more and more overborne, the South saw principle being converted into starvation and ruin. If its head was held high, there was less and less body to hold it.

Of course, readers versed in history can say that they knew about these matters. Yet, emerging as they do in the course of Foote's recurrent returns from battles to the opposing capitals, these interpretations become actualities that are at once economically and unforgettably etched in the reader's mind.

They are unforgettable because of the particular perspective of Foote's whole narrative. If one puts the war not only in the foreground but *as* the foreground, it no longer seems the result of political forces but is itself the very means of political force. *It* is the violent action to which politics and history have surrendered; by being narratively true to its dominance, Foote implicitly reveals a superior political vision of those four years. The war was, in all its intensity and bloodiness, the superior reality of that long moment to those who fought it and to Lincoln, who ultimately presided over it. He was not indulging in mere self-serving rhetoric when he said at Gettysburg that the world would little note nor long remember what he said but could never forget what the soldiers did. Because his own death sealed the conclusion of all the battles and because he himself had the language equal to his large vision of the nation, there are many who feel that his language is more permanent than the battle, but that is only because the battle has not yet found itself in language. If we had to wait a hundred years for Lincoln's vision to begin to be fulfilled in the action of history, we have also waited—not passively but actively through attempt after attempt—for that battle and all the battles of the war, to find the writer equal to their reality. For me, Shelby Foote is that writer.

Knowing both historically and imaginatively the full reality of the war, he does not have to be for or against it; instead, he believes in the war, believes in it enough to believe that the men who fought it were as real as its reality. His great task as a writer is to render their reality. That rendering draws on all his skill as a novelist and at the same time requires all his energy as a reader of all the Civil War histories and narratives that have preceded him. His novelistic skill is deployed in two ways. First, he has literally to mobilize his immense panoramic action in a linear narrative. Thus, he has the difficulty not only of moving from battle to battle in cumulative sequence but also of determining a sequence for actions that took place almost simultaneously in time but in far different space. The deep structure of such a subject all but requires the "meanwhile back at the ranch" transition, which is as old as Homer. Yet such a transition implies subordination of one action to another; it also subverts the true nature of historical process, implying as it does a fictive closure of events. Equally important, it denies the very nature of the war as Foote envisions it. He sees the whole cumulative force of the war as pushing forward; thus, the retroactive moves he perforce has to make in order to bring his war forward in all theaters of action are necessarily at variance with his deepest recognition of the war's forward thrust. Although there might be retreats on any given field, both sides went relentlessly forward not so much toward each other—though there were furious encounters of opposing forces—as in the powerful direction the war took, a direction beyond the management or even victory of either side. There could be no real "meanwhile back at the ranch," since such a transition implies that things in one place are not affected by actions in another. But Foote knows that this was a war in which telegraphic communication all but instantly relayed results of one action to the opposing nerve centers of Washington and Richmond and from thence out to the extremities. Yet he also knows that the war cannot be reduced to this acceleration, since there were men still laboring with muzzle-loaders to the extent that breech-loading carbines could not make headway against them, and the presence of Federal balloon observers did not keep Jackson from becoming obscurely lost until he burst in fury upon Hooker's flank. All the troop transport by train did not annihilate the old inertial resistance of land and weather any more than all the machines of war could quite obliterate the recalcitrant individual soldier. The old order of making war and the old resistance of nature to technology were as much in conflict with the new technology as the South was in conflict with the North. How else could the war have been so very big and very long?

Yet all these conflicts, ideologically and historically large though they are, remain for Foote the subordinate and implicit aspects of the struggle. The battles themselves are, and must be, the explicit conflict. They are the violent resolution of the irresolvable political and historical conflicts. The measure of Foote's achievement is that he fully recognizes the violence and at the same time never forgets that it is human violence—more human than politics and history because it is so mortal.

Foote's forward movement in his narrative sequence is directly into that mortality. Although the necessities of his scope and comprehensiveness require him to make temporal retrograde movements in his narrative, these are offset by the breadth and intensity of his cumulative and panoramic action. Beyond that, Foote possesses sufficient narrative resources to make the most telling references to his past narrative. He tolls anniversaries of past battles or deaths of commanders; in the midst of narrating one action, he interpolates reminders that it is taking place simultaneously with another action that he has already dealt with; he emphasizes the haunting repetition of action—the returns to Manassas, to Fredericksburg, to the Wilderness; he amasses cumulative references to past battle behavior in building the characters of his commanders. These rhetorical tactics not only keep the whole mass of his accumulating narrative in mind; they sustain his narrative strategy of treating past battles and past narrative as the reserve force of lived experience. Thus, the reader's experience tallies with the dominant strategy of Grant and Lee and Sherman, whose remarkable reading of each battle became the experience on which they relied as they moved on and on into the terrible responsibility of command.

If Foote's problem in relation to his own narrative past is to mobilize it by means of the lifelines he keeps throwing back to it, thus attaching an immense reserve force to his own forward movement, he has a vastly different relation to his future. The broad and deep outlines of his great subject are known. Almost every reader knows that the South will begin with victory at First Manassas, that Jackson will be brilliant in the Shenandoah Valley, that Pickett's charge will fail at Gettysburg, that Grant will win Vicksburg on the same day, that he will ultimately come east and push relentlessly forward to Appomattox, and that Lincoln will die in the aftermath. The vast majority of the relatively limited audience sufficiently interested and arduous enough to contemplate these three massive volumes will know much more. Such knowledge and such inevitability suspend for both writer and reader possibilities of novelistic suspense. A writer who knows this inevitability too well will allow his knowledge to over-determine both his judgment of participants and his selection of narrative incident and direction. Such overdetermination results in a cheapened authority—cheapened because the authorial advantage of hindsight is deployed to foreknow the future. Knowing the conclusion too easily, the writer forgets that the participants did not know it.

Yet the writer of historical narrative who tries to suppress the inevitability of the "future" is more and more seduced into faking suspense and excitement by tuning up descriptions, dramatizing action by making it "colorful"—in other words, by making it read "like a novel." Although Foote had written novels before entering on this monumental project, and though he uses many novelistic resources in his narrative, he never resorts to such techniques to gain excitement, for the simple reason that he never doubts the reality of his subject. Instead, his whole effort is to get into that subject by using all the resources of the historian. The result is that he pushes deeper and deeper into the conflict even as he pushes forward through it. Knowing fully the inevitability he confronts, Foote displaces both the prejudgment of character that rests on foregone conclusions and the narrative excitement that gains novelistic suspense with a plenitude of both action and evidence. Thus, the reader who knows all about Grant and Lee, or about Stuart and Sheridan, finds that he does not know about Henry Sibley's campaign through Texas into New Mexico, about Richard Taylor's brilliant Red River campaign, about Isaac Newton Brown's remarkable achievements in the naval war on the Mississippi, about William Cushing's incredible efforts to torpedo the Confederate ironclad *Albemarle,* about the battle of Mobile Bay, about the intricate Florida campaigns, about Pea Ridge, about Buck Van Dorn's death, or about a hundred other engagements and ironies that were vital parts of the war.

Foote does not try to make these "minor" events major so much as he allows his narrative to discover their importance, and discover it not merely by covering it but by integrating and weaving it into the comprehensive web of inclusion. Thus, the reader, or this one at least, is perpetually astonished at how little he knows and at the same time profoundly gratified by his mounting grasp of the largeness, fullness, and pervasiveness of the Civil War. And throughout this massive narrative comprehension, Foote maintains clarity of progression without visible resort to showing off or belittling others for

neglecting these episodes and incidents that flanked the central theaters of action. Instead, he gives to every action he comprehends the
great vitality of his imaginative embrace. If he knows that they are
subordinate in any conventional view of the war, he also knows that
they are actions—participations in the general conflict—just as he
knows that subordinates, all the way down to privates, participated in
the individual battles. And if he remembers that some of these actions
are diversions from the main lines of the struggle, he does not forget
the diversionary delight that is incipient in them.

To appreciate Foote's comprehensive coverage is to be brought
back to my point about his impartiality and to be brought forward
from the balance, continuity, and comprehensiveness of his structure
to his treatment of character. For if structure and sequence are at the
heart of narrative, so also is character. And character, as his initial
portraits of Davis and Lincoln fully signal, is utterly central for Foote.
If the war was a clash of forces, institutions, and ideas, it was fought
by men. Although the war with its battles was larger than the men and
though in a deep sense it made or broke or killed them, they nonetheless fought it. Because battles are violent efforts toward decision,
because the Civil War was decisive in the extreme, and because we
helplessly know the outcome, the same inevitability that both we and
the writer encounter in relation to action and incident is operative in
relation to character. Once we know a battle is going to be lost, the
evaluative mechanism that runs like a constant dynamo in our minds
begins to take precedence in relation to the persons fighting it.
We helplessly conceive the completed action, to which we know
the conclusion, in terms of prejudgment masquerading as detached
judgment.

There is no way for the historical narrator to evade this problem
completely; it goes with the territory. Even Bruce Catton, an able,
lucid writer committed to genuine narration rather than thesis, confronts the decisive Confederate victory at Ball's Bluff with the following paragraph:

> [McClellan] did not have to wait much longer [for a larger object
> than his having won the goodwill of the army], for the Army of the
> Potomac was about to suffer one more public disgrace, and the shock
> of it would force a change—and, in the end, would arm and perpetuate
> a bitterness that would be felt to the last day of the war and beyond. On
> October 21 [1861], a small Federal detachment was routed in an en-

gagement at Ball's Bluff, on the Virginia side of the Potomac thirty-five miles upstream from Washington. The engagement had little military significance, but it was one more dreary licking. The Confederates inflicted heavy losses and they killed, in hot battle action, a prominent Union commander—Colonel Edward D. Baker, an unskilled soldier but an orator and politician of much renown, a member of the United States Senate, and for years an intimate friend of Abraham Lincoln.[1]

Here is extremely serviceable prose, but it reverses the order of narrative in order to put the meaning of the battle before the battle. We are not told just what the significance is—other than that it will perpetuate a bitterness much more significant than the battle itself, which is *militarily* insignificant. Catton then proceeds to give an extremely condensed version of the battle and concludes by showing that the "disgrace" of the defeat led Zachariah Chandler, Lyman Trumbull, and Ben Wade to see the president and demand some decisive action from the senile Winfield Scott and the overcautious McClellan. Their pressure led to the retirement of Scott—which thoroughly suited McClellan, since he was promoted to general-in-chief.

By putting the battle in a secondary position, Catton is able to put the unspecified significance in the primary position, thus making it the withheld narrative action. That significance is the promotion of McClellan, which had been the larger object for which the Young Napoleon was waiting at the outset of Catton's paragraph. But that decision has great cost for Catton, since he has to return to the battle of Ball's Bluff a hundred pages later, showing how those three abolitionist senators went on to lead the Joint Congressional Committee on the Conduct of the War, the first action of which was summarily to investigate the possibly treasonous behavior or Brigadier General Charles P. Stone, who was in command at Ball's Bluff. And here again Catton concludes that the charges leading to his imprisonment and the wreckage of his career were unfounded.

Foote's narrative is far different. He begins with the battle itself in the larger context of McClellan's confrontation with Joseph E. Johnston, his Confederate counterpart. Both of them were cautious and at the same time immensely popular, and Johnston had just tricked

1. Bruce Catton, *Terrible Swift Sword* (New York, 1963), 88–89. Vol. II of Catton, *The Centennial History of the Civil War*, 3 vols.

McClellan by retreating under cover of Quaker guns (logs painted to look like cannon) that held McClellan sufficiently at bay while Johnston conducted his retrograde movement. Smarting under the public criticism of his exposure, McClellan, upon hearing that Johnston was apparently preparing to evacuate Leesburg, determined to find out whether the Confederates were really retreating in that sector. He therefore sent one division, under McCall, up the Virginia side of the Potomac to make a reconnaissance and ordered Stone's division, stationed on the Maryland side, to assist. McCall "halted at Dranesville, ten miles short of Leesburg, content to do his observing from there." But Stone, "who read his instruction as permission to push things—believed that the best way to discover the enemy's strength was to provoke him into showing it." He thus sent two regiments across the river at Edwards Ferry and his others across at Harrison's Island, three miles upstream in order to envelop whatever opposition might exist.

> Here the operation was necessarily slow, being made in three small boats with a combined capacity of 25 men. By dawn one regiment was on the island looking out across the other half of the river at the wooded Virginia bank. It reared up tall there, over a hundred feet steep and mean looking; Ball's Bluff it was called, and from beyond its rim they heard a nervous popping of musketry, each shot as flat and distinct as a handclap, only more so. They were Massachusetts boys, and they looked at one another, wondering. No one had told them on the drill field or bivouac that the war might be like this. They continued the crossing, still in groups of 25, herded by their officers, and took a meandering cowpath up the bluff toward the hollow-sounding spatter of rifle fire.[2]

Foote goes on to show that the rifle fire is coming from an exchange between another Massachusetts regiment that, having crossed the river earlier and engaged the Confederates in the bush, has retreated to the edge of the bluff. Both are reinforced by a Pennsylvania regiment under Colonel Edward D. Baker. Foote carefully outlines Baker's character, showing his longtime friendship with Lincoln, whom he had known in Illinois before going to the Mexican War, his participation in the California Gold Rush, and his subsequent election

2. Shelby Foote, *The Civil War: A Narrative* (3 vols.; New York, 1958–74), I, 104–105. All subsequent citations are to this edition and will be given parenthetically in the text.

as an Oregon senator. Baker could have had a major general's commission but remained a colonel in order to stay in the Senate, where he was Lincoln's chief spokesman from the Far West. He had ridden in the presidential carriage on inauguration day and introduced Lincoln for the inaugural address. A fine speaker who loved to quote poetry to the troops, he was eager for the battle that was taking shape and greeted the Massachusetts colonel who had brought his troops up the bluff with a quotation from "The Lady of the Lake." Minutes later the man who on the Senate floor "had called for a sudden, bold, forward, determined war received it in the form of a bullet through the brain, which left him not even time for a dying quotation" (I, 106).

Foote does not stop with Baker's death, but narratively pursues the battle action as Shanks Evans' Mississippi and Virginia regiments drive the retreating Federals back down the bluff and into the water, pouring fire "into the huddled, leaping, rout of blue-clad men as fast as they could manipulate ramrods and triggers." The horror of the developing scene caused some Confederates to pause momentarily, but only momentarily, before they rushed to the rim of the bluff, where they poured a furious fire that lashed the water "until the surface boiled 'as white as in a great hail storm,' one participant declared." The panicked soldiers leapt into the small boats and swamped them, and one flat boat "was scrambled into until it was almost awash . . . but presently, live men ducking and dodging and shot men falling heavily on the gunwales, it capsized, and thirty or forty were drowned" (I, 107).

This, then, was, as Foote narrates it, the battle that Catton sees as a bungled fumble of no military significance. It is not merely the concentration of novelistic ability, producing a graphic account of the battle, that distinguishes Foote's account. Rather, his deployment of the battle as the primary cause of a narrative sequence distinguishes his conception of the war. The war itself, in this early stage of his narrative, is revealed in the very act of becoming the reality that generates political response. Thus, Baker, who has declaimed on war, is drawn into the conflict he has weakly imagined—and slaughtered. Equally important, there are men out there *on both sides* who, though nameless, are as real as Baker. They are at once more deadly yet as frail as Baker proves to be. That is what those bullets, charges, and retreats are all about. Foote's great strength is to conceive the action of that reality as both the gripping and generative force of his narrative sequence.

He is then in position to pursue his sequence. The news of Baker's death galvanizes the Senate into indignation at the same time that it reduces Lincoln to helpless tears at his sense of personal loss. Out of the indignation comes the Joint Committee on the Conduct of the War, whose first act is to scapegoat the hapless Stone. And from that initial step, the committee, with all the virulence of the generating battle, can implicate and threaten anyone suspected of sympathy for the enemy. At the same time, Lincoln, still struck to the heart with his personal loss, yet faced, only eleven days after Ball's Bluff, with the task of telling McClellan of his promotion to the place of the aging and increasingly discredited Scott, shows fatherly concern for the Young Napoleon even as he knows that this youthful and ambitious general has coveted the rank of general-in-chief. He knows how McClellan has snubbed Scott not only because he has seen it but also because McClellan has patronizingly lectured him on the nature of military science. For all his knowledge, Lincoln yet shrewdly feels both the burden and responsibility that his commission places upon McClellan's youthful and ambitious shoulders:

> "Well," Lincoln said, "draw on me for all the sense I have, and all the information." Still wondering, however, if McClellan was as aware of the weight that had been added as he was of the weight that had been taken away, he returned to the point. "In addition to your present duties, command of the army will entail a vast labor on you."
> "I can do it all," McClellan told him. (I, 110)

Such is the conclusion of this particular sequence. It leaves Foote ready to proceed with McClellan's farewell to General Scott, to giving a masterful appraisal of Scott's Anaconda Plan (which Foote believes essentially represented the strategy that Lincoln and Grant would materialize more than three years later), and to go on to all that McClellan could not do. It also leaves him in position, 150 pages later, to show how the Joint Committee on the Conduct of the War had spawned a progeny of committees to implicate anyone suspected of treason. When the Lincolns lost their son Willie, and Mrs. Lincoln's ensuing hysteria, coupled with her southern parentage, subjected her to rumors of disloyalty, Lincoln himself, aware of the mounting slander and accusations, came unexpectedly to a secret session of a congressional investigating committee to announce in a sad voice: "I, Abraham Lincoln, President of the United States, appear of my own volition before this committee of the Senate to say that I, of my own knowledge, know that it is untrue that any of my family hold treasonable communication with the enemy" (I, 252).

These are the far-reaching consequences of Ball's Bluff, and Foote's sequence shows how the battle, far from being a fumble, was itself of vast military significance in that it brought the war home to both the president and Senate, thus intensifying and widening the conflict by spawning a militant indignation in the political sector that accelerated a change in command and led ultimately to the grief-stricken heart of the president who had lost a real son. My selection of this sequence is likely to conceal what is perhaps the finest quality of Foote's writing: his essential restraint. The words may seem all wrong in light of Foote's dramatic intensity and vividness of description, but this sequence is but a thread in his comprehensive narrative web, and its tensile strength lies in Foote's refusal to call overt attention to his own connective operations and designs. The battle itself is where he finds the impetus, and he lets the battle do its work.

Since battle is both the primary form and force of his subject, he does not see the battles as fumblings or mistakes. They are the massed action of planned and designed group conflict. Those who plan, direct, and attempt to execute them confront a concentrated field of violence and contingency that tests foresight for possibilities of spontaneity, probes courage to its roots in fear, and tries life in the presence of death—and all this violent contingency is organized into a cumulative sequence of increasing magnitude and deepening deadliness that yet has a life of its own.

To comprehend the sequence brings us always back to the humanity of Foote's vision of men at war. They are never so much wrong or right as they are human. Take McClellan, for instance—and another comparison of narratives. K. P. Williams in his impressive five-volume *Lincoln Finds a General*—an account of Grant's emergence to supreme command as comprehensive in its account of northern military strategy as Douglas Southall Freeman's seven volumes on Lee and his lieutenants were comprehensive of the Confederate generalship—conducts what amounts to an all-out assault on McClellan in order to prepare the way for Grant's superiority. Despite his mastery of battle plans and his wonderful maps of battles, Williams' narrative design locks him in a fixation on McClellan's faults: his caution, his perennial overestimate of enemy numbers, his vanity, his ambition. And Williams' sympathy with western warriors causes him to assume a defensive stance in relation to the hapless Pope, whom he uses to continue his attack on McClellan.

Foote knows all of McClellan's weaknesses—every one—and exposes them, not, however, by argument but through narrative. He tells of McClellan's laughing at Stanton's depiction of Lincoln as the "original gorilla" and of his keeping Lincoln and Stanton waiting at the door of his house while a wedding party is in progress, only to have a servant inform the president after an hour and a half that the general has retired for the night. Yet Foote's very narrative at such moments is charged with a consciousness of much more than mere exposure of McClellan's behavior. Stanton, who, after all, had also sneered at Lincoln, was with him, showing that he was playing both sides of the street. And a reader of this narrative will have been educated beyond sentimentality to recognize that Lincoln's humility had its own strategic side. Foote's Lincoln was perfectly capable of a consciousness of Stanton's double-dealing and could have taken a particular pleasure in having his company as the two endured McClellan's snub.

Beyond that, Lincoln knew how much he needed McClellan. For McClellan had organized the army, and he was loved by the men. Foote knows, or rather his narrative knows, that these were not small but great accomplishments. There *was* something warm about him, and if Lincoln was set about with enemies in front and rear, so was he. Moreover, McClellan was able. His troop dispositions during the Seven Days were strong; if he overestimated enemy strength at that time, he was hardly helped when Lincoln and his war cabinet took forty thousand men away from him to defend Washington. Foote's narrative moves into the thicket of all these contradictory forces, showing that McClellan's fear of Johnston and Lee's numbers was no more irrational than Lincoln's fear of what Foote beautifully calls the Shenandoah shotgun, out of which Lee might at any moment send Jackson blasting toward the Capitol. When McClellan's enemies persuaded Lincoln to yield to their wish for his removal, they got Pope, a hard fighter who had brilliantly succeeded at Island No. 10 but who proved a vastly simpler figure for Lee to fathom. Arrogantly and insensitively telling his new forces that he came from the western theater, where his soldiers had seen only the backs of their enemies, and advocating war on southern civilians as well as on southern soldiers, he succeeded only in arousing a contempt coupled with a devastating intelligence in Lee, who wrote to Jackson, "I want Pope to be suppressed."

After Pope's disaster at Second Manassas, there was no one but McClellan. If Stanton could say to Lincoln that anybody would be better, Lincoln could wearily reply: "Anybody may do for you. I need somebody" (I, 242). McClellan was *somebody,* and Foote's full treatment of his long travail reveals it. When, after Antietam, he was again, and finally, relieved of command, his request to his adoring troops that they fully support Burnside disclosed, if nothing else, not only that the charges and fears of his disloyalty were groundless but also that there was a grace and generosity about him that cannot be reduced to vanity. Yet throughout the extended treatment of Mc-Clellan's command, Foote never finds himself defending or attacking McClellan. Instead, the narrative exposes his character at the same time that it comprehends it. And again it is the action of the battles that decides the issue. They are sufficiently indecisive to disclose his caution, even his fear—which is intimately related to his love for his troops—but they are not defeats and demoralizations of his army. He retains to the end a glamor upon the panoplied field of battle that his imagination spent itself in organizing.

Seeing Foote's balanced structure and comprehensiveness of scope, seeing his conceptual vision of battle as the inescapable action and reality of the Civil War, and seeing, too, his capacity to describe that action in such a way that it discovers the character of the participants—the generals, the politicians, the men—seeing all this still leaves the texture of the narrative to be accounted for. And here again it is not sufficient to praise Foote's "art," as if he had merely applied his novelistic skill to his great subject. Just as his concern with battle action involves him in a truly conceptual vision of the war, his profound research into and knowledge of historical detail is completely wedded to his narrative skill. Thus, the texture of his narrative is a translation of all his enormous reading of prior texts into a living and not merely a lively account of the action. He unfailingly sees both the ground and the actors in his battles in such a way that his capacity to make things appear—to create the images of his scenes and actors—is the very current of his narrative.

There are no illustrations in his volumes—indeed, illustrations would be an affront to the narrative he accomplishes—because he must have looked so long and searchingly at photographs as to have resolved them into verbal vision. Here is his description of Lee.

> On horseback, deep-chested and long-waisted, with his big leonine head set thick-necked on massive shoulders, he looked gigantic. Partly that was the aura. It must have been; for when he dismounted, as he often did, to rest his horse—he had a tender concern for the welfare of all animals, even combat infantrymen, aside from those times when he flung them into the crackling uproar of battle like chaff into a furnace— you saw the slight legs, the narrow hips, and realized, with something of a shock, that he was no larger than many of the men around him, and not as large as some. The same contrast, above and below, was apparent in his extremities; the hands were oversized and muscular, the feet tiny as a woman's. He was in fact just under six feet tall and weighed less than 170 pounds. Quickly, though, you got over the shock (which after all was only the result of comparing flesh and perfection. However he was was how you preferred him) and when you saw him thus in the field your inclination was to remove your hat—not to wave it, just to hold it—and stand there looking at him: Mars Robert. (I, 585–86)

This is unabashedly an idealized portrait, as the prose frankly acknowledges. As a matter of fact, Foote immediately follows it by referring to less flattering accounts of Lee by Robert Toombs and the editor of the Charleston *Mercury*. But there are so many insights in it, not least of which is the parenthetical recognition that Lee's gentleness does not obscure the fact that he was able, ready, and willing to sacrifice his men to the furnace of battle. The fierceness and gentleness are borne out by the large trunk of the rider, whose horse obscures the delicacy of the lower body. And finally, the descent into the solid facts of weight and height that lead to the mysterious generosity of the figure who leaves preference to his beholder, but a preference that gives back authority to the figure who is not Marse Robert, as we have always seen it spelled, but Mars Robert, whose name at once pronounces the gentle patriarch yet designates the mailed essence of the warrior.

If the idealism of this particular portrait is rare for Foote—and it is—the vividness is not. There are literally hundreds of unforgettable images of the officers who led men to battle. There is of course Grant, walking always with his body pitched forward; and Sherman, "red bearded, tall and thin, with sunken temples and a fidgety manner"; and Judah P. Benjamin, Confederate secretary of war and later secretary of state, whose rotund, smiling face stood always between the administrative dispatch with which he kept his desk cleared and the military men who approached him and upon whom he exercised his talent in dialectics with a "precision of logic that could lead men where they would not go, making them seem clumsy in the process"; and the redoubtable Edwin M. Stanton, who had once snubbed Lincoln before the war and whose moral savagery in dealing with men who were culpable was offset by "the joy he took in fixing a frightened general or petitioner with the baleful glare of his black little near-sighted eyes behind small, thick-lensed oval spectacles"; and Jackson, dust covered on horseback in the Seven Days, "the dingy cadet cap pulled so far down over his face that the bill almost touched the lemon he was sucking"; and Philip Kearney, who had lost an arm in the Mexican War, riding in the darkness into A. P. Hill's men at Chantilly and, upon being called on to surrender, whirling his mount and "leaning forward on its withers with his arm around its neck" as he tried to escape, only to be shot down in the dark, where the Confederates found him "lying one-armed in the mud, the back of his coat and the seat of his trousers torn by bullets"; and Charles S. Winder, sick with fever but leaving his ambulance at Cedar Mountain, where "tall and wavy-haired, he kept his post . . . calm and cool-looking in his shirt sleeves," until "a shell came screaming at him, crashing through his left arm and tearing off most of the ribs on that side of his chest" (I, 58, 222, 244, 487, 644, 600–601).

Unforgettable as these images are, it is the voices of the war in Foote's narrative that are to me the most haunting. When Winder lies quivering on the ground, for example, a staff lieutenant rushes to him to ask, "General, do you know me?"

> "Oh yes," Winder said vaguely; and his mind began to wander. The guns were banging all around him, but he was back at home again in Maryland. In shock, he spoke disconnectedly of his wife and children until a chaplain came and knelt beside him, seeking to turn his thoughts from worldly things.
> "General, lift up your head to God."
> "I do," Winder said calmly, "lift it up to him."

> Carried to the rear, he died just at sundown, asking for the welfare of his men, and those who were with him were hard put for a comforting answer. (I, 601)

And when Kearney's body is brought into the Confederate lines, A. P. Hill, looking on the man he had known in the old army, remarks: "Poor Kearney. He deserved a better death than that." Foote's sensitivity to this and similar moments reminds us, even in the midst of violence, that there was yet civility in the Civil War.

It is not generals alone who speak in this narrative. Foote finds voices everywhere in his search through the records. During the Yazoo fight between the *Carondelet* and the Confederate ironclad *Arkansas,* the badly damaged *Carondelet* fires back: "The return shots glanced off the *Arkansas'* prow, doing no considerable damage except to one seaman who, more curious than prudent, stuck his head out of a gunport for a better view and had it taken off by a bolt from an 8-inch rifle. The headless body fell back on the deck, and a lieutenant, fearing the sight would demoralize the rest of the guncrew, called upon the nearest man to heave it overboard. 'Oh, I can't do it sir! It's my brother,' he replied" (I, 552).

These examples in no way suggest the range of the voices in these volumes. There are also the speeches of Lincoln and Davis, reminiscent of the crafted speeches in Thucydides' history of the Peloponnesian War. Davis' speeches have the oratorical formality of state speeches, yet in Foote's carefully orchestrated context, they disclose a genuine stateliness. And Foote hears the music in Lincoln's speeches and places them so ably in his narrative that no reader will miss it. Beyond the political speeches, there are the rallying cries to battle, ranging from the bluntness of Bedford Forrest demanding surrender unless his opponents wish him to give them no quarter, to the martial flourish of Sherman addressing his troops during the course of their destructive march across Mississippi. Then there are the taunting cries of the men of the armies, whether in the midst of battle or during the lull between. Finally there is the irrepressible humor of the soldiers, which Foote catches superbly. There is, for example, the southern soldier, suffering from the "Tennessee quickstep" from having eaten green corn, who boasted that "he could hit a dime at seven yards." And when John Pope announced that his headquarters were in the saddle, there was the wry observation that his headquarters were where his hindquarters should be. Then there is

Lincoln's humor, forever present, indicating how rich his musical range really was. He had a penchant for unerringly discovering appropriate barnyard imagery and activity with which to illuminate or explicate the behavior of politicians and generals. But I think my favorite Lincoln joke has to do with Stanton, whose prancing and bouncing put Lincoln "in mind of a Methodist preacher out west who got so wrought up in his prayers and exhortations that his congregation was obliged to put bricks in his pockets to hold him down. 'We may have to serve Stanton the same way,' Lincoln drawled. 'But I guess we'll let him jump a while first'" (I, 245–46).

There are two reasons for the great effectiveness of these voices in the narrative. First, they are embedded in the narrative in such a way that they wonderfully serve it, giving it the tenor of dramatic authenticity without once reducing it to scenes of dramatic dialogue. Second, these speeches are never footnoted, a fact that has drawn complaints from some reviewers. I must confess that there were times when I wished for footnotes that might have conveniently located the sources of certain speeches or anecdotes. Yet I think that Foote was boldly right in dispensing with them. As he says in his bibliographic note to the first volume, "Accepting the historian's standards without his paraphernalia, I have employed the novelist's methods without his license." By freeing himself from footnotes, the speeches and anecdotes are freed from their prior textuality to become voices in this text. Any reader familiar with the *Official Records* or histories and memoirs of the Civil War will recognize some or even many of these voices, though no such reader, I venture to say, will read these volumes without *hearing* the war far better than ever before. And no reader, whether reading about that war for the first time or the hundredth time, will doubt Foote's assertion that "nothing is included here, either in or outside quotation marks, without the authority of documentary evidence that is sound." I am glad that Foote made the assertion, but he would not have had to. The authenticity of his narrative, coming from its comprehensiveness, its discipline, its clarity, its graphic conception and vision, and its capacity both to see and hear the action of the moving forces, produces a living and informed faith in the reader: living, because the reader will never have felt the war so vividly and intimately; informed, because he will never have known or seen it so illuminatingly.

But these volumes illuminate more than those four years. They

were written during the twenty years (1954–1974) when the Civil
War centennial approached, came, and passed and when a southerner, who succeeded to the presidency by virtue of an assassination,
sought, and largely achieved, a political realization of Lincoln's unforgettable vision of Gettysburg, which was in turn a monumental
rededication, on a field almost still bloody, of Jefferson's original
vision in the Declaration. And yet, almost simultaneously, this same
southerner carried out a moral and ideological imperialism, also inherited from the Civil War, leading us into the Vietnam War and
finally resulting in a radical disunion in the body politic as well as a
radical aversion to war. That aversion, flourishing under the umbrella
of nuclear threat, makes war "unthinkable," as we are told by those
who imply that the old "conventional" wars were easy to fight. Those
who, easily willing to think the unthinkable, emerge with visions of
technological deterrents multiplying with ever-increasing "refine-
ments" that inevitably assume the identity of Star Wars. The one side
reduces history to simplicity, voiding the old wars of their terror and
courage; the other futuristically invents machines that make the warrior obsolete. Both are fantasy.

These same twenty years witnessed the exhaustion of the great
movement in art and literature denominated as the *modern,* which
came to full fruition in World War I, when a whole civilization experienced the expression of a profound nihilism in the very trench warfare—really initiated, as readers of Foote will discover, by Longstreet before Chancellorsville—presently referred to, with unbe-
lievable complacency, as conventional war. The modern has died into
the postmodern, the very term disclosing the devastation wrought by
one period on another. What was profoundly dislocating and revolutionary in the fracturing of representation and reference has run its
course into acutely self-reflexive forms on one hand and into an
instantaneous technological communication and information system
on the other, both of which combine to displace narrative and de-
construct the self. In the flood of images, fact, and language pouring
from the information system, the novelistic imagination has pursued
paranoid strategic retreats into structures of discontinuity as a means
of escaping narrative plot.

It is surely of great critical importance that, during these twenty
years, Shelby Foote, coming from the world of the novel, should have
narratively discovered a larger, wider, and more complete Civil War

than anyone before him. He discovered it precisely because narrative
was never device or technique but vision itself, a means of seeing,
through language, a historical reality that he never doubted. The
ground of the battlefields was still solid beneath his feet; the weather
of Mississippi, Tennessee, Georgia, and Virginia—and, yes, of
Texas, Louisiana, Arkansas, Missouri, Kentucky, Alabama, Florida,
Maryland, and Pennsylvania—was present to his senses: and the war
itself must always have been living for him, so that he never had to
bring it to life but had to reach the sure life it had in his mind and blood
and bone. To reach it, he went relentlessly outward to the fields, the
woods, the weather—how well he realizes that Napoleon's fifth element of war was mud—and to the records, letters, memoirs, and
histories, there to quarry out the lives, actions, character, and, above
all, the battle of a nation for its life.

And so he sees at the end of his narrative the two figures, Lincoln
and Davis, with whom he began—the one victorious at the moment
of his death, yet his death the very measure of the loss in victory; the
other captured, imprisoned, abused, yet unreconstructed and, some
might say, unvanquished. But Foote knows better than easily to use
that word, which was to become a shibboleth for southerners, most of
whom had not faced the fury of Lincoln and Grant's arithmetic of
war. Having recorded both the valor and defeat of the nation that
fought and died, and having recorded, too, the death of Davis' own
children, he comprehends how profoundly Davis represented his nation. Yet if Davis was defeated, he remained unyielding, ready to
challenge in court the constitutionality of secession. And no court,
supreme or otherwise, was ready to face the challenge. Yet beyond
Davis' refusal to renounce his cause, he lived long enough to say to a
reporter who asked him for the underlying motivation that might
account for four years of war, "Tell the world that I only loved
America."

To read this great narrative is to love the nation, too—to love it
through the living knowledge of its mortal division. Whitman, who
had seen, in the amputated limbs heaped beneath a tree at Fredericksburg, the true dismemberment of the body politic and who intimately
knew and loved the bravery and frailty of the soldiers, observed that
the real Civil War would never be written and perhaps *should* not be.
For me, Shelby Foote has written it. Unlike Thucydides, he was not a
participant in the war he narrates; but like him, he is boldly sure that

his subject is as great as any in the past and that, as a writer, he is equal to it. He never says so much, but the writing—which he wonderfully calls his "devocioun"—emboldens me to say that this work was done to last forever.

INDEX

Abolition, 20, 121

Adams, Henry: *Education*, 12, 25–26, 30, 63, 144–63; a model life, 25; life as history, 25; life into art, 25; third-person strategy, 25, 128, 156, 163; self as history, 25–27 *passim*; self-division, 26, 165; Adamic vision, 28; and Gertrude Stein, 30–31; quoted, 63, 109–10, 137, 142, 147, 148, 153, 157, 161, 189n; and James, 109–10, 168; and Mark Twain, 114; and autobiographical convention, 127–28; "The Dynamo and the Virgin," 144; as historian, 146; *Mont Saint Michel and Chartres,* 146, 148, 151–52; and linear form, 152; and ironic vision, 157–58; and failure, 158–60; as Hamlet, 161; dynamic self, 164; self as unity of thought, 165; theory of history, 165; the Dynamo and the Virgin, 165–66; and autobiographical suicide, 166; and Foote, 191

Adams, John: quoted, 146; mentioned, 29

Adams, Marian Hooper: monument, 26; suicide, 160

Adams, Samuel, 18

Alexander, E. P., 109

American Revolution, 16–19 *passim*

Anderson, Quentin, 92

Anderson, Sherwood, 131

Antiwar culture, 191

Aquinas, Saint Thomas: *Summa,* 150; and Adams, 150–52 *passim*

Armstrong, Samuel, 132

Articles of Confederation, 41–42

Augustine, Saint, 4, 14, 15, 28, 108, 128–29, 165

Autobiography: and New Criticism's failures, 1–3, 34–35, 55, 121–23 *passim*, 145; open form, 2, 23, 124; and canon, 3, 8; convention, 3, 126–28 *passim*, 168; and biography, 3; and "I," 3, 34, 40, 79, 88; and slave narrative, 3; conflicting views of, 4; not a genre, 12; defined, 12–14; and fiction, 12–13; and history, 12–13; as term, 12, 14, 31, 33, 103; and self-made life, 19; as modern term, 14, 103; and revolution, 12, 20; and representative life, 22; and Adams, 25–28, 29–31; and Franklin, 28–29; as self-generation, 29; autobiographical and biographical consciousness, 31; as metaphorical suicide, 109; and minority and nonliterary culture, 123–24; ghost-written autobiography, 125; as-told-to autobiography, 125; only genre taken for granted, 126; first person as problematic signifier, 126–27; exemplary, 134; life versus form, 168; and death, 168; language as medium, 168 *See also* Confession; Memoir; Self in autobiography

Autobiography of Malcolm X, 11, 124–25, 129. *See also* Haley, Alex

Bacon, Delia, 125

Bacon, Francis, 125, 152

Badeau, Adam, 109

Baker, Edward D., 201–204

Baldwin, James: *Notes of a Native Son,* 123

Barker, Gus, 184

Battles and Leaders of the Civil War, 110

Benjamin, Judah P., 209

Benjamin, Walter, 101, 118

Bildungsroman: and *Two Years Before the Mast,* 71

Biography: its goal, 13; Boswell and Johnson, 14; presence in autobiography, 129; as metaphorical murder, 129. *See also* Autobiography

Bishop, Jonathan: 79, 80n, 84n, 92

Blackmur, R. P., 122, 144

Black Muslims, 129

Bloom, Harold, 79–81

Boswell, James: *Life of Johnson,* 14; and Gertrude Stein, 31

Boyd, Julian P., 53

Brady, Matthew, 103

Brown, Isaac Newton, 199

Buckner, Simon Bolivar, 119

Buell, Don Carlos, 113

Burke, Edmund, 46